Management and Planning in
the Leisure Industries

Management and Planning in the Leisure Industries

Edited by
Ian Henry

MACMILLAN

First published in 1990 by
THE MACMILLAN PRESS LTD
Houndmills, Basingstoke, Hampshire RG21 2XS
and London
Companies and representatives
throughout the world

ISBN 0–333–48533–5

A catalogue record for this book
is available from the British Library.

Printed in Hong Kong

10   9   8   7   6   5   4   3
00 99 98 97 96 95 94 93 92

Contents

3   The Management of Human Resources in the Leisure Industries

Robert J. Brown

4   Financial Management and Leisure Provision

Mike Stabler

5 Leisure Management and the Law

Valerie Collins

Part II THE CONTRIBUTION OF SOCIAL THEORY TO AN UNDERSTANDING OF LEISURE POLICY, AND LEISURE MANAGEMENT AND PLANNING

6 Analysing Leisure Policy

Fred Coalter

List of Figures

Notes on the Contributors

Robert J. Brown is a director of Moran, Stahl & Boyer, a consultancy group which specialises in intercultural management. He was previously Senior Lecturer in Industrial Psychology in the Business School at the Polytechnic of North London, where he was also the Course Director of the Diploma in Management (Leisure). He has spent time in many leisure environments as a consultant on human resource issues, and has supervised a range of research projects into personnel management and industrial relations problems.

Fred Coalter is Director of the Centre for Leisure and Tourism Studies at North London Polytechnic. He has been involved in leisure research for over a decade at the Polytechnic of North London, the Tourism and Recreation Research Unit, University of Edinburgh, and the Centre for Leisure Research, Moray House College, Edinburgh. During that time he has been responsible for a wide range of research projects dealing with topics as diverse as football hooliganism, access to countryside recreation, and the rationale for public sector leisure provision.

Valerie Collins graduated in law and is currently a Senior Lecturer in law at Trent Polytechnic. A keen participant in sport, she has combined her sporting interests with the practical experience of having worked in a sports centre to produce a text, *Recreation and the Law*, and several articles in this subject area.

Ian Henry is currently Lecturer in Leisure Studies and Recreation Management at Loughborough University, having previously taught in this field at Bradford and Ilkley College, and Leeds Polytechnic, following practical experience as a sports centre manager and as head of Leisure Services in a Metropolitan District. He graduated initially in English and philosophy from the University of Stirling and subsequently received a master's degree and doctorate from Loughborough University in recreation management. He has written widely in the fields of leisure policy, management and planning, and has a particular interest in comparative leisure policy.

John Spink is Senior Lecturer in Community Studies at Bradford and Ilkley Community College. His teaching interests lie in the fields of urban studies, urban geography, and planning. He is a professionally qualified town planner, and his recent research has related to urban development processes and their implications for recreation. He is a co-author of *Understanding Leisure* and *Leisure and Urban Processes*.

Mike Stabler, at one time employed in local government and subsequently in commercial management, is a lecturer in economics at the University of Reading, specialising in property, land and construction management. His research interests have mainly been concerned with the economics of the environment, recreation, sport and tourism. He has conducted a number of projects on the financing and management of leisure resources and has also published on data and methodological problems of leisure research. He is currently studying the economic structure of the tourist industry with particular reference to the impact of its operations on tourist destination areas.

Introduction

This book is intended to provide a guide to theory and practice in key areas of leisure management and planning in the leisure industries, for undergraduates, HND students, and those on post-experience and postgraduate courses. It is divided into two parts. Part I consists of five chapters on substantive areas of practical interest to leisure managers. Chapter 1 reviews the structure and development of the leisure industries in the public, voluntary and commercial sectors. Chapter 2 reviews leisure planning practice in the commercial and public sectors. Chapter 3 analyses the development of different approaches to human resource management, and their application in leisure organisations. Chapter 4 considers the application of key concepts and techniques in financial management and their implications for leisure managers. Chapter 5 considers the structure of legal responsibilities placed on leisure managers, highlighting specific implications for managers of leisure facilities and services. Each of these chapters brings together material on managerial practice relating it to the specific concerns of leisure management in a way which has not been available in the past to those studying in the leisure management field.

Part II of the book has rather different goals. Much of the literature in the leisure studies field (as opposed to leisure management) is premised on developments in social theory, which has had its own trajectory over the 1970s and 1980s. Links between the predominantly prescriptive concerns of leisure management (theories about how to 'improve' managerial practice), and the analytic concerns of leisure theory (how best to understand and explain leisure and other related sociopolitical phenomena) have not normally been made explicit. Chapters 6 and 7 of the book seek to redress this imbalance and to make clear the relationship between management theory and practice on the one hand and, on the other, explanations of the nature of wider social practices. The chapters deal with an analysis of leisure policy, and the relationship of sociopolitical schools of thought to leisure management and planning theory. This smaller section of the text is therefore aimed predominantly at those students with an interest in pursuing a study of leisure management and planning in its wider social and political context.

Each chapter of the book is introduced with a set of aims reflecting the content and thrust of the particular chapter, enabling the reader to review in some detail the material covered before embarking on detailed reading and study. At the end of each chapter brief notes of guidance in relation to further reading are given. It is also intended that a series of case studies in management and planning in the leisure industries will be produced to complement Part I of the text.

IAN HENRY

Acknowledgement

The photograph on the front cover of this book of water activities in West Edmonton Mall, Alberta, was kindly supplied by Professor Sue Glyptis of Loughborough University.

Part I
The Leisure Industries and Management and Planning Practices

1 The 'Mixed Economy' of Leisure: The Historical Background to the Development of the Commercial, Voluntary and Public Sectors of the Leisure Industries

Fred Coalter

Introduction: Learning the lessons of History

The purpose of this chapter is to situate our discussion of the nature and significance of management and planning in the leisure industries by highlighting the context within which the leisure industries and leisure policy have developed. An historical perspective is important for three reasons. First, in respect of the public sector, many of the contemporary facilities, which account for a large proportion of local government current expenditure, are products of decisions taken in the nineteenth century – for example, many urban parks, museums, swimming baths and libraries date from the 1870s–1890s. Such provision, and the inherited financial commitments often lead to 'facility inertia', reducing the capacity to develop new provision. Secondly, such facilities represent a 'philosophical legacy', or conventional wisdom, concerning the appropriate divisions between the public, voluntary and commercial sectors. These attitudes are currently coming under close scrutiny as proposals for 'compulsory competitive tendering' for the management of public sector leisure provision raise fundamental questions about their appropriateness.

Finally, attitudes and policies regarding leisure have been historically variable, usually reflecting particular social, economic and political circumstances. It is therefore useful to recognise that management decisions are taken within a broader social and economic context and that apparently neutral 'technical' decisions often have political implications.

These issues will be illustrated by looking at four broad historical periods in which policies for leisure were the subject of political debate, institutional reform and provision and in which the various roles of the three sectors were consolidated. The intention is not to provide a 'history of leisure policy' but rather to illustrate various themes underlying the development of contemporary provision and policy.

The four periods are:

1. The nineteenth century, in which the major themes are industrialisation and the emergence of modern leisure.
2. The first third of the twentieth century (approximately 1900–39), which can be characterised as laying the foundations of the Welfare State.
3. Post-1945 to the mid-1970s, in which the major themes are the emergence of the welfare state, containment of work and the problems of affluence and recreational welfare.
4. Contemporary structures: economic constraints, recreation as welfare and the reassertion of market principles.

The Nineteenth Century: Industrialisation and the Emergence of Modern Leisure

The idea of leisure as 'free time', a specific period separate from work and characterised by notions of 'freedom' and 'choice', is largely a product of the social and economic changes in the late eighteenth and early nineteenth centuries. In pre-industrial societies the relationship between work and non-work was an 'organic' one in which popular sports and pastimes were often linked to work-related or seasonal events, and were rooted in rural and parochial social systems. Unlike the elements of individual choice and self-expression regarded as central to modern leisure, these activities were characterised by communality and collectivity (Malcolmson, 1973; Cunningham, 1980; Bailey, 1979).

Such an 'organic' relationship could not survive the rapid process of social, economic and cultural change associated with industrialisation and urbanisation. A series of social, economic and political events served to undermine the social relationships which sustained such 'popular cultural' forms as fairs, bull-running, cock-fighting, mass football games and so on.

First, unplanned urbanisation led to the increasing enclosure of previously common land and the reduction of the amount of open space required for many of the traditional pursuits. Simply in terms of the physical environment previous popular cultural activities therefore became difficult if not impossible to pursue. The rapidity of such changes are indicated by the fact that between 1750 and 1851 the number of cities in Great Britain with populations of over 50,000 rose from 2 to 29.

Secondly, the emergence of the factory system separated the place of work from home, labour from recreation. In addition, the factory system of production – with the optimum economic operation of industrial plant requiring predictable and intensive use – required new forms of work organisation and discipline. The systematic organisation of work into specified places and times again served to undermine the time consuming popular recreations.

However such changes were uneven and occurred over a long period of time – depending on regional variations in the extent of urbanisation and the expansion of the factory system. The resultant changes, and the emergence of new forms of leisure, were also not simply the result of structural changes but were reinforced by legislation and national and local government policies.

In addition to being undermined by urbanisation and industrialisation popular pastimes were systematically suppressed by the public authorities. For example, magistrates banned wakes as threats to public order and the Highways Act 1835 introduced fines for the playing 'at football or any other game or any other part of the said Highway to the annoyance of any passenger' (Malcolmson, 1973). Because of these actions Malcolmson (1973) suggests that the roots of public policy for leisure lay in repression, as the state attempted

> to back up the workings of the free market, to complement the discipline which was inherent, though not always entirely effective

in the market economy.

The concerns of the state can be seen to be twofold – public order and work discipline. Large public gatherings of rowdy crowds in urban areas raised the spectre of the French and American revolutions and the possibilities of assaults on the existing order. Further, much state activity was based on the recognition of the interdependence between work and non-work time. The rational and systematic ordering of work into specific places and times also required the reciprocal organisation of leisure. Therefore, from the middle of the nineteenth century the state was involved in regulating and rationally organising the temporal parameters of leisure. Various Factory Acts and Bank Holiday Acts served to organise leisure into specific and defined time periods and to undermine pre-industrial practices such as 'Saint Monday' (extending the weekend by taking Monday as a holiday).

However the concerns of public policy were not wholly repressive or prohibitive. Like much of social policy, that which concerned itself with work and work disciplines contained elements of both control and liberation. For example, the Factory Acts served also to limit over-exploitative employers and to serve as a formal recognition of the legitimacy of the idea of free and private time separate from work.

Further, the roots of much modern leisure legislation and provision is to be found in a concern for public health and sanitation in urban areas. As we have noted already, the growth of urban areas had greatly reduced the amount of open space and the unplanned urban developments contained little open space provision. This exacerbated the problems of the over-crowded, unhygienic and unsanitary conditions of much urban living.

Contemporary reformers argued that open, fresh air and exercise would improve the general health and fitness of the community and the workforce (improving productivity). Such utilitarian concerns with health resulted in three broad responses – attempts to resist closures, provision of urban open spaces and the public provision of bath and wash houses.

In 1841 Parliament voted monies to support the establishment of urban parks – the 'lungs of the city' – and in 1847 legislation was passed enabling local authorities to provide public parks. Such utilitarian concerns with health were also evident in the 1846 Baths and Wash Houses Act.

However social policy concerns not only related to the public health and fitness of the workforce but also with the moral welfare of the working class, with the content of their leisure. These concerns – which are evidenced in such legislation as the Museums Act 1845 and the Libraries Act 1850 – are usually referred to as the 'rational recreation movement'. The concern of this movement was to provide alternatives to the perceived degeneracy of working class social life, to provide a cultural content for leisure time.

Here the rationale for provision was based on a 'merit good' argument. Intervention was based on the presumption that consumers were not the best judges of their own (or society's) welfare. Private preferences were viewed as distorted as compared with a normative definition of socially beneficial behaviour (Gratton, 1980). In this regard Mellor (1976) has noted that the majority of nineteenth century public facilities were provided not in response to popular demand, but because they were regarded as socially desirable. The normative purposes associated with provision often were reflected in the rules and regulations defining the 'proper' use of facilities (for an example relating to urban parks see Walker and Duffield, 1982).

The 'rational recreation' movement is interesting for two reasons. First, it serves to illustrate the limitations of the direct role of the state. Despite the fact that the 'problem of leisure' was to find new modes of regulation and social integration, the direct involvement of the state was limited and often reluctant. Although much of the involvement was repressive or regulatory – legal suppression of popular customs, legislation to regulate and license drinking and gambling, legislation on working hours – more generally laissez-faire arguments were dominant. There was a reluctance to become involved directly and the various Acts (Museums, Libraries, Baths and so on) were not mandatory, but merely permitted local authorities to make provision where they so desired.

Although competition in the latter half of the nineteenth century, based on 'municipal pride', served to overcome reluctance to spend rate income on recreational provision, the development of many of the facilities depended on private philanthropy. This brings us to the second aspect of the 'rational recreation' movement – its largely private and voluntary basis. The organisation and provision of 'rational' recreational opportunities and the 'leadership' which was regarded as essential were left largely to the efforts of the voluntary sector.

The 'rational recreation' movement was in reality not a coherent organisation, but was a broad ideology shared by a wide and heterogeneous range of voluntary organisations, often funded and controlled by middle-class philanthropists. The main concern of this movement was with the moral welfare of the urban working class and with the content of working-class leisure. Rather than simply suppressing various 'pre-industrial' leisure forms these reformers sought to provide wholesome, self-improving 'rational' activities as alternatives to what they regarded as irrational and degenerate behaviour (most especially the public house and drinking). For example the Church of England, through Sunday School recreation programmes, attempted to provide alternative attractions in the form of day trips and educational visits. Mechanics' Institutes were established to provide education classes and the Reverend Henry Solly founded the Working Men's Club movement as an alcohol-free meeting place. A movement referred to as 'Muscular Christianity' promoted the newly codified games of association football and rugby as a means of fostering the virtues of self-discipline, deferred gratification, teamwork and the subordination of individual interests to the greater collective good.

The concern of both the state and the middle class with the moral welfare of the working class contained an ambiguity which is also present in contemporary social policy for leisure – a humanitarian concern for social welfare and the quality of life was combined with a class-based concern with social control. Social and economic change had undermined previous modes of social integration – the new urbanising society was producing social fragmentation and class polarisation with an increasing fear that this would lead to social unrest. In this context many reformers believed that 'properly managed, leisure could be used not simply to civilise the working class ... but also to remake society, to halt the drift towards atomisation' (Cunningham, 1980).

From this perspective 'public' leisure facilities – parks, museums, libraries – and voluntary leisure associations could provide the basis for a new civic culture in which conciliation and consensus would be achieved. Leisure was an area in which social and economic inequalities would cease to be important.

To view these initiatives merely as efforts at 'social control' is however, to misrepresent the ambiguities in the 'rational recreation' movement. Among the self-improving, artisanal sections of the working class there was in the first place a concern to promote temperance and to adopt modes of behaviour and disciplines regarded as necessary for political and social progress (Hargreaves, 1984). Secondly, the rational recreation movement largely failed to reach its 'target groups'. Those elements of the urban working class which did participate did so on their own terms (Cunningham, 1980; Bailey, 1979). For example, middle-class sponsorship of Working Men's Clubs was accepted until alternative forms of finance were established – paradoxically often via the profits from the sale of alcohol.

Thirdly, although the 'problem of leisure' was to find new modes of regulation and social integration, the direct involvement of the state was limited and often reluctant. Apart from its repressive and regulatory aspects state policy tended to consist in permitting and encouraging local government or voluntary effort. Most of the legislation relevant to the provision of public leisure facilities was permissive – local government was not required but merely permitted to spend rate income on libraries, wash houses, parks and so on. Often the provision depended on private philanthropy, to provide books for the libraries or land for urban parks.

However by the end of the nineteenth century we can discern the broad elements of a public policy for leisure. These elements were to form the basis of much subsequent policy (Coalter *et al.*, 1988):

- **Urban deprivation:** A belief that recreation provision could contribute to the improvement of the quality of life in urban environments.
- **Physical health:** This was related to the problems of urban deprivation and a concern for the health and productivity of the work force. However, on occasions, such as the aftermath of the Boer War, there was a more widespread concern with the 'health of the nation', and its fitness to fight.
- **Moral welfare:** A concern with the content of working-class leisure, symbolised by the campaigns against the pub and alcohol.
- **Social integration, social control and 'community':** 'Public' space and 'public' facilities could be used to establish a socially integrative, civic culture transcending social and economic inequalities and counteracting tendencies toward social fragmentation. This was based on an ethos of 'participation' which has remained a constant theme in public policy. Participation is viewed as confirmation of a broader social consensus.
- **Self-improvement:** The emphasis on physical and moral health and socially integrative recreation, mixed with a strain of puritanism, meant that an ideology of self-improvement dominated public policy and provision.
- **Limits of public provision:** Despite political rhetoric, there was a marked reluctance to become directly involved in leisure provision. While the state set the outer limits of leisure behaviour and morality, through prescriptive legislation and licensing, the development of leisure policy was left to the permissive powers of local government, voluntary effort and the commercial sector.

This last point concerning the commercial sector is a very important one. One reason for the relative failures of the rational recreation movement was that in the latter half of the nineteenth century voluntary organisations and public provision increasingly had to compete with the new 'entertainment industries'. In addition to the continuing importance of public houses, new forms of commercially provided leisure opportunities were becoming available – professional football, railways and excursion trips, piers and, most important of all, the music hall (Bailey, 1979).

In the latter half of the century large-scale capital investment was undertaken in order to build larger halls. Increases in real income and free time encouraged the increasing capitalisation of leisure facilities and the consumption of commercially provided goods and services. Cunningham (1980) suggests that the large size and public nature of the new commercial leisure organisations made them acceptable to authority. They ceased to be threateningly 'privatised' and were open to public supervision, licence and control. Leisure and the commercial market for leisure goods and services became an important element of the broader capitalist market.

Early Twentieth Century

The three sectors of the 'mixed economy of leisure' – the public, voluntary and commercial – consolidated and extended their roles in the early years of the twentieth century. Various state reforms established the ideological and legislative roots of the 'welfare state'. Legislation such as the Unemployed Workman's Act 1905 and the National Insurance Act 1911 demonstrated the beginning of an acknowledgement of collective responsibility for the welfare of disadvantaged individuals and groups.

In terms of more leisure-specific legislation, several initiatives concerned with urban and rural land use formally acknowledged the growing importance of recreational provision for the public. For example, the Town Planning Act 1909 listed recreational open space as a category of land-use to be recorded and the Forestry Commission, established in 1919, was the first governmental body to have a statutory duty to make provision for recreation.

In the 1930s two pieces of legislation of major historical significance were passed. The Physical Training and Recreation Act 1937 established the Fitness Council to distribute grants to both local authorities and voluntary bodies, to assist in the provision of facilities for physical recreation. The Act was motivated in part by the instrumental concerns with the 'health of the nation' and a fear that the nation was physically unprepared for a war with Germany (Evans, 1974). The solution remained that of merely encouraging local government to make provision and strengthening the voluntary sector. Nevertheless, although the scheme was ended by the outbreak of war, the Act also established the principle of state funding for recreation for its own sake.

The state's willingness to pass legislation to increase public recreational opportunities was also evident in the Access to the Mountains Act 1939. This Act was passed in response to a widespread campaign for access to the countryside which included mass trespasses in the Peak District. The eventual Act was a limited measure. For example, amendments to the original bill included the deletion of the recommendation that trespass should cease to be a civil wrong and the creation of a system for establishing access was so complicated and expensive that it proved unworkable (Hill, 1980). However, although the Second World War ensured that the Act was not implemented, it is of historical significance. Although greatly modified from its original intention it established the principle of recreational access to uncultivated mountains and moorlands which has consistently remained in all subsequent legislation (Sidaway *et al.*, 1986).

It is also significant that these two Acts were both passed as result of public pressure and organised voluntary group activity. The period up to 1939 was characterised by an expansion of the voluntary sector in recreation and its development on a national scale. For example, the National Association of Boys' Clubs (1925), the National Playing Fields Association (1925), the Central Council for Recreative Physical Training (eventually the Central Council for Physical Recreation, CCPR) (1935) and the Ramblers' Association (1935) all reflected the 'rational recreation' ethos. They sought to pressurise central and local government to take a more positive attitude towards a policy for leisure and themselves made a major direct contribution to the provision of recreational facilities.

More generally this period exhibits apparently paradoxical develop-ments. On the one hand it was characterised by economic depression and high levels of unemployment and on the other there were spectacular developments in modern leisure forms.

Although total unemployment was high its incidence varied greatly between regions – with much being concentrated in the North of England, Wales and Scotland. For those in employment there were reductions in working hours, although Jones (1986) suggests that the actual increase in leisure time may have been reduced by increased overtime working. Paid and unpaid holidays increased and by 1939 60 % of the working population had paid holidays.

These changes and increased prosperity for some, mostly white collar groups, encouraged the continuing commercialisation of leisure. Capital investment in stadia for mass spectator sports such as professional football increased and new technologies led to the development of the cinema as a natural extension of the music hall. According to Jones (1986) the cinema was arguably the main leisure institution of the 1930s.

Wireless produced both commercial opportunities and another area for state intervention and regulation – licences increased from 2 million in 1926 to 9 million in 1938 (Jones, 1986). The British Broadcasting Corpora-tion was established in 1927 with a board of governors appointed by the government, which also controlled its income by setting the level of the licence fee. The policies of the BBC were essentially conservative and educative, aiming to educate the populace and to improve popular cultural tastes – 'rational recreation' on the radio.

By the end of the 1930s many features of the modern mixed economy of leisure were established – a vibrant and often highly organised voluntary sector, a commercial sector which provided both leisure services (cinema, travel) and leisure commodities (cars, bicycles, newspapers) and the basis of state involvement through grant aid to voluntary sector bodies (such as the CCPR) a legislative recognition of growing recreational demands (Access to the Mountains Act 1939) and the beginnings of a recognition of the potentially significant role of the state in providing recreational opportunities. The role and significance of the state was to be given a major impetus by the Second World War and the post-war reconstruction programme, often referred to as the establishment of the Welfare State.

The Welfare State and the Development of the Commercial, Voluntary and Public Sectors in Leisure

The massive increase in centralised state direction and control of all aspects of social and economic life during the Second World War combined with a wartime desire for a more equal society to lay the basis for the post-war reforms and the emergence of the Welfare State. The Labour government after 1945 passed legislation reforming and improving access to education, health, social security, unemployment benefit and so on. These reforms established access to a range of welfare services as a 'right of citizenship'.

The extension of rights to the sphere of leisure was more limited, although one of the few statutory obligations on local authorities to provide for leisure was contained in the Education Act 1944. This stated the value of 'recreative social training' and placed a duty on local education authorities to provide adequate further education facilities for 'leisure time occupations in organised cultural training and recreational activities ... for any person over compulsory school age'. As such wording indicates, much of post-war leisure policy remained within the rational recreation tradition and often adopted elitist formulations.

For example, in 1946 the Arts Council was established by Royal Charter to continue the work of the Council for the Encouragement of Music and the Arts (CEMA). This had been established in 1940 by the Pilgrim Trust to support the arts as a contribution to the nation's morale and to emphasise and reinforce notions of collective identity and purpose. However the policies of the Arts Council were rooted in elitist views of 'fine art' and critics suggested that the Arts Council very early abandoned CEMA's popularising approach in favour of 'few but roses' (Hutchinson, 1982).

Such a conservative approach was also present in the National Parks and Access to the Countryside Act 1949, which established the National Parks Commission with powers to designate areas of scenic beauty as National

Parks. The Commission was charged with the dual duties of preservation of natural landscapes and of producing opportunities for outdoor recreation. Although this Act was the culmination of a long struggle for access to the countryside its contribution was limited, with a priority given to conservation (Shoard, 1980; MacEwan and MacEwan, 1982).

Therefore, although the immediate post-war policies for leisure were framed within a general, diffuse commitment to the extension of rights of citizenship, their effective contribution to the democratisation of opportunities was relatively limited.

In the post-war period a major expansion occurred in the area of self-organisation and self-help in leisure with a substantial, if uneven, growth in the voluntary sector. Rises in real wages and small increases in non-work time (usually reductions in the working year rather than the working week) fuelled increased memberships of a variety of recreational and quasi-recreational organisations. For example, the English Golf Union tripled its membership between 1960 and 1976 (from 131,208 to 398,170) and the Ramblers' Association membership rose from 13,770 in 1968 to 31,950 in 1975 (Sports Council, 1986). Reflecting the growth in car ownership and increased mobility, the membership of the Camping and Caravan Club of Great Britain grew from 92,000 in 1965 to 157,000 in 1975 (Sports Council, 1986).

Problems of definition, the often unstable and transitory nature of many of these organisations and lack of systematic data makes it extremely difficult to measure the nature and scale of the voluntary sector. For example, Hoggett and Bishop (1986), in a study of two small areas in Bristol and Leicester, found a wide range of organisations such as military modelling, naturalists, amateur dramatics, aquarists, morris dancing, metal detecting and rat fancying. Newton (1976), in a study of voluntary sector activity in Birmingham, found approximately 3,000 such organisations. Although precise information is difficult to obtain it is not unreasonable to suggest that, in terms of the provision of leisure opportunities, the voluntary sector may be the most important sector in the mixed economy of leisure.

Of course the growth of this sector has not been uniform, with certain types of organisation experiencing decline and with their geographic distribution being uneven (Gratton and Taylor, 1987). Although most sporting organisations have experienced rapid and continuing growth (Sports Council, 1986) other, less activity-specific groups have declined. For example, membership of traditional organisations for women declined during the 1970s, with Women's Institute membership declining by 20% and the Townswomen's Guild by 32%

Current political thinking, with its emphasis on the reduction of direct public provision or management of services, places increasing emphasis on the role of the voluntary sector and the notion of 'voluntarism'. We will look at such policies later in this section but before that we must now turn to look briefly at the changing and expanding role of the commercial sector.

In a sense the growth in the nature and variety of out-of-home voluntary organisations appears to be in contradiction to developments and trends in the commercial sector. During the post-war period the commercial sector in leisure experienced both expansion and decline as the use of leisure time became more and more dominated by home-centred, 'privatised' forms.

Throughout the 1960s and 1970s rises in real wages, new technologies in both the industrial and service sectors, reductions in working hours and low unemployment served to create a new mass consumer market. The growing importance of consumerism in any understanding of leisure raises many of the same difficulties experienced in the voluntary sector of demarcating leisure and 'non-leisure'. Many goods have a dual function: while not being strictly leisure goods, their use may facilitate leisure – for example, washing machines and other domestic aids. Others, such as 'do-it-yourself', home improvements and central heating serve to make homes more comfortable and attractive places to spend leisure time. Cars purchased for non-leisure reasons (travel to work, taking children to school) also have obvious leisure uses. Other consumer durables have more direct leisure purposes – televisions, stereos, records, tapes and latterly videos.

Increased leisure opportunities faced older forms with competition and attendances at some traditional out-of-home entertainments declined. For example, annual attendances at professional football declined from 41 million in 1948–49 to 25 million in 1975–76 and cinema attendances declined from 21 million weekly attendances in 1956 to 1 million in 1984 (although by 1987 attendances had risen by 41% on the 1984 figure to average 75 million ticket sales per annum).

However other out-of-home opportunities emerged, reflecting changing social tastes and aspirations. For example, as increased leisure time occurred in the form of longer annual holidays this fuelled the growth of a travel industry to cater for both the home and overseas holiday markets. Between 1951 and 1979 holidays spent in Britain rose by 60% and holidays taken abroad rose by 700% (Open University, 1981). As with all such changes, however, the spread was not even throughout the population – in 1977, 41% of the population did not take a holiday (over 4 nights away from home) (Open University, 1981). Changing social habits led to rises in such things as eating out.

The decline in some traditional industrial sectors meant that the emerging leisure markets became a relatively attractive investment for capital. In such circumstances one of the main features of the commercial sector in leisure has been the increasing processes of market concentration. For example, in the United Kingdom 5 companies control 63% of the record market, 9 companies control 95% of the paperback book market, 3 companies control the majority of cinemas and 3 groups provide for over

70% of daily newspaper readers. Further, companies who initially concentrated on one aspect of service provision diversified to cater for a wide variety of leisure opportunities. For example, Granada owns television production, broadcasting and rental companies as well as bingo clubs, cinemas and theme parks; Grand Metropolitan owns 5 breweries which operate 4,700 pubs, hotels, betting and gaming clubs, wine and spirit businesses; First Leisure owns piers, holiday camps, leisure centres, discos, squash, snooker and health clubs, bowling alleys and theatres.

This degree of concentration and the domination of large sections of commercial leisure markets by so few companies has led critics to question the extent to which choice between real alternatives actually exists (Clarke and Critcher, 1985).

The growing commercialisation of leisure and the domination of leisure time by the home-based activities and various forms of electronic media mean that the role of the public sector in leisure provision is a relatively minor one – restricted largely to sport, recreation and the arts. Nevertheless public policy and provision in these areas has a significant influence on opportunities and patterns of provision and participation. Further, public policies often have important implications for both the commercial and voluntary sectors, variously constraining or facilitating their operations. The rest of this chapter will therefore concentrate on an analysis of the development of the contemporary framework of public sector institutions and strategic shifts in policy. Although it is recognised that much public policy may have 'leisure effects' – transport, housing, broadcasting, level of welfare benefit – and that state regulation controls large areas of leisure activity – gaming laws, licensing, VAT on entertainments – we will concentrate on the traditional areas of public subsidy and provision – sport, the arts and countryside recreation.

Throughout the post-war period there was a cross-party 'social democratic' consensus about the proper role of the public sector, and this underlay the gradual expansion of public provision and welfare services. Politicians both encouraged and responded to electoral pressures for an expanding range of publicly provided goods and services. Within this broad climate of opinion a relatively amorphous notion of a 'social service' combined with a local government commitment to 'service development' to increase public sector investment in leisure provision. The general commitment was given an impetus by the reorganisation of local government in 1974, which abolished a number of small district councils and created larger local government units. Leisure provision was in the first place a beneficiary of the rush of spending by the local authorities to be abolished by reorganisation. Secondly, the new larger local authorities adopted policies of corporate planning and many established unified service departments, resulting in a more comprehensive and unified approach to leisure planning and provision.

At national government level policy considerations and institutional reform resulted from a perception of the fundamental nature of economic and social change. New production technologies, increased industrial productivity, reductions in formal working hours, high employment levels and rises in real wages were presumed to be fuelling a 'leisure explosion'. It was suggested that there was a shift from a production-based industrial society to a 'post-industrial' society dominated by the service sector. Whereas the nineteenth-century 'problem of leisure' had been to construct industrial work disciplines, the modern problem was viewed as adjusting to new levels of affluence and increased leisure time – the 'containment of work'.

The general perceptions of the nature of social and economic change and the need for a governmental response is summarised by the 1966 report of the Advisory Sports Council as follows:

> We have entered an era of dramatic evolution in our material progress ... more and more people are acquiring greater leisure and the means to enjoy it ... consequently we are faced with the need for better, more abundant and sophisticated facilities for our leisure activities.

The implication was that citizenship rights were to include access to a range of recreational opportunities and much of the rhetoric of leisure policy was within a social welfare perspective. For example, the 1975 White Paper, *Sport and Recreation*, stated that 'in a society which enjoys substantial leisure time' the provision of recreational facilities was 'part of the general fabric of the social services'. The recognition of the limitations of the voluntary and commercial sectors led to the acceptance of an increased role for public involvement and investment. This was required because the capital requirements for certain types of facility were beyond the resources of the voluntary sector and the low profitability would fail to attract commercial investment.

Initially the strategic commitment was to cater for existing demand – to provide new sporting facilities, to reconcile the interests of conservation with increased recreational use of the countryside. However, once it was accepted that access to recreational opportunities was a right of citizenship, continuing inequalities in participation led to the definition of certain groups as 'recreationally deprived' and to the production of policies of 'recreational welfare'.

If citizenship was to be a reality then public provision must provide equal opportunities for all. As in the nineteenth century, a vague ideology of a 'natural' if latent 'community' underpinned many of the policies. All that was required was the removal of constraints to participation – as Bacon (1980) and Pearson (1982) argue, much policy and provision occurred within an ideological formulation that denied the significance of social class, and gender differences.

The aim of social policy shifted from catering for expressed demand to democratising access. 'Sport for all' (McIntosh and Charlton, 1985) and the 'democratisation of culture' (Green, 1977) became the rhetoric of social policy for leisure.

However, as with most social policy, these initiatives combined a desire to cater for new freedoms with a concern for social integration and social control. The effects of the social changes underlying the new 'leisure democracy' (Roberts, 1978) were not unambiguous. The welcoming of the new era was combined with a fear about the deleterious effects of the new freedoms (most especially among male working-class youth). Many of the new freedoms and choices were the result of the decline of traditional communal and economic constraints. Yet such changes also contained the possibility of diminished social controls as the influence of traditional community and family structure declined. The nineteenth-century concerns with the socially disruptive effects of social and economic change re-appeared in the rhetoric of leisure policy from the mid-1970s onwards.

Contemporary Structures and Policies

The broad orientation of leisure policy has shifted since the mid-1970s, from one of recreational welfare to one of 'recreation as welfare'. In the language of economists recreational provision was supported because of the 'externalities' or benefits which were associated with it. In particular, provision for sport was to be supported because of its supposed contribution to the reduction of vandalism and delinquency and ability to compensate for wider social and economic deprivations (for a critical assessment of some of these arguments see Coalter, 1988). The pragmatic emphasis on recreation as welfare was reinforced when rising unemployment (especially among young people) seemed to indicate that the 'containment of work' was to become the 'collapse of work' (Jenkins and Sherman, 1979). Rising unemployment, deteriorating urban environments and growing social unrest placed the issues of integration and control in the centre of the leisure agenda (Carrington and Leaman, 1982). These concerns were vividly illustrated in the 1975 White Paper, *Sport and Recreation*, which stated:

> By reducing boredom and urban frustration, participation in active recreation contributes to the reduction of hooliganism and delinquency among young people ... the social stresses on many young people today are enormous... If we delay too long in tackling the causes of these stresses constructively, the problems which arise from them will be magnified, and the cost of dealing with their results greatly increased. The need to provide for people to make the best of their leisure must be seen in this context (DoE, 1975).

This shift, from a social democratic concern with citizenship and welfare to a 'harder pragmatism', was reinforced by changing economic circumstances and fiscal policies. The economic crisis of the mid-1970s and the Labour government's approach to the International Monetary Fund

(IMF) for a loan led to growing restrictions on public expenditure. This 'new realism' was to be reinforced by the election in 1979 of a Conservative government, led by Margaret Thatcher, committed to monetarist economic policies and a reduction in public expenditure. Further, it was ideologically committed to the primacy of the market in the allocation of most goods and services. This laissez-faire approach stresses a minimal and residual role for public subsidy and provision and an increased role for the voluntary and commercial sectors, with individuals taking greater responsibility for personal consumption and welfare.

Such perspectives led to growing pressure to reduce dependence on state subsidies. Within the Sports Council and Arts Council this led to greater emphasis on the role of commercial sponsorship. Central government sought to reduce the levels of local government spending via a variety of initiatives such as the imposition of spending limits, penalties for overspending, rate capping and the proposal for the Community Charge (Poll Tax). More generally, government encouraged local authorities to increase economic efficiency and to reduce subsidies by increasing charges for certain services (for example, leisure provision). This has led to the compulsory process of 'competitive tendering' whereby local authorities are required to compete for the management of their leisure services against commercial bidders.

Many of these changes are reflected in the changing policies of the national leisure agencies, and it is to those that we now turn.

The current public sector structures for sport, arts and recreation were largely established in the late 1960s and early 1970s and reflected a number of concerns and interests – pressure from the voluntary sector, a perception of the need for new institutions to meet the challenge of changed social and economic conditions and a growing emphasis on systematic strategic planning.

Government policies for leisure are developed largely 'at arm's length' – through a system of quasi-independent bodies. The governmental and quasi-governmental institutional structures for sport, arts and recreation is characterised by its fragmented nature and apparently ad hoc policy development (Travis *et al.*, 1978). Some commentators regret this, suggesting that it prevents the development of an integrated and coherent leisure policy, while others suggest that such structures reflect the various interests, problems and dynamics which characterise the differing spheres of leisure (Coalter *et al.*, 1988).

There are a number of possible explanations for a reluctance by Government to become directly involved in policy formulation:

- **Overload**: Governments face increasingly complex problems of administration and management, making comprehensive, rational decision-making impossible. A solution is sought by delegating responsibility to quasi-government bodies.

- **Lack of government expertise**: As the range of government responsibilities increases there is an inevitable lack of expertise in particular areas. Policy decisions are therefore delegated to professionals or experts with a comprehensive knowledge of these areas.
- **Depoliticisation**: A 'liberal' version of this explanation is that judgements and policies concerning sport, recreation and artistic merit are regarded as being inappropriate areas for party-political judgements. They are viewed as pluralist areas (Roberts, 1978) in which a wide range of interests exist and it is necessary to have independent experts as a 'buffer' between such areas of policy and party-political judgements. For example, it is often asserted that aesthetic judgements concerning what art to fund is a non-political issue which is the province of experts.

A more radical version suggests that the function of quasi-governmental bodies is to 'depoliticise' social class issues, insulating them from the realm of adverserial policies and reducing them to purely 'technical' decisions made by professional experts. Some critics suggest that this is the process underlying the role of the Sports Council in seemingly redefining problems associated with inner city unrest and unemployment within the terms of leisure and sports provision (Carrington and Leaman, 1982; Coalter *et al.*, 1988).

Another version of such an explanation is that the 'arm's length' principle is used to distance government from areas where there is little political capital to be gained and much political danger. The quasi-independent body thereby manages any pressures and diverts them from government. The role of the Countryside Commission in seeking to reconcile the competing interests of agriculture, conservation and recreation might be regarded as illustrating this perspective (Coalter *et al.*, 1988; Cripps, 1979).

Sports Council

The roots of the Sports Council lie in the concerns of the voluntary sector (CCPR) with Britain's relative lack of international sporting success and with domestic issues relating to the politically deleterious effects of social and economic change. Attitudes towards work were changing, problems with youth symbolised the declining authority of the family. Sport, recreation, leadership, guidance and increased participation could all contribute to the reinforcement of social solidarity in times of rapid social change.

The CCPR established the Wolfenden Committee to address such issues, and its 1960 report pointed to a national shortage of recreational and sporting facilities. The proposed solutions under the slogan 'recreation for all', were greater aid to the voluntary sector, an increased role for local authority provision and the establishment of a Sports Development Council. The function of such an independent council would be to distribute grants and ensure the independence and plurality of sporting organisations.

The proposal for a Sports Development Council was rejected by the then Conservative government on the basis of a mixture of traditional Conservative commitment to a minimal state intervention, a concern not to 'politicise' sports administration and a desire to preserve the role of the voluntary sector – the role of the state should be 'supportive but non-directive' (McIntosh and Charlton, 1985; Coalter *et al.*, 1988).

The Labour government elected in 1964 was committed to a broadly ranging programme of reform and administration and an increase in strategic and corporate planning to enable a more rational use of resources and meeting of needs. Within this context the Advisory Sports Council (ASC) was established in 1965 to assist government in the rational and systematic planning of sport. The role of the ASC was to 'advise government on matters relating to the development of amateur sport and physical recreation, to foster co-operation among statutory authorities and voluntary organisations and to establish priorities for expenditure'. A system of Regional Sports Councils (RSCs) was established to facilitate regional co-ordination and determine future requirements for sporting facilities.

The policies of the ASC were essentially demand-led, aimed at encouraging local authorities to extend provision and opportunities for the inevitable rise in sporting and recreational demands in an increasingly affluent society. It provided research information concerning facility deficits, the nature of sporting demands and advised on relevant provision. However the ASC, via the allocation of grant-aid, had a more direct influence on the voluntary sector (the governing bodies of sport). During this period there was an intimate relationship between the ASC and the CCPR with the latter providing staff for the RSCs, and its Director General being seconded as the first Director of the ASC. Despite its concern to encourage local government planning and provision the main thrust of its early policies was to promote and modernise the voluntary sector and improve its efficiency and ability to promote sporting excellence.

These relationships and policies were to change gradually as a result of the establishment of an Executive Sports Council in 1971. On the premise of a lack of civil service and expertise (and a desire to keep as much as possible 'outside government') the Conservative government established the Sports Council as a quasi-independent government organisation. It was to be responsible not only for developing sporting excellence and catering for expressed demand but, more significantly, to provide sport and recreation 'in the interests of social welfare and the enjoyment of leisure among the public at large'. Whereas the ASC's function was to advise government on sporting issues, the Sports Council's Royal Charter required it 'to have regard to any statements of policy' of the government – a requirement which has led subsequent critics to suggest that the Sports Council often acts as an agent of government rather than an independent voice for sport (Howell, in Coalter *et al.*, 1988; Hargreaves, 1984). Certainly, in terms of social welfare concerns and urban policy, Sports Council initiatives have paralleled government policies more closely than either the Arts Council or Countryside Commission.

The slogan of the Sports Council, 'Sport for All', marked a shift from concentrating on supply to the promotion of demand (McIntosh and Charlton, 1985). The Sports Council adopted a more promotional and campaigning stance, seeking to educate the population as to the value of sport and to motivate previously non-participating groups.

Such policies were in part a result of a recognition that formal provision for expressed demand had failed to cater for large sections of the population. A growing recognition of social, cultural and economic obstacles to participation led to the adoption of the rhetoric of 'recreational welfare'. The 1975 White Paper, *Sport and Recreation*, provided a major impetus to such policies with its references to recreation provision as being 'part of the general fabric of the social services' and the need to recognise the existence of 'recreational disadvantage'. The White Paper also reflected wider concerns about economic uncertainty, inner city decline and the possibility of increased social instability. Recreational welfare and recreation as welfare were often inseparable as sport and recreation began to play a more prominent role in urban social policy. For example, in 1977 the Urban Programme was extended to include recreation provision (DoE, 1977a) and other government initiatives emphasised its importance in combating multiple deprivation – *Quality of Life Experiments* (DoE, 1977b), *Recreation and Deprivation in Inner Urban Areas* (DoE, 1977c).

The Sports Council endorsed such policies and its 1974–75 *Annual Report* referred to the ability of sport to act as 'a sociable and socialising activity, adding an important dimension to an integrated community life. It can bridge gaps between ethnic groups and cultures ... ameliorate social problems such as juvenile delinquency'. By 1981, following the urban riots, the Council was even more firmly convinced of the efficacy of 'recreation as welfare', referring to the urgent need to put more sports leaders on the streets because of 'the deteriorating situation in terms of unemployment and the problems caused by social unrest in the inner cities' (Sports Council, *Annual Report Report*, 1981–82).

The mid-1970s also produced two significant shifts in the methods advocated by the Sports Council. In the first place, a recognition that large-scale, conventional sports facilities failed to attract certain sections of the population led to an emphasis on more 'relevant' and accessible forms of provision. Such provision did not have to be purpose built but could be achieved by converting existing local facilities. This approach, stressing maximum and cost effective use of resources, was also congruent with the climate of financial constraints being imposed on local government spend-ing. Secondly, social service models of 'outreach' work were adopted. Those not reached by conventional promotion and marketing were to be integrated by 'putting sports leaders on the streets' to provide 'leadership' and 'motivation'. Increasingly more systematic methods of 'targeting' particular groups for 'positive discrimination' were adopted and, following the urban riots of 1981, the Sports Council established the Action Sport scheme. This sought to deploy 'street motivators' to penetrate particular communities or groups which previous initiatives had failed to reach (Sports Council, *Annual Report*, 1982–83).

Having regard to government priorities (as required by the Royal Charter) the Sports Council's policy orientation therefore gradually shifted from developing a social policy for sport to addressing issues concerning the role of sport in urban and social policy. In terms of grant-aid such a shift was not immediate and throughout the 1970s and early 1980s the Sports Council funding allocations continued to favour governing bodies and elite participation (Gratton, 1980; Sports Council, *Annual Report*, 1979–80; Sports Council, 1982).

Nevertheless, the growing congruence between government and Sports Council policy was reinforced in 1978 when the Council acted as an agent of government, agreeing to administer funds ear-marked for specific purposes (£802,500 for deprived urban areas; £1.7 million for the Football and the Community scheme). This led critics to suggest that the Sports Council had compromised its independence which is based largely on the ability to decide its own grant allocations.

More fundamental shifts, especially with regard to relationships with the voluntary sector, occurred after the election of a Thatcherite Conservative government in 1979. This government's emphasis on managerialism, stricter forms of financial accounting and commercial sponsorship led to strategic shifts in the Council's administrative philosophy and policies. Its strategy document, *Sport in the Community: The Next Ten Years* (Sports Council, 1982), announced the intention to shift its funding priorities towards a more concerted attempt to ensure greater levels of participation (for both recreational welfare and recreation as welfare motives). As part of this reorientation and an increased emphasis on corporate planning, funding for governing bodies became conditional on ensuring that their policies reflected the Council's priorities and made a contribution to their achievement. Rather than responding to the self-defined needs and policies of particular organisations the Council was now insisting that these organisations 'have due regard' to its own policy objectives. Rather than providing a framework for voluntarism (via funding, advice, administrative support) the Council now adopted a much more directive role. This was in part the result of an acknowledgement that not only were such bodies not representative of all sports participants but also they often made only a limited contribution to promoting mass participation. Such policies have exacerbated long-standing tensions with the representative body of the organised sporting sector – the CCPR – as to who is the true voice of British sport.

These policies were reinforced by a letter in November 1987 from the Minister of Sport (Colin Moynihan) to the Director of the Sports Council. In this letter the Minister asked a series of questions about the nature of the Council's role and questioned whether or not the Council should disengage from supporting elite competitors and concentrate more on encouraging community provision and areas and groups with special needs.

Recent changes in Council membership and the retirement of senior staff (allegedly opposed to new policy directions) have led to accusations that the Council has departed from its traditional balance of interests. Perhaps paradoxically, as the Sports Council has increased its efforts to promote mass participation (the latest initiative being the 'Ever Thought of Sport?' campaign), has emphasised the role of sport in the solution to broader social problems, has promoted the growth of sponsorship and illustrated the economic importance of sport (Sports Council, 1987) and imposed a 'pattern of purpose' on the organised sports bodies, its own future is now being questioned.

Arts Council

We have already noted that the Arts Council was established in 1946 to continue the wartime work of CEMA. The rationale for such a quasi-independent organisation was that party-political judgements should not influence aesthetic and artistic judgements and that artistic excellence should not be dependent on the profit motives of the market place. Therefore, unlike the Sports Council, which dealt almost exclusively with amateur sports organisations, the Arts Council, by funding professional artists, supported a quasi-commercial market for art. Certain similarities exist in the rationale for the support of 'excellence' in both sport and arts – they were regarded as contributing to national morale and, via emulation, could lead to increased public participation.

The original Royal Charter required the Arts Council to increase public access and to promote the development of a greater knowledge, understanding and practice of 'the fine arts exclusively' – thereby narrowing its focus and retreating from CEMA's more popularising approach. A policy of 'few but roses' led to a stress on developing centres of excellence and a responsive rather than initiating funding stance. This in turn led to a metropolitan bias with funding and provision becoming concentrated in London, with the Council taking responsibility for grant-aiding The Royal Opera House, Royal Shakespeare Company, English National Opera and National Theatre (from 1963). Such funding, eventually accounting for about one-third of the Council's total budget, introduced a good deal of flexibility into the Council's grant-aid policies due to the political impossibility of removing subsidies from these organisations. This metropolitan bias was accentuated by the closure of its regional offices during the 1950s.

The response of the voluntary sector and the role of philanthropy to these moves is of interest. Just as the Pilgrim Trust had provided the initial funding for CEMA so another charitable organisation (Gulbenkian Foundation) funded various voluntary organisations enabling the establishment of the Regional Arts Associations – which the Arts Council eventually agreed to fund in 1961 (Coalter *et al.*, 1988).

A White Paper, *A Policy for the Arts*, was produced in 1965 by the recently returned Labour government. As part of a broad reform of economic, social and cultural institutions the White Paper led to the appointment of a minister with special responsibility for the Arts, substantially increasing funding and the broadening of the focus from 'fine arts' to arts generally. Jazz, photography and dance were accorded limited recognition and the new Chairman, Lord Goodman, announced what appeared to be a significant change in policy. Although the improvement of standards and quality were important 'it is not our paramount consideration ... the major emphasis is on creating new audiences for the arts' (quoted in Coalter *et al.*, 1988).

This policy, referred to as the 'democratisation of culture', was based on liberal ideas of the civilising nature of traditional art and that it should be available to all. As with the Sports Council there was a growing realisation that mere formal provision was not enough to ensure participation – education and increased knowledge were necessary. However as such educative policies were being contemplated (if not properly funded), the community arts movement began to question the nature of the art to be 'democratised'. Rather than the dissemination of traditional art forms downward the community arts movement proposed 'cultural democracy' – the broadening of the definition of what was to count as 'art' and the proposal that all should have the opportunity to participate in the production of art rather than be mere consumers. Rather than seeing art as some material product (painting, play, music) the community arts movement stressed art as participation, involvement and process.

The uneasy relationship between the Arts Council and the community arts movement was in part resolved in 1979 by delegating responsibility to the Regional Arts Associations and local government, emphasising their essentially local character.

Part of the Arts Council's reluctance to become involved with community arts may be explained by its focus on professional rather than amateur artists and its essentially demand-led strategies. Unlike the Sports Council the Arts Council has rarely been directly concerned with the social composition of audiences. It concentrated largely on maintaining professional theatres, artists, writers and performers, leaving questions about audience composition to its subsidised clients. Therefore, unlike the Sports Council, the Arts Council placed a low priority on recreational or cultural welfare. Further it largely rejected policies based on ideas of recreation as welfare – such 'social policy' concerns were regarded as outside its remit. For example the Chairman of the Arts Council was explicit in stating that, because of a limited budget, it was important that the Council did not 'stop doing our job in order to do somebody else's job' (quoted in Coalter *et al.*, 1988).

As with the Sports Council the election of the Thatcher government in 1979, committed to monetarist policies and reduction of public expenditure, had an effect on the practices of the Arts Council. Many 'New Right' philosophers and politicians agreed that the market should decide what art should be produced and that subsidies merely provided unpopular or 'bad art'. It responded to changed economic and ideological circumstances by placing an increasing emphasis on commercial sponsorship and the importance of business and managerial expertise. This was in part achieved via a series of new appointments to the Council (and a few well-publicised departures of opponents to the new orientation). In 1983 Luke Rittner, previously in charge of an organisation called Business Sponsorship of the Arts, was appointed Secretary General.

Historically the Arts Council has shown a reluctance to plan for art, regarding bureaucratic direction and control as inappropriate to the world of artistic expression. However, in responding to the government's policies the Council produced a major review of its work, *The Glory of the Garden*, which outlined a more directive approach. This proposed a change in its funding policies from the traditional 'response funding' to one of 'challenge funding'. This took the form of a challenge to its clients and potential clients to obtain matching funding, with the implication that the money should be already available as part of the grant application. Although this did not amount to a formal planning procedure it was nevertheless designed to 'establish a pattern of purpose' whereby organisations become more self-sufficient and are encouraged to propose initiatives in line with the Council's publicised plans (a policy shift similar to that which occurred in the Sports Council). *The Glory of the Garden* also proposed a decentralisation of policy-making by devolving responsibility for funding to the regions. However, without substantial changes in funding priorities and with the abolition of the Metropolitan Counties (major funders of the arts) the economic position of the regions has not improved.

Like the Sports Council, the Arts Council has increasingly emphasised the externalities associated with the arts as well as their aesthetic value. Public subsidies to the arts are now argued for because of the economic importance of the arts in providing jobs, generating taxable income and attracting foreign tourists (Myerscough, 1988). While not opposed in principle to increased commercial sponsorship, many are concerned that commercial considerations will mean that the glamorous, safe and successful art forms will be supported to the detriment of new and experimental forms. The fear is, further, that if commercial sponsorship grows it may not simply supplement public funding but replace it in certain areas.

Therefore, like the Sports Council, the Arts Council in responding to a government committed to market forces and hostile to public expenditure has undergone substantial changes in its policies. These changes have affected the balance between the Council, its clients and the market. The former liberal policy of supporting, encouraging and responding to its clients has shifted to a more directive stance and the original intention to remove artistic production from the commercial demands of the market (Williams, 1981) has been greatly modified.

Countryside Commission

Throughout the 1950s and 1960s increased leisure time, rises in real wages and the spread of car ownership led to greatly increased levels of informal countryside recreation. For example, although adequate survey data is not available admission figures at 45 National Trust properties show that between 1955 and 1978 there was a 7 per cent rate of growth (Patmore, 1983). This gave rise to growing concern about the possible effects of recreation on the countryside and the need to reconcile the interests of agricultural production, conservation and recreation. This was a major theme in the 1966 White Paper, *Leisure in the Countryside*, which referred to the problem of reconciling the recreational demands of townspeople with the requirements of those who lived and worked in the countryside. Concern with the reconciliation of interests was central to the Countryside Act 1968 which established the Countryside Commission.

The Commission replaced the National Parks Commission and was given wider powers and responsibilities for all countryside areas in England and Wales. Unlike the Arts Council and the Sports Council the Countryside Commission was not created as a quasi-independent government body but remained as part of the Department of the Environment until 1982. Further, unlike the Arts Council and Sports Council, whose main aims included the promotion of participation in leisure activities, the role of the Countryside Commission was to meet expressed demand and to seek to reconcile this with the interests of agricultural and conservation – the role was not to encourage people to go to the countryside, to 'identify, tap and encourage latent demand' (Adrian Phillips, quoted in Coalter *et al.*, 1988).

The initial response to the increasing demand for countryside recreation was to view it as a problem to be contained. It was viewed as a 'Fourth Wave' (Dower, 1965) – a social change sweeping across the countryside with the same radical effects as urbanisation, the growth of the railways or suburbanisation. The fear was of 'access in excess' (Fitton, 1979).

A central theme of the 1966 White Paper was therefore the need to direct town-dwellers away from remote countryside by providing specially managed country parks closer to the main centres of population. Although the creation of such parks was to be the responsibility of the County

Councils the Commission had a major role to play in encouraging and supporting such developments. Although such policies undoubtedly contributed to the extension of recreational opportunities, critics also suggest that they indicate that from the beginning the Commission's policies were dominated by the 'conservation imperative', which also had to have 'due regard' to the economic needs of agriculture. It was within these conflicting pressures that the Commission sought to develop policies for recreational access to the countryside. In terms of relationships with the various interests the Commission has had much stronger links with the agricultural and conservation bodies, such as the Council for the Protection of Rural England, or with those with a dual conservation–recreation role, such as the Ramblers' Association, than with those solely concerned with sports or outdoor pursuits.

Further, being part of a government department raised a number of dilemmas for the Commission as it sought to reconcile the roles of being both a government agency and a pressure group representing interests often in conflict with government (Cripps, 1979). The Commission found itself at a public inquiry opposing government plans for the M25 route throught the Kent Downs Area of Outstanding Natural Beauty, seeking to amend the National Parks and Access to the Countryside Act 1949 to require a public inquiry following the government's refusal to designate a Cambrian National Park and opposing the wholly voluntary approach to landscape conservation in the Wildlife and Countryside Act 1981. Such conflicts and restrictions on financial management and staff appointments led the Commission to push for 'independence', which was achieved in 1982.

The Council's approach to its remit has undergone a number of broad shifts throughout the 1970s and 1980s. Like the Sports Council it is largely dependent on the co-operation of local authorities to implement policy (in an area which is not a mandatory local government function). The Commission seeks to influence local government via a mixture of financial incentives, technical information, establishment of suggested standards for provision and demonstration projects.

The initial approach was to work through the formal planning process and seek to get conservation and recreation issues included in structure and local plans. However the limitations of this approach (agricultural use of land is exempt from planning control) and the realisation that it was not an appropriate system for dealing with many smaller scale countryside issues led the Commission to propose policies of 'countryside management' (Sidaway *et al.*, 1986).

This shift in policy was also motivated by a partial shift in the Commission's concerns as the fear of 'access in excess' was replaced by a concern for the deleterious effects of agricultural change. Intensive agricultural production and demands of new farming technology were leading to a transformation of the landscape with a loss of trees and hedgerows and reduction in access opportunities.

However, faced with the economic imperatives of agriculture (encouraged by EEC farming subsidies), and the planning exempt status of farming land, the Commission could only adopt the mixture of voluntarism and agreement which was the basis of the countryside management approach. This entailed using the powers of local government to enter into voluntary agreements with landowners to provide financial assistance and help in undertaking landscape conservation and facilitating informal recreation. To encourage the adoption of this approach the Commission financed the Upland Management Experiments in the late 1960s and experiments in the urban fringe in the early 1970s.

This mixture of voluntarism and financial incentives was extended to recreational access via provisions in the Countryside Act 1968 which provided financial assistance to landowners who entered into access agreements. The provisions in the Act for compulsory access orders have seldom been used, in part indicating the low priority given to recreational access by local government and the power of the farming interests.

The Wildlife and Countryside Act 1981 represented a further attempt to intervene in market forces via a mixture of financial incentives and voluntarism. This legislation was concerned with conservation rather than access and represented a small step away from the laissez-faire approach in which 'stewardship' of the countryside was left to private landowners. The Act permitted local authorities to enter into management agreements with landowners and to provide them with financial compensation for refraining from particular types of development (usually in ecologically sensitive areas). This legislation led to a number of abuses as it provided an incentive to threaten to develop otherwise uneconomic land.

Although the Commission formally accepted the Act they had expressed reservations during the consultation phase that depending solely on voluntary agreements might not be enough and that 'government should give themselves the power to act should voluntary processes break down' (Countryside Commission, *Annual Report*, 1979). This realisation that voluntarism or agreement might not be enough is at the root of the dilemmas faced by the Commission in its attempts to reconcile the various interests of agriculture, conservation and recreation – to seek to use persuasion to ameliorate the effects of the economic imperatives of agricultural production. In such circumstances the interests of conservation and even more of recreation are inevitably marginalised. For example, in its 1979 *Annual Report*, referring to the Ministry of Agriculture, Fisheries and Food, the Commission stated that it had 'cause to regret a lack of regard for conservation and recreation in Ministry policy and practice'.

Because of this the Commission has long argued for the need for a Royal Commission to investigate the possibility of co-ordinating government policies for agriculture, conservation and recreation. In the absence of a broadly-based economic and social strategy for the use of the countryside then the economic imperatives of agricultural production will be paramount. Some recent changes, such as a reduction of EEC subsidies and the imposition of production quotas, have led to some agricultural land being taken out of production and there is a growing debate about the potential of recreational use and tourism as an 'alternative crop'. However, whatever the result of such changes and initiatives the Commission will continue to seek to reconcile unequal interests in a system which will remain dominated by the strategic demands of profit and production.

A further constraint on the Commission is its dependence on local government to implement its policies. However, continuing financial constraints on local government and the non-mandatory status of recreational provision, place severe restrictions on the Commission's effectiveness. One response has been to place an increased emphasis on 'voluntarism' and the role of the voluntary sector. The Commission, via grant-aid, has sought to strengthen the administrative structure and effectiveness of this sector to achieve its predominantly conservationist goals (e.g., British Trust for Conservation Volunteers, Royal Society for the Protection of Birds).

The scope for commercial sponsorship is much less in this area than in sport and the arts. However a Commission-promoted initiative, 'Operation Groundwork', has sought to obtain commercial funding for small-scale environmental and access improvement work in the urban fringe. This initiative seeks to create a partnership between local voluntary groups, local authorities and the commercial sector. Significantly, and reflecting the current government's philosophies, the initiative has been established as a Trust, outside the formal structures of local government, 'privatising' certain aspects of provision. This process has been reinforced by the establishment of a Groundwork Foundation aimed at attracting commercial sponsorship. However, despite these developments, the attractiveness of conservation and informal recreation to commercial sponsors seems likely to be limited.

Despite these various initiatives the questions remain as to whether the root issues in the countryside are the reconciliation of differences, the need for greater co-ordination and co-operation or, as MacEwan and MacEwan (1982) suggest, whether 'the authorities have the ultimate power to control major land use decisions'.

In many ways the effectiveness of the quasi-independent government bodies in leisure depends on their ability to appear to be independent of government – to 'depoliticise' issues. However in all cases they are required 'to have regard to' government priorities. Having taken those priorities on board, their capacity to 'represent' the interests of their organised lobbies (sporting, artistic, recreational) has become increasingly restricted. Critics have suggested that rather than representing the interests of their various constituencies to government these agencies are in danger of representing the interests of government to their constituencies. However, it is mistaken to view increased government influence or direction as indicating an increased concern with 'leisure policy'. Rather, increased directiveness represents a more general attempt to restructure aspects of the state apparatus, to reduce general levels of public subsidy and to introduce market principles to aspects of social policy.

Local Government: Current Dilemmas

Despite the strategic importance of the quasi-independent government bodies local government, as direct provider and subsidiser, still remains the largest public sector provider of leisure opportunities (expenditure amounted to £1,882 million in 1985–86). However local government is also experiencing the ideological pressures and economic constraints outlined above. Pressures to reduce public subsidies, to increase economic efficiency, to define and measure performance effectively (see Sports Council, Greater London and the South East, 1988), and to become more consumer-led have resulted in the Local Government Bill 1987 introducing compulsory competitive tendering for the management of a range of services. This process has been extended to leisure services, with local authorities being compelled to draw up tenders and compete with commercial companies for the right to manage public sector facilities.

Such policies may transform the rationale for and practice of local government leisure provision. Already some authorities are entering joint venture schemes with commercial companies and the potential role of leisure provision in economic development and job creation increasingly are being emphasised. Leisure and cultural facilities are being used to create an environment attractive to new or relocating industries and leisure-based initiatives in areas like the London and Bristol docks are used to regenerate inner city areas and attract tourist income.

Policies of recreational welfare undoubtedly have increased opportunities for a number of targeted groups, although there remain substantial differences in participation rates among social and economic groups. However, despite the 1975 White Paper's designation of leisure services as part of 'the general fabric of the social services' they have occupied an ambiguous position between ideologies of welfare ('need') and ideologies of the market ('demand' or 'profit'). This ambiguity is due in part to an ideology of leisure as being a private sphere in which individual choice and responsibility is paramount and in which the notion of 'need' (the basis of welfare provision) is difficult to define. This may mean that the welfare elements of leisure services may become more difficult to defend. Increased emphasis on a 'managerialist' approach and a concern with 'efficiency' (income maximisation, financially optimal use of resources) may undermine the 'equity' objectives of social policy (Gratton and Taylor, 1985).

This of course is not a necessary outcome of such changes. An efficient use of resources may mean that subsidies are concentrated on those groups least able to pay the full economic cost of participation. However as Gratton and Taylor (1985) point out, the traditional supply-side approach (subsidising activities or facilities) is not the most efficient or equitable method. They suggest that equity (and efficiency) might better be assured by demand-side subsidies which are targeted to identifiable disadvantaged groups. However, such a scheme would be administratively complex and if simple economic imperatives became the driving force of local government leisure services the emphasis may be placed on the maximisation of income and use (irrespective of the social composition of participants).

It would seem that the new policy developments – which entail not only an economic emphasis on efficiency and reduction of subsidy but also an ideological commitment to the reduction of the scale of public sector provision – represent an historic shift in the rationale for leisure services. Concerns with recreational welfare would seem to be weakened by a broad shift towards a more market-oriented, income maximising approach to the delivery of leisure services. It would seem that the dilemmas between ideologies of welfare and the market, which have characterised leisure services may be resolved in favour of the market. In this chapter we have sought to trace the foundations of, and shifting balance between the major sectors of, the leisure industries in Britain. In doing so we have highlighted the nature of contemporary pressures on public and voluntary bodies to achieve more 'commercially viable' positions. Thus the adoption of a more entrepreneurial approach to management and planning in the public and commercial sectors should be anticipated. In the chapters which follow, therefore, one can expect to find a blurring of the distinctions between management styles and approaches adopted in the different sectors in leisure.

Further Reading

A number of texts deal with the historical background to the emergence of leisure and provision in the nineteenth century. Of these Cunningham (1980), Bailey (1979) and Malcolmson (1973) cover a range of perspectives and are among the most readable. The inter-war period is less well covered, Jones (1986) being one of the few texts to have a central focus on the history of leisure for that period.

There are a number of items cited in the references which deal with leisure and leisure policy in the public sector, usually by reference to the area of activity, such as the arts (Hutchinson, 1982; Myerscough, 1988), sport (McIntosh and Charlton, 1985; Hargreaves, 1984), countryside recreation (MacEwan and MacEwan, 1982, Shoard, 1980). As the commentary in the chapter suggests, there is considerably less attention paid to the voluntary sector, or even the commercial sector, though Hoggett and Bishop (1986), and Gratton and Taylor (1987) provide notable exceptions.

Some of the major arguments of this chapter are rehearsed more fully in Coalter *et al.* (1988). Interestingly contrasting accounts of the development of leisure and the nature and significance of policy are given in Roberts (1978) and Clarke and Critcher (1985).

References

Advisory Sports Council (1966) *Report*, London: HMSO.
Bacon, A.W. (1980) *Social Planning, Research and the Provision of Leisure Services*, Centre for Leisure Studies, Salford University.
Bailey, P. (1979) *Leisure and Class in Victorian England*, London: Routledge.
Bramham, P. and Henry, I. (1985) 'Political Ideology and Leisure Policy in the United Kingdom', *Leisure Studies*, 4 (1).
Carrington, B. and Leaman, D. (1982) 'Work for Some and Sport for All', *Youth and Policy*, 1 (3).
Clarke, J. and Critcher, C. (1985) *The Devil Makes Work: Leisure in Capitalist Britain*, London: Macmillan.
Coalter, F., with Duffield, B. and Long, J. (1988) *Recreational Welfare: The Rationale for Public Sector Investment in Leisure,* London: Avebury/Gower.
Coalter, F. (1988) *Sport and Anti-Social Behaviour: A Literature Review, Research Report no. 2, Scottish Sports Council, Edinburgh.*
Countryside Commission (1979) Annual Report, Cheltenham, Countryside Commission.
Cripps, J. (1979) *The Countryside Commission: Government Agency or Pressure Group?*, Town Planning Discussion Paper, 31, University College, London.
Cunningham, H. (1980) *Leisure in the Industrial Revolution*, London: Croom Helm.
Department of the Environment (1975) *Sport and Recreation*, London: HMSO.
Department of the Environment (1977a) *Policy for the Inner City*, London: HMSO.
Department of the Environment (1977b) *Leisure and the Quality of Life: A Report on Four Local Experiments*, London: HMSO.
Department of the Environment (1977c) *Recreation and Deprivation in Inner Urban Areas*, London: HMSO.
Dower, M. (1965) *The Challenge of Leisure: the Fourth Wave*, London: Architectural Press.
Evans, J. (1974) *Service to Sport: The Story of the CCPR 1935–1972*, London: Pelham Books.
Fitton, M. (1979) 'Countryside Recreation: the problems of opportunity', *Local Government Studies* July/August.
Gratton, C. (1980) 'Efficiency and Equity: Aspects of Public Subsidies to Sport and Recreation', paper presented to Sports Council/SSRC Research Council Seminar, *Economics of Leisure*, University of Kent.
Gratton, C. and Taylor, P. (1985) *Sport and Recreation: An Economic Analysis*, London: E. & F.N. Spon.
Gratton, C. and Taylor, P. (1987) *Leisure Industries: an Overview*, London: Comedia.
Green, M. (1977) *Issues and Problems in the Decentralising of Cultural Planning*, Centre for Contemporary Cultural Studies, University of Birmingham.
Hargreaves, J. (1984) 'State Intervention in Sport and Hegemony in Britain', paper presented to the Leisure Studies Association, International Conference, *People, Planning and Politics*, Brighton.

Hill, H. (1980)   *Freedom to Roam*, London: Moorland Publishing.
Hoggett, P. and Bishop, J. (1986)   *The Social Organisation of Leisure: A Study of Groups in their Voluntary Sector Context*, London: Sports Council/ESRC.
Hutchinson, R. (1982)   *The Politics of the Arts Council*, London: Sinclair Browne.
Jenkins, C. and Sherman, B. (1979)   *The Collapse of Work*, London: Eyre Methuen.
Jones, G.S. (1986)   *Workers at Play*, London: Routledge.
MacEwan, A. and MacEwan, M. (1982)   *National Parks: Conservation or Cosmetics?*, London: Allen & Unwin.
McIntosh, P. and Charlton, V. (1985)   *The Impact of Sport For All Policy 1966–1984 and a Way Forward*, London: Sports Council.
Malcolmson, R.W. (1973)   *Popular Recreations in English Society, 1700–1850*, Cambridge: Cambridge University Press.
Mellor, H. (1976)   *Leisure and the Changing City 1870–1914*, London: Routledge.
Myerscough, J. (1988)   *The Economic Importance of the Arts in Great Britain*, London: PSI.
Newton, K. (1976)   *Second City Politics*, Oxford: Clarendon Press.
Open University (1981)   *Popular Culture and Everyday Life*, U203 Popular Culture: Block 3, Units 1 and 11, Milton Keynes: Open University Press.
Patmore, A. (1983)   *Recreation and Resources,* London: Basil Blackwell
Pearson, N. (1982)   *The State and the Visual Arts*, Milton Keynes: Open University Press.
Roberts, K. (1978)   *Contemporary Society and the Growth of Leisure*, London: Longman.
Shoard, M. (1980)   *The Theft of the Countryside*, London: Temple Smith.
Sidaway, R. *et al.* (1986)   *Access to the Countryside for Recreation and Sport*, Sports Council/Countryside Commission.
Sports Council (1979–80; 1981–82; 1982–83)   *Annual Report*.
Sports Council (1982)   *Sport in the Community: the Next Ten Years*, London: Sports Council.
Sports Council (1986)   *Digest of Sports Statistics*, London: Sports Council.
Sports Council (1987)   *The Economic Impact and Importance of Sport in the United Kingdom*, London: Sports Council.
Sports Council, Greater London and South East (1988)   *Regional Recreation Strategy*, London: Sports Council.
Travis, A. *et al.* (1978)   *The Role of Central Government in Relation to Local Authority Leisure Services in England and Wales*, Centre for Urban and Regional Studies, University of Birmingham.
Walker, S. and Duffield, B. (1982)   *Urban Parks and Open Spaces: A Review*, London: Sports Council/ESRC.
Williams, R. (1981)   *The Arts Council: Politics and Policies*, London: Arts Council.

2 Planning for Leisure: The Commercial and Public Sectors

Ian Henry and John Spink

Introduction

In this chapter we seek to identify key features of planning activity in both the public and commercial sectors of the leisure industries. Although there are distinctive literatures for planning in both sectors, clearly planning as an activity, and theories about planning as a process, enjoy common features. Planning is an activity which involves the attempt by an actor or actors to establish conditions which are likely to be favourable to the achievement of some desired outcome. This may involve providing a community with facilities and services through which some of its members can meet some of their wants or 'needs', or it may involve the development of strategies which allow a commercial organisation to exploit profit opportunities in certain market segments. In both cases there exists in the literature a range of material indicating how the planner should go about achieving those aims (though much of this is not specific to the leisure field). Such literature may be *prescriptive*, indicating how planners ought to plan, or it may be *evaluative*, analysing how in fact planners do go about developing plans. This review will draw on both types of literature, but the reader should bear in mind that evaluating these types of commentary involves the use of different criteria.

Treatment of *leisure* planning in the literature can be described as somewhat unsystematic and fragmented. This chapter therefore attempts both to redress the imbalance in sources specifically dedicated to leisure planning and to explore the relationship between planning activity in public and commercial sectors by juxtaposing arguments and materials germane to both sectors. The framework adopted involves a discussion of *systems and structures* of planning, *styles and techniques* adopted, and the pressures on and *potential* for leisure planning in both the public and commercial sectors of the leisure industries.

Organisational Goals and Planning

In dealing with leisure planning in both sectors, the chapter will largely restrict itself to consideration of *organisational planning* in the commercial sector, and with *statutory planning* for communities, or 'town planning' in the public sector. However it should be evident that organisational planning (i.e., planning to achieve goals set for a given organisation) is as necessary in the public sector, be it planning to achieve goals for a local authority department or a leisure quango, as it is in commercial sector organisations. One of the serious difficulties encountered in undertaking comparison of planning in public and commercial sector organisations is that of the difference in the aims or 'missions' of organisations in the two sectors. Generally a commercial organisation's performance can be measured (in terms of prescriptive managerial theory) in terms of profit in, for example, calculating the return on investment achieved. Where an organisation operates in the not-for-profit sector, as is the case with many public sector leisure organisations, performance cannot be evaluated by reference to such readily quantifiable indicators. If planning therefore involves striving to reach a specified set of goals, the nature of the differences in goals between the two sectors should be identified.

Figure 2.1 shows a mission statement, the overall aim of a major multi-national company operating in certain leisure and other related consumer product and service markets. The Grand Metropolitan Group consists of a number of divisions operating in fields such as brewing, international hotels and tourism and gaming as well as consumer products. The achievement of aims embedded in its mission statement is to be accomplished through the work of each of the divisions for which objectives are set in terms of projected sales, market share, profit margins, return on investment, and so on. Although the statement gives expression to a number of subsidiary conditions necessary for the achievement of the mission (such as respecting the environment in which the company operates) nevertheless the primary goal is profitability – to produce 'a consistently high quality and growing return to its owners'. The objectives or strategies of individual divisions can therefore be evaluated by reference to the long-term aim of maximising profitability of the group as a whole.

By contrast, the aims of a public sector body such as the Countryside Commission are laid down in legislation. Figure 2.1 cites the general functions of the Commission as described in the Countryside Act 1968. In place of a hierarchy of goals with profit clearly established as the primary aim, the functions as listed express potentially conflicting responsibilities of conservation on the one hand, and access and recreational opportunity on the other. The same difficulties could be illustrated by reference to the aims of other leisure quangos (the Arts Council and the Sports Council) or by reference to the goals of local government provision. The point of

Figure 2.1 Aims of private and public sector leisure organisations

Grand Metropolitan PLC: Mission Statement

The management of Grand Metropolitan is dedicated to conducting the affairs of the Group in such a way that the value of its business is maintained, while it produces a consistently high quality and growing return for its owners.

Our chosen field of activity is consumer products and services in the food, drink and personal services sectors. We add value to our products and services by building brands in order to achieve good margins and sustain profitability over time.

Our objective is to source our revenues equally between the domestic market of the UK, the domestic market of the USA, and the international market, in order to guard our assets and profits from economic and political risks.

The core business sectors in which we operate are appropriate to the existing and developing skills of our management and workforce. Our aim is to produce a balance between mature and developing businesses, between those which are cash generating and cash demanding, and between our fixed and tangible assets, such as property, and intangible assets such as brands.

The size and spread of the interests of the Group enable us to commit considerable resources to the development of new businesses, the building of brands, and to sustain the operation of businesses during adverse market conditions.

We seek to be a good neighbour, to behave in an exemplary manner towards customers, employees and shareholders, and to respect the environment in which we operate.

Countryside Commission: Statement of the Aims and Functions

The functions conferred by this Act on the said Commission . . . are to be exercised for the conservation and enhancement of the natural beauty and amenity of the countryside, and encouraging the provision and improvement, for persons resorting to the countryside, of facilities for the enjoyment of the countryside and of open-air recreation in the countryside.

Figure 2.1 is to underline the fact that, if one accepts profit maximisation as the primary aim of a commercial organisation, a coherent and unified hierarchy of objectives can (at least in principle) be operationally defined, in quantitative terms, and their achievement can therefore be readily monitored. The situation is somewhat different for the public sector organisation where goals are expressed in qualitative terms, where they incorporate potentially conflicting goals, from which it is difficult to establish clear unambiguous measures of performance. Thus planning in such not-for-profit organisations is inherently more problematic than is the case in commercial organisations.

Planning for local communities as opposed to public or private sector organisations is even more problematic. Prescriptive management theory provides us with the premise of a primary objective in the form of profit maximisation for the commercial firm, while public sector organisational aims (albeit qualitative and perhaps inconsistent) may be spelt out in the constitution of those organisations. However, in the case of planning for a particular community, the goals themselves, as well as the means of achieving those goals, are the subject of debate.

Leisure Planning in the Commercial Sector

The Structure of Planning in the Commercial Sector

The structure of commercial leisure has, in common with many other industrial sectors, been subject to considerable structural change. The size of firms operating in this field, the nature of their investments, and the leisure forms provided, have evolved with industrial change. We have identified elsewhere (Haywood *et al.*, 1989) a number of key features in the recent history of leisure markets. Such factors include the growing significance of large-scale multinational organisations operating in the leisure markets, diversification of such large companies across a wide range of markets both within the leisure sphere and other areas of industry, and vertical integration with larger firms becoming attracted to small-scale outlets for service provision such as squash clubs, health clubs, and snooker halls. A brief review of some of the activities of the major quoted companies on the stock exchange operating in the leisure area will illustrate such trends. Nevertheless the leisure industries still incorporate a range of different types of organisation, and planning will tend to vary from one such type to another.

Although it is possible to identify where a formal responsibility lies in public sector (town) planning, and therefore to identify those responsible for planning, the same clearly cannot be said for the commercial sector. Responsibility for public sector planning of this type is enshrined in legislation so that, for example, certain types of local authority are formally charged with responsibility for development control or the production of structure plans. In the commercial sector, however, who carries out planning activity and what techniques or styles are employed will be dependent on the specifics of the type of market and the firm concerned. One way of conceptualising this diversity is to employ an approach based on contingency theory. The basis of this approach is founded in the argument that the style and techniques of planning adopted and the responsibility for planning activity will be contingent upon the nature of the organisation, its social, political, economic and industrial environments.

Building on a typology by Mintzberg and Waters (1985) which identifies five ideal types of commercial organisation operating in particular environments, Bowman and Asch (1987) identify planning approaches and structures which are consistent with each of these ideal typical organisational structures. These amount to hypotheses about the location of responsibility for planning in commercial organisations and these ideal types can be illustrated with reference to the leisure industries.

The Simple Structure

This description relates to small organisations, with uncomplicated organisational structures, typically headed by a single entrepreneur or head of organisation who is responsible for planning activity. Examples of this type of organisation might be found in a commercial health studio, squash club or sports retail outlet (or a small chain of such businesses). Because such organisational structures are generally small and uncomplicated, control and influence is centralised in an autocratic or charismatic leadership. Formal, simple, planning techniques may be employed but strategies may simply reflect the unarticulated vision of the entrepreneur, or a charismatic leader.

Machine Bureaucracy

This type of organisational structure, which incorporates the classic traits of bureaucratic organisational form, with formalised hierarchical responsibilities, tends to be associated with highly routinised forms of production as in manufacturing of mass products such as sports equipment. Power and influence tends to be concentrated at the apex of the organisation, and formal responsibility for planning is therefore concentrated in the hands of the formal leadership.

This type of organisational form is best suited to a stable environment, when the need for strategic changes in direction can be readily identified and such changes implemented in a timescale which does not place pressure on the organisation for immediate action. Rigid structures and communication channels militate against swift response to organisational crises, or the adoption of innovative planning solutions. The fact that decision-makers are far removed from those responsible for implementing strategy may provide difficulties when problems in implementation of plans emerge. This type of organisation and environment is that classically associated with formalised corporate planning, a highly routinised, hierarchical, 'rational' and detailed approach providing relatively fixed plans.

Professional Bureaucracy

In this type of organisation bureaucratic, hierarchical organisational structure is tempered by the power of professionals within the organisation who are able to legitimate their authority by reference not to their position within the organisational hierarchy but by reference to professional skills, and professionally recognised qualifications. This type of organisation, Mintzberg *et al.* argue, is suited to operation in stable, but complex environments. The complexity of the environment demands the specialist expertise of the professional, but stability means that there is no necessity for swift response to changing economic, political or social environments. Such strategic responses to change are difficult to effect given the power of professional autonomy enjoyed within the organisation by experts in their own field.

This type of organisation may be more common in the *public* sector in leisure. The Arts Council would be a typical example of a professional bureaucracy, with the expertise to judge particular areas of work vested in specialist officers dealing with particular areas of the arts, such as dance, drama, visual arts, etc. Indeed one of the Arts Council's difficulties in responding to the changed political and economic situation from the beginning of the 1980s with the incoming Conservative administration of Mrs Thatcher was the difficulty of obtaining a clear redirection of strategy, given the power of the arts experts within the organisation. Each of these professionals could argue that their own area of the arts would be irreparably damaged by a significant reduction in funding. In an unstable environment therefore the professional bureaucracy is likely to experience problems in deciding on a co-ordinated response to changed organisational circumstances. Given that planning is the responsibility, de facto, of professional specialists operating in complex areas, there are difficulties also in establishing performance criteria for such organisations.

Divisionalised Structures

This type of organisational form is typical of large-scale organisations which operate in diverse markets, often through diversification having itself been adopted as a strategy to combat the potential dangers of operating in single, highly competitive, product markets. A typical divisionalised structure has, for example, been employed by Mecca Leisure, which has separate divisions for Social Clubs, Entertainment and Catering, UK Holidays, and Other Activities. Detailed planning and strategy tends to take place within divisions which are seen as the most appropriate units for deriving strategic responses to the volatile markets within which these organisations operate. Planning is co-ordinated across divisions, not by centralised control which would undermine divisional autonomy, but through the training and development of divisional managers, involving the inculcation of organisational ideology.

While the central administrative units of these divisionalised structures manage the portfolio of divisions, controlling the allocations of revenue and capital, developing control systems and profit targets, and appointing key divisional personnel, the divisions themselves manage the range of products for which they are responsible.

Although this type of divisional structure is fairly common amongst the larger conglomerates in the leisure industries, a number of criticisms have been levelled against this approach to business planning. It is argued, for example, that the process of annual review of divisional performance encourages divisional managers to take the short-term view in order to avoid criticism for underperformance. Comparison between divisions will provide the basis for future investment decisions and thus managers will be encouraged to place emphasis on those indicators of comparison which are usually quantifiable, rather than on important qualitative criteria such as reputation for a quality product. However, it is perhaps misleading to portray divisional managers as entirely independent since they are often in an inferior position to central administration which can apply pressure to conform to expected norms.

The Adhocracy

This final organisational structure is associated with dynamically changing and complex environments in which young organisations operate in a highly organic, unformalised way with work structures growing up around problems to be addressed by the organisation rather than by formal design or organisational structure. Typical of this kind of organisation are some of the newer leisure consultancy companies. Such companies have tended initially to form open structures with planning or strategy emerging through the directions taken by particular work groups rather than reflecting predetermined strategic goals. The volatile nature of the environment, particularly during the period in which the organisation is making its reputation, militates against the adoption of formal planning approaches. Problems of planning in such organisations are predominantly problems of co-ordination, rather than of implementation. In such contexts organisational goals may be insufficiently clear and may be displaced by the personal goals of actors involved in the shaping of decisions.

These five ideal typical organisational forms are indicative of the range which exists within the leisure industries and suggest how and where particular responsibilities for planning lie. However, little has been said about the planning techniques adopted in the business planning process. Indeed in some of the examples cited above there is little by way of a formal approach to planning and formal techniques may not be adopted, but rather planning goals simply 'emerge' from the activities of the organisation.

Styles and Techniques of Planning in Commercial Sector Organisations

In this section we will deal selectively with planning at three levels – planning of products and services; planning at the 'business unit' level; and planning at the corporate level in large-scale commercial sector leisure organisations. Our treatment of planning techniques is invariably selective since little consideration will be given for example to personnel planning or financial planning strategies, partly because of lack of space, and partly because these are points of reference in Chapters 3 and 4 in this volume on human resource and financial management. Furthermore, we do not deal specifically with planning implementation and with day to day operational planning. (Readers are referred to more general texts on planning for detailed treatment of some of these topics in Further Reading indicated at the end of the chapter.)

Product Planning

One of the concepts fundamental to planning at all levels in both sectors of the leisure industries is that of the product life cycle. The development, adoption, growth and decline of products within their markets, it is claimed, follows a particular pattern (illustrated in Figure 2.2). This pattern is said to be relatively similar in a wide range of cases whether the product (or service) constitutes a major form of personal investment such as a car, or a minor form such as a type of drink. In each case sales of the product will tend to follow the same pattern or life cycle, with similar phases – introduction of the product into the market, growth in sales (which may be sustained or short-lived), the tailing off of growth as the product reaches maturity, and when sales have peaked the decline of the product, with sales perhaps stabilising on a lower plateau at a residual level. Clearly not all product sales conform strictly to this pattern. Some products or services (the terms are treated as synonymous for our purposes in this chapter) go on to decline only for sales to pick up again as tastes change and products are 'recycled', while others have sales growth patterns which are sporadic. Product failures may also never get beyond the introduction stage, being withdrawn from or rejected by the market. Nevertheless the overall pattern established in the life cycle diagram in Figure 2.2 is one which it is claimed applies to the majority of products or services which get beyond the stage of introduction to the market place.

Figure 2.2   Simplified representation of the product life cycle

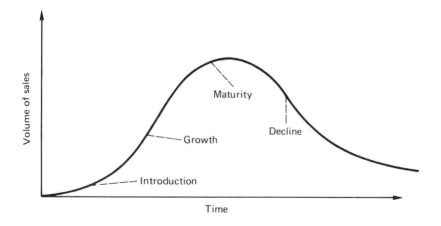

There is, however, an obvious limitation to the application of the product life cycle in business planning. Although we may expect product sales to follow this general pattern, we are unable to specify the dimensions of the axes against which this pattern is drawn. We cannot specify the length of time a product will take to reach saturation sales and fall into decline, nor the height or gradient of the sales curve in growth, maturity or decline stages. What, then, it might be asked, is the practical application of this concept for business planning? It is perhaps easiest to answer this question by reference to a practical illustration of the way in which an understanding of the product life cycle will inform planning decisions about the level of investment in a product, or about product withdrawal and product replacement decisions.

The leisure industries are in many ways more subject to fads and fashions than other product markets. By their very nature leisure products and services will have lower 'functional' value than those products such as foodstuffs, educational equipment, pharmaceuticals, etc. which meet economic or physiological needs. Leisure goods and services are said to have more 'expressive' value than many utilitarian products – that is, through the purchase of such goods and services the buyers are able to express something about themselves, to establish an identity they wish to portray. Thus wearing sports-related leisure clothing may be taken as a symbol of a healthy lifestyle, of youth and exuberance. The adoption of particular brand names in clothing denotes quality and cost, and knowledge (of what is fashionable) and therefore provides status. This is not to say that leisure products have no functional value. Clearly jogging shoes and athletics wear, for example, facilitate healthy exercise, promoting healthy lifestyles which are functional. Similarly functional goods which may well be necessities of one sort or another can also have expressive value. Transport for many people is a necessity, but, for example, four-wheel drive recreational vehicles used predominantly in a suburban setting for domestic purposes and urban travel to and from work, may be interpreted as expressing an attachment on the part of the owner to the image of an outdoor, activity-based lifestyle. However, though expressive and instrumental value may attach to both leisure and non-leisure products, there is a dominant emphasis on the expressive in many leisure product markets which fosters volatility of taste in those markets. Style, fashion, expressive value are intangibles which corrode quickly. To wear yesterday's fashions defeats the object of the exercise of attempting to be fashionable, and yet style or fashion can change overnight. Leisure markets can thus present opportunities for high volume turnover, but also present risks of overinvestment in what may turn out to be short-lived fads.

As we have noted, though the shape of product life cycles may be broadly similar, the dimensions against which the cycle is drawn may be radically different for different products. Thus the hula-hoop, the skateboard, or Rubik's cube had relatively short life cycles while professional football as a product would seem to have spanned a century or more, attaining maturity during the middle decades of this century. This is not to say that football's decline is terminal, but certainly for products and services in a period of decay the process is not easily reversed.

As a planning tool the product life cycle suggests a strategic orientation at each stage of development. In the *introduction* phase sales will be relatively low in value and therefore profits negligible. Product promotion is likely to be aimed at innovators in the market, and promotional effort will be high. Promotional effort will normally focus on the product which is new rather than a 'brand', since there are normally few competitors at this stage. This orientation is likely to change in the *growth* stage. Here the major objective is to spread adoption of the product from innovators to the mass market. This also requires intensive promotion, though perhaps aimed at the 'brand' or the company providing the product, rather than at the product per se, since public awareness of the product will be growing and competing brands are likely to be developing. The *mature* stage of the life cycle is reached when growth slows and sales begin to reach saturation point. The emphasis at this stage is likely to be on increasing market share in order to increase sales, often by promoting 'brand' or company loyalty. Finally *decline* sets in as sales decrease and the producer is faced with either abandoning the product or service, or attempting to arrest decline by product improvements, pricing strategies and/or heavy promotional strategies.

These stages can be illustrated by reference to a number of leisure product markets. The compact disc market has for example moved through the introduction stage occasioned by the development of new technology, to that of growth. The theme park market would seem to have reached maturity, with worries about saturation of the market beginning to emerge. The market for bingo has been a product market in decline for some years, and it is to this example which we now turn.

There has been concern among those involved with bingo for a number of years about declining attendances and the ageing of the playing public. Among the strategies enjoined to halt the decline has been the adoption of a joint, computer-linked 'National Game' for very high prize money involving co-operation across companies. This required an amendment to the legislation which had previously limited the size of prize money, an amendment successfully secured by the passing of a bill in 1986 after intensive parliamentary lobbying. As we have noted, in a static or declining market one strategy by which individual companies can sustain sales and profits is by increasing market share. The two market leaders in this field, Mecca and Top Rank, have been successful in many localities in squeezing, particularly small-scale, operators. Larger prize money, better equipped, more stylish and comfortable surroundings, together with price concessions on alcohol and catering have allowed the larger companies to increase market share.

A third type of strategy employed has sought to counter the trend of increasing age in the clientele of bingo players. Mecca for example has employed Samantha Fox as a promotional figurehead to give their product a younger image. The impact of this campaign is limited by the fact that legislation prevents advertising beyond the point of sale, so that the campaign is likely to reach only those who use or pass existing bingo establishments. Nevertheless the campaign is clearly seen by the company as worth the investment involved.

A final strategy in terms of product planning which is worth highlighting is that of planning product replacements. As products are in periods of growth or early maturity, replacement products may be introduced so that they may begin to reach a position of reasonable profitability as the original product begins to decline. This strategy allows a company to sustain profitability despite the demise of major products. In the case of bingo, serious consideration of alternatives to the traditional form of the game was given by Mecca Leisure when the product had already entered the stage of decline. An experimental replacement product was introduced in the form of 'quadro' a computerised (and therefore 'modern') game which was an individualised variant on the traditional game. The aim here was to develop a product which would counter the old-fashioned image of the bingo hall, and would emulate some of the appeal of the arcade games. The experiment was not a success, perhaps because the very social nature of the experience sought by those attending the bingo hall was undermined by this individualised high tech alternative.

Business Unit Planning

The concept of the product life cycle is an important building block for commercial planning decisions. Moving beyond decisions at the individual product level, it provides a key element in the rationale for business unit decision-making. The business unit may be a division within a wider corporate organisation or may be a single enterprise operating in a single market or a limited set of product markets. The two primary tools of planning to be discussed here are those of the product-market development matrix, and traditional SWOT analysis.

Product-market Development Matrix

Figure 2.3 illustrates a series of alternative strategies for sustaining performance which may be adopted by managers. This two-dimensional analysis which originated with Igor Ansoff (Ansoff, 1965) has been further developed by a number of writers (cf. Hofer and Schendel, 1978). However, at its simplest the matrix identifies four options, one in each cell, which might be adopted by managers operating at the business unit level.

Market penetration involves attempting to increase sales of existing products to existing markets. Such strategies may involve encouraging existing clients to use a product or service more intensively, may involve enhancing market share by taking custom from competitors, or may encourage non-users in a particular market segment to take up the

Figure 2.3   The product–market development matrix

PRODUCTS/SERVICES

	Existing	New
Existing	Market penetration	Product/Service development
New	Market development	Diversification – Related – Unrelated

MARKETS

product. *Market development* represents the strategy of attempting to attract new markets or segments to existing products. This may involve the adoption of a new geographical territory, or of new target markets. *Product or service development*, by contrast, involves the development of new products for existing client groups. Where an organisation feels that it knows its market well, or where new products or services meet needs related to those met by existing product lines, then it may make sense to pursue new development with clients having established brand or company name loyalty.

Finally, *diversification* as a strategy involves developing new products for new markets, and can be subdivided into two major types. Related diversification is a process whereby an organisation seeks to obtain ownership or control of its suppliers, or of the companies responsible for distributing its products. Similarly it may seek to make use of its technological expertise or knowledge of markets by diversifying into technologically or market related areas. Thus the Head Corporation entered the market for the manufacture of metal tennis rackets having established its expertise in metal alloy technologies in its original business of manufacturing sailing masts. The second type, unrelated diversification, involves a move into product markets which have little connection with the existing business activities of the organisation. Such a move is often associated with spreading risk across a range of markets and/or escaping from markets in decline. Thus for example Pleasurama, originally with its base in the London casinos market, diversified in 1987 into other unrelated leisure interests such as hotels and tourism in the UK and Europe in order to insulate itself against currency fluctuations and any sudden downturn in the casino market.

SWOT Analysis

The product–market matrix outlines a number of possible directions to be taken by a business unit. However the particular direction to be taken by those responsible for planning is likely to be guided by an analysis of the strengths and weaknesses of the organisation and the opportunities and threats presented by its environment. SWOT analysis (Strengths, Weaknesses, Opportunities, Threats) is a conceptual tool of clear relevance to the business planner. The twin foci of this type of analysis are, on the one hand, the internal features of the organisation, availability, quality, utilisation and control of organisational resources, and on the other, the key dimensions of the external environment, including assessment of social values, political developments, economic technologies, technological change, and shifts in the nature of the market within which the organisation is operating.

Figure 2.4 illustrates some of the features of the analysis of the organisation's external environment. Using the example of a business unit operating in the brewing industry, some of the following points might emerge from an analysis of opportunities and threats.

- **Political forecasting:** The Conservative government's commitment to competition and the strength of its current electoral position suggest that it would be wise to consider the implications of its policy programmes. So, for example, when it is declared that the Department of Trade and Industry is considering proposals for the introduction of legislation to loosen ties between tenant landlords in public houses and breweries (*Sunday Times,* 17 July 1988), firms operating in this market should monitor the proportion of business they conduct with such outlets. Public houses owned by the breweries would be unaffected by the proposed legislative changes, and therefore assessment is required to establish whether there would be a need to protect existing outlets by ensuring ownership, or whether opening up of other outlets controlled, but not owned, by other brewers would constitute a market opportunity for expansion.

  From the other side of the political spectrum, concern has been expressed by some politicians about the dangers of alcoholism. Labour MP Tony Banks, for example, has argued that consideration should be given to the introduction of mandatory health warnings for alcohol advertising and packaging, similar to those required of tobacco products. The effect of public awareness of health issues in the case of smoking has clearly suppressed the tobacco market and therefore concentration of resources in the alcohol products area may prove a risky strategy in the longer term.

- **Economic environment:** One of the major factors which UK industry is having to come to terms with in the period leading up to 1992 is the opening up of a unified European market which brings with it both

46

Figure 2.4 Analysing the external environment: a business unit in the brewing industry

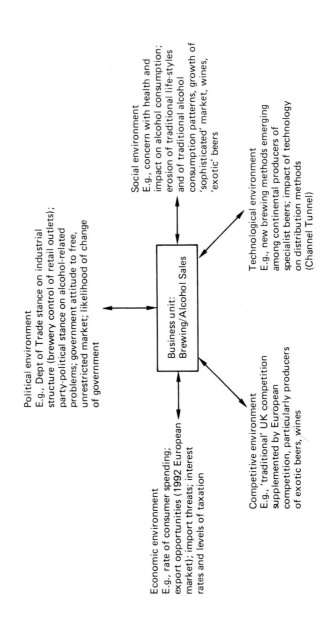

Political environment
E.g., Dept of Trade stance on industrial structure (brewery control of retail outlets); party-political stance on alcohol-related problems; government attitude to free, unrestricted market; likelihood of change of government

Social environment
E.g., concern with health and impact on alcohol consumption; erosion of traditional life-styles and of traditional alcohol consumption patterns, growth of 'sophisticated' market, wines, 'exotic' beers

Business unit:
Brewing/Alcohol Sales

Technological environment
E.g., new brewing methods emerging among continental producers of specialist beers; impact of technology on distribution methods (Channel Tunnel)

Economic environment
E.g., rate of consumer spending; export opportunities (1992 European market); import threats; interest rates and levels of taxation

Competitive environment
E.g., 'traditional' UK competition supplemented by European competition, particularly producers of exotic beers, wines

potential opportunities and problems. In the beer market, for example, the strength of competition from countries such as Belgium, which have a tradition in the production of a wide range of specialist beers for specific tastes, will be substantial. Similarly mass-produced draught beers from Belgium, the Netherlands, Denmark, and West Germany, seem likely to increase competition for example in the lager market. Reduction of tariffs on whisky seem likely to boost further the healthy export position for whisky-based products.

Further elements of the economic environment which are likely to receive consideration include taxation and interest rates. The Conservative administration has displayed a concern to reduce taxation levels in order to foster investment in the UK but this has to be offset against that government's propensity to employ interest rates as a means of controlling consumer expenditure.

- **Competitive environment:** The European market may also mean increased competition in securing suppliers or distribution outlets, while innovations such as the Channel Tunnel may have a marked effect on the speed and cost of delivery of substitute products.
- **Technological environment:** Given the opening up of European markets brewers might anticipate the introduction of specialised brewing techniques of their European counterparts (e.g., fruit-based beers produced and marketed in the Benelux countries) either under licence from foreign firms or by those concerned to compete with such organisations. Other technological developments in the production of draught low alcohol beer and lager may well require a response from competitors, while technological developments such as the 'Chunnel' are likely to affect distribution of the product and reshape catchment areas.
- **Social environment:** A key feature of changing social values evidenced in emerging lifestyles in the 1980s is a concern with health and the impact of increased awareness of the impact on health of certain products and activities. This factor has promoted considerable interest by the industry in products which minimise the negative effects of alcohol, such as low (or no) alcohol bottled and draught beers and lagers and soft drinks. Traditional drinking patterns in the UK have already been reshaped to some degree, with the growth of expenditure on wines and spirits and the relative (though not absolute) decline in beer sales.

The features of the external environment for the brewing industry cited here invariably constitute a selective rather than an exhaustive list of factors. As with any form of planning the major difficulty encountered is the inability to predict with any level of certainty the anticipated changes discussed. Nevertheless for any leisure organisation this type of assessment will be an essential feature of the planning process. The three steps in this element of the process are first to identify salient features of the environment within which the organisation operates, secondly to evaluate the importance of the individual factors; and thirdly to estimate the likelihood of the potential changes identified actually coming about.

As we have noted, external analysis of opportunities and threats should be complemented by internal analysis of strengths and weaknesses of the organisation. In earlier sections of this discussion of commercial sector planning the focus of discussion has been restricted to a consideration of product planning. However, an organisation's products and services are simply one element in the resources available to it. In any assessment of the strengths and weaknesses of the organisation a review of the full portfolio of resources is undertaken. Not simply products, but human resources, plant and buildings, materials, financial resources, and marketing should thus be considered. Figure 2.5 provides an example of the nature of the analysis which might be undertaken by a business unit operating in the brewing industry, in evaluating its strengths and weaknesses (see Chapter 4 for details of financial ratios and their application). It is not possible to give comprehensive treatment to the forms which such evaluation might take and therefore a number of key questions to be addressed are cited for each set of resources considered. Although direct reference is made here to a particular type of business unit, the questions to be addressed should be of a generic relevance to any form of business concerned with the production of services or products.

One should stress that such a list of questions, or even categories to consider, is not exhaustive and will vary in emphasis according to the area of the leisure industries under scrutiny. The object of an assessment of the strengths and weaknesses of an organisation is to develop a plan which builds on strengths, while eliminating or reducing weaknesses. However, it should be noted that strengths taken in combination may be incompatible. For example, a reputation for high quality, durable products may be incompatible with the needs of an organisation operating in a low price high volume product market.

These two approaches to planning at the business unit level, product–market matrix and SWOT analysis, taken together, offer management criteria against which to evaluate the performance of the organisation in its own product markets without generating specific advice on which particular strategy should be developed. They constitute aids to decision-making rather than 'rules of thumb' for selecting a particular strategy. In moving on to planning at the corporate level we move beyond consideration of how to plan in order to improve a given business unit's performance, to consideration of which business units a corporate organisation should plan to invest in, or divest itself of, and why.

Planning at the Corporate Organisational Level

As we have noted, UK leisure markets are dominated by the activities of a number of large-scale, multinational, corporate organisations. One of the

Figure 2.5 Evaluating the strengths and weaknesses of a business unit in the brewing industry

Product mix: What products are being developed and/or sold by the organisation? At what stage in the product life cycle are each of these products? Is there a sufficient balance in the blend of products between traditional beers/lagers and new products such as non/or low alcohol beers, 'exotic' beers, etc.?
What size is the market within which the products are sold?
What is the nature of competition within each of the product markets and what is the competitive situation of each of the products?

Financial resources: What are the profitability, liquidity, gearing and activity ratios of the organisation and how do these compare with those of other brewing concerns?
How are financial data used in the analysis of performance for the various elements of the organisation?

Human resources: What level of qualifications, skills, and expertise is available within the organisation at all levels, from management to 'shop floor'? Is there, for example, sufficient production expertise or knowledge of new beer markets available to the organisation for it to undertake its own development and production of new products, or to buy in appropriate products produced by specialist concerns?
What is the 'culture' of the organisation, and is this appropriate for the environment of the organisation?
How does the organisation compare with other brewing units in terms of pay, conditions, fringe benefits, relations with trades unions, etc.?

Material resources:
Are the buildings, plant and other factors relating to technology sufficiently modern, well located and adaptable to operate effectively in production terms? Is the level of investment in replacement sufficient? Do anticipated new markets require the development or purchase of new plant to accommodate new or different brewing processes?
Are supplies secure and reliable?
Are stock control systems effective?
Are production control systems effective?

Marketing:
Does the organisation have a coherent set of marketing plans? Are target markets appropriate?
Are elements of the marketing mix coherently constructed for each of the product markets within which the organisation operates?
Does the organisation have a positive image in terms of quality, value for money, efficient service, etc? How does it compare with those of other brewers and their products?
Is sufficient effort made to obtain market intelligence and to disseminate research findings?

largest of these is Grand Metropolitan which operated in 1986 with six divisions – Brewing (including ownership of Budweiser, Carlsberg, Fosters, Websters, WatneyMann and other leading brands); Consumer Services (including Mecca Bookmakers, food retailing in pubs and restaurants, and health care); Foods; US Consumer Products (including pet foods, and health and fitness equipment); International Hotels; and International Wines and Spirits. This kind of corporate profile allows the organisation to move into profitable areas of industry in different economies and different currencies, maximising (or at least increasing) return on investment. However, such a complex portfolio of businesses clearly requires some planning at the strategic level. The major tool for planning at this level is portfolio analysis.

Perhaps the best known of the approaches to portfolio analysis is that based on the nine cell General Electric matrix (named after the company in which it was first applied in the late 1960s). It is a matrix constructed along two dimensions (see Figure 2.6), which are composite measures of 'industry attractiveness' and 'competitive position'. The way each of these composite measures is constructed is illustrated in Figure 2.7. Taking the horizontal dimension first, the competitive position of a business is assessed in a four stage process. The first step in the process is to identify factors which significantly influence the competitive position of the businesses to be compared within the portfolio. These are likely to include

Figure 2.6   Portfolio analysis: the nine cell General Electric matrix

COMPETITIVE POSITION

		Strong	Average	Weak
	High	Winners	Winners	Question marks
INDUSTRY ATTRACTIVENESS	Medium	Winners	Average businesses	Losers
	Low	Profit generators	Losers	Losers

factors associated with analysis of (internal) strengths and weaknesses of those businesses, such as market share (expressed as a proportion of the share enjoyed by the market leader), location and/or distribution, product or service quality, pricing position, knowledge of market and expertise within the business. The next stage in the process is to identify the importance of each of these factors in relation to its contribution to the competitive position of the business unit. This is accomplished by assigning each of the factors a weighting (indicative of its relative importance) so that the total of all weightings added together is one. The third step is the rating of each business unit to be compared on a scale of 1 to 5 in terms of the strength of its position for each of the factors (with 1 being very weak and 5 being very strong). In the fourth step the rating of the business unit is then multiplied by the weighting for each factor and finally the products of rating by each factor summed to provide an overall index of competitive position. A similar process is adopted for the vertical dimension, as illustrated in Figure 2.7.

Figure 2.7 Estimating industry attractiveness and competitive position for portfolio analysis

Competitive position factor	Weight	Rating	Value	Industry attractiveness factor	Weight	Rating	Value
Market share	0.3	4	1.2	Market size	0.2	4	0.80
Location/distribution	0.2	3	0.6	Projected growth market	0.12	1	0.12
Product/service quality	0.2	2	0.4	Profitability	0.4	4	1.60
Knowledge of market	0.15	4	0.6	Nature of existing competitors and likelihood of entry of others	0.18	1	0.18
Market awareness and image of product/service	0.1	2	0.2	Technological investment required	0.1	3	0.30
Production/service delivery skills in existing workforce	0.05	2	0.1				
Total competitive position score			3.1	Industry attractiveness score			3.00

When the indices of competitive position and industry attractiveness have been constructed the business units to be compared are assigned to an appropriate position in the overall matrix. Businesses which appear in the three bottom right hand cells are those which are ripe for disinvestment or will require a significant effort to improve their competitive position. 'Winners' are those businesses which appear in the top left hand cells representing the business units most likely to generate profits in the medium term for the corporate portfolio.

However, even this apparently complex assessment of a portfolio of businesses is relatively crude, and as Hofer and Schendel (1978) point out, further detailed evaluation is required before decisions should be made on the allocation of corporate resources or the divesting of businesses. These include assessment of the portfolio in terms of balance between winners, losers, question marks and average businesses; consideration of the external environment of each business, including the identification of opportunities and threats, key trends and competition; consideration of short-term and long-term profit and risk for each business.

An example of a situation in which portfolio analysis would have been usefully applied is provided by the case of the selling off by Grand Metropolitan of its social club (bingo) and nightclub interests in a management buyout in 1986. Mecca Leisure represented a set of business units in the 'profit producers' category which were clearly likely to be less profitable in the future without further investment. The profit potential of the division of Grand Metropolitan was less attractive to the multinational than other alternative opportunities for investment. The social club business, based on a product in decline, was attached to a number of other leisure services, in particular a number of night club/discotheques which though profitable were also likely to be subject to changing trends in leisure markets. The management of this division of the corporate company, however, was sufficiently convinced that profitability could be sustained at an acceptably attractive level for their own purposes and therefore bought the interests of the corporate company in this division. The result has been that the parent company has received funds from the sale which it has been able to invest in other business areas, while the new Mecca Leisure company has been able to sustain profitability.

Leisure Planning in the Public Sector

One of the distinctions, it is claimed, between the public and private sectors in leisure provision is the bias in public provision towards maintaining facilities or planning their location, so that public agencies become more product oriented. Swimming baths, libraries, parks and leisure centres are administered and organised with a focus on the activity or facility provided. The private sector, with its profit coming directly from the customer, is far more likely to be concerned with the experience, its impact on participants, and thus become more leisure-process or consumer oriented. The emphasis in public sector planning on land use, facilities and location, underlines this distinction in approach between public and private sectors. Access and infrastructure become the focus, perhaps to the neglect of individual needs and satisfaction. Given the division within leisure between the worthy, uplifting and morally approved and what may be seen as more enjoyable and entertaining, it is no surprise that the public sector becomes preoccupied with organising the former, while the private sector comes to dominate the provision and profits from the latter.

In leisure, as in any other area, planning needs to be seen as goal oriented, purposive activity, encompassing a range of processes by which a desired future can be envisaged and ultimately achieved. This conscious attempt to influence future outcomes is in general terms simple and uncontroversial but in operation is ultimately evaluative and political in content and method. Of necessity, planning involves the identification or selection of desired goals or ends, and also ways of achieving these (see Figure 2.8).

Figure 2.8 The means–ends distinction in planning

ENDS	Future state, Set of goals Normative, evaluative (political) Programme objectives, Desired aims
MEANS	Methods, bureaucratic and technical, Efficient, rational, effective Operational (professional)

Theorists since Max Weber have recognised the functional division of ends and means, and the problem of separating these in reality and practice. The divisions easily overlap and blur the separation ideally envisaged, so that bureaucrats, civil servants and professional planners may rapidly be drawn into defining objectives and setting agendae (i.e., dictating ends) which are more properly the concern of the political domain. This division of function has long been assumed in British central and local government. The assumption that politicians (who are amateur, subjective, partial, short-term and sectional), have different roles from officials (who are professional, objective, rational, long-term, public interest centred, consensual and orderly), has been central to most systems of public planning.

Within the British system most public sector planning has focused on attempts to achieve predetermined goals within the environment by the use of statutory town and country planning controls on land use and development. Although there have been ambitious attempts to narrow the perspective solely onto leisure by formulating strategic plans designed specifically for recreation, like the Regional Recreation Strategies of the Regional Councils for Sport and Recreation, these and other specialised plans have foundered for lack of resources. Most resources in the public sector remain within the context of town and country land-use planning. It is this approach to public sector planning which is therefore the subject of the rest of this section of the chapter.

Town and country planning in Britain envisages 'planning' as directing the environment towards particular ends by reconciling conflicts over the use of land, by improving the environment and attempting to provide for 'better' life-styles (Faludi, 1973). Planning is seen as the arrangement of land uses, and also the method by which this conscious pattern is encouraged. There is thus a concentration on spatial arrangements. The relationship between site and building are seen to generate positive and negative effects, advantages and disadvantages. It is the ordering of this arrangement of leisure activities and other land uses which has been the historic focus for town and country planning in Britain.

The Structure of Planning in the Public Sector

In the United Kingdom, town planning developed out of what was discerned as the chaos of Victorian market-led urbanisation. The reality of squalor and inefficiency contrasting with utopian ideals of philanthropists and social reformers was seen to support the need for formal intervention by government. Initially, political intervention was for physical and sanitary improvement, gradually increasing in scale from individual houses to slum streets and finally to whole districts of insalubrious housing. The intellectual justification for this assumption of power came from ideas of physical and environmental determinism (that conditions determined the moral and physical nature of inhabitants) backed by the contemporary concern for fitness and nationhood. Environmental improvement was thought to have positive effects on human mortality, morality and social order. Within this supportive climate increasing government intervention in urban areas was gradually accepted. This mixture of mot- ives – humanitarian, utopian, functional and determinist – has persisted in public and political attitudes towards the environment through much of the twentieth century (Ravetz, 1986; Cherry, 1982; Reade 1987).

The ambitions of the legislators are clearly set out in the preamble to the first Housing and Town Planning Bill in 1909:

The object of the Bill is to provide a domestic condition for the people in which their physical health, their morals, their character and their whole social condition can be improved .... The Bill aims in broad outline at, and hopes to secure, the home healthy, the house beautiful, the town pleasant, the city dignified, and the suburb salubrious. It seeks, and hopes to secure, more and better homes, better houses, prettier streets, so that the character of a great people, in towns and cities and villages, can be still further improved and strengthened by the conditions under which they live.

These motives, linked to the assumption that there is a socially desirable pattern of land use, different from that which would be generated by market forces, have tended to persist as the rationale for continuing and increased public intervention through statutory urban planning. Planning was held to resolve competing claims, to allocate 'best' uses, and to preserve and select positive environmental features, with each succeeding piece of legislation. Coupled with concerns over 'profitable' or 'fruitful' leisure, planning legislation was utilised to ensure supplies of play spaces and recreation facilities.

Inter-war legislation did little other than to attempt vainly to reduce urban 'sprawl' which was seen as 'blighting' rural areas (Figure 2.8). Preservation of green spaces came early as a major planning objective. Not until 1947 with the establishment of development plans for towns and shire counties were the physical realities of sites for playing areas, parks, public open space, libraries, shops, and all other land uses recorded in topographic 'plan' form. These 'blueprints' for the future, along with the National Parks and Access to the Countryside Act 1949, fitted the idealism and resolve of a Labour administration establishing a welfare state of public order and provision. Future development was to be planned, according to the rules of the 1947 Act, with sites indicated, boundaries clarified, and the benefits of development organised and utilised in the public interest.

The 1947 Act formed the central feature of British town and country planning throughout the post-war period. Control of land-use was seen as the basis of government intervention in the environment, with all 'development' (construction of buildings, or significant change of use of buildings or land) needing authorisation from local authorities, working in coordination with the minister. This system formed the basis for contemporary urban planning despite later amendments. It preserved an orderly pattern of land uses along existing lines as well as promising potential for future expansion. It reinforced exclusivity of areas. Residential districts could not be invaded by unwanted industrial users, and established city structures were reinforced by this type of detailed plan-making. Only agricultural land was excluded from control, partly a heritage of planning's roots in urban squalor and Victorian cities. By the 1960s this system came to be seen as too rigid in its 'blueprint' approach, with perpetuation of existing patterns and limited capacity to cope with rapid growth.

Growing political attention to socio–economic change and wider urban and suburban problems showed the limitations of the 1947 approach (Figure 2.9). The Countryside Act 1968 represented such changes with its designation of country parks, picnic sites, nature trails and bird sanctua-

Figure 2.9 State intervention: town and country planning and leisure

	1800–1900	1918–19	1919–39	1939–45	1960s	1980s
Chronology State	Laissez-faire 'property'		Minimal intervention 'conservative' depression reconstruction	Welfare state reformism austerity consensus	Corporate state — Modernisation	'Enterprise' small state — Crisis — Monetarism
Planning Acts Objectives	1909 Improve health and housing		1919 1932 Reconstruct Stop sprawl Protect 'Country'	1947 Reform Socialise Control	1968 Organise Develop Integrate growth	1980 1986 Minimal state Reduce public sector Encourage private development
Forms	Possible schemes for new building		Schemes for 20,000+ population	Physical plans (6in. to mile) Development controlled	Socio-economic Diagrammatic plans	Enterprise Zones Simplified Planning Zones
Aims	Improve		Restrict	Construct	Reorganise	Facilitate
Leisure	Private provision		Protection of some green spaces	Detailed planning of amenity provision	Broad outline of amenity provision	Market supported Decentralised provision
Implications	Commercially profitable facilities Public and private benefaction of leisure spaces		Largely ineffective attempts to check urban sprawl and preserve rural areas	Reconstruction of town centres Land-use structured Specific allocation of leisure spaces	Liveable cities aim General land-use implications	Pressures on central spaces Job creation supported in tourism and leisure

ries. The Town and Country Planning Act 1968 divided planning powers between the two tiers of local government in establishing Structure Plans, designed to indicate the broad pattern of strategic land use at county or regional level, and Local Plans operating at district level. Structure Plans were meant to be general statements on land use issues lasting 10–15 years, while the district-based interpretations in Local Plans would provide the detailed basis for development control by local councils.

Despite some modifications and the exclusion of certain limited areas (like Enterprise Zones, Urban Development Areas, Simplified Planning Zones, etc.) in 1980 and 1986, this remains the system in operation today. Some aspects, like the need for permission from a local authority for 'development' and the need to conform to a published statutory Local Plan, stem from the 1947 Act. Other aspects, like the creation of a generalised, broadly-based strategic structure plan for a county or sub-region, date from the 1968 changes. The development plan system currently in operation has thus evolved as shown in Figure 2.10.

Figure 2.10   The development plan system

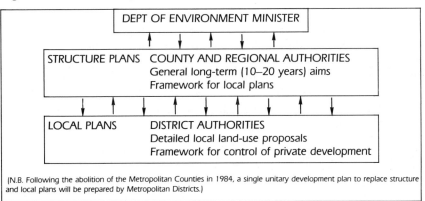

(N.B. Following the abolition of the Metropolitan Counties in 1984, a single unitary development plan to replace structure and local plans will be prepared by Metropolitan Districts.)

The Structure Plan in association with its relevant Local Plans constitutes the development plan for any area. It forms the basis for decisions by local authorities on development of land and buildings, subject to final possible arbitration by the Secretary of State for the Environment. Decisions by the minister may well prove just as significant as published plans. If there is consistent reversal of local decisions on contentious issues such as green belt building, or out-of-centre shopping, then authorities will be reluctant to refuse permission to develop or to act contrary to the implicit intention of Whitehall. Central government is thus a significant element in this system and has powers of veto and final appeal which can be used effectively to by-pass decisions made locally. (For more detailed description of the system and its operation see Kirby and Carrick, 1985.)

Emphasis on leisure and recreation in structure plans and local plans varies according to the nature of the area involved. Until relatively recently recreation and tourism assumed low priority in the range of key issues or policy objectives adopted, but as awareness of the employment potential of these spheres has grown, so more plans have come to emphasise the functional implications for jobs and for image building.

At Structure Plan level most authorities adopt an approach similar to that of the West Midlands:

> Provision for recreation is an important element of the Strategy. Access to a wide range of leisure opportunities is a major component in the quality of life. It also contributes to the attraction of living within the County and can thereby help to arrest the outward migration of population, which is a major concern. The provision of recreation facilities, particularly those serving a regional, national or international market, has potential economic benefits both directly in generating additional jobs and also in promoting the image of the West Midlands County (West Midlands County Structure Plan Review, October 1979, p.77).

Other county authorities emphasise the particular resource concerns of their areas. North Yorkshire's key issues include consideration of:

- the extent to which priority should be given to the provision of recreation facilities and the manner in which available resources should be deployed
- the extent to which North Yorkshire should be expected to cater for the recreational demands of non-residents and
- the extent to which further provision should be made for caravans, (North Yorkshire County Council, Structure Plan, Written Statement, 1979, p.85).

As might be expected, areas of extensive tourism and recreation, like Cumbria, tend to emphasise the issues of provision and environmental conflict in their strategies, while authorities less commercially involved develop fewer leisure issues and objectives. A similar contrast is observable in local plans for resort towns. Tourist pressures figure largely in local plans for places like Lynton and Lynmouth (Local Plan, 1982), Clacton (Local Plan, 1982), Haworth, West Yorkshire (Local Plan, 1979), often expressed as concern over the conservation of historic townscapes threatened by unsympathetic commercial development. Some local plans focus entirely upon recreational potential, in the form of Subject Local Plans. Greater Manchester authorities developed the Medlock Valley Subject Local Plan in 1982, with objectives of recreational development and co-ordination in an extensive area running through several heavily populated areas.

The variety of possible approaches reflects the prominence of tourism and recreational issues locally. Readers would be advised to consult the relevant county-wide Structure Plan, and Local Plans, in their local library or planning department, to see which issues have been identified, prioritised, and which strategy adopted for their particular area. Generally, leisure issues have not been emphasised in statutory plans, except where commercial development pressures have been strongest, or where tourism has formed a substantial component of the local economy. With growth in leisure spending and a service oriented local economy, increasing emphasis at least on the economic aspects of leisure development has been apparent.

Styles and Techniques of Planning in the Public Sector

As the development plans system has evolved, so methods of planning adopted by authorities have changed to reflect the context and content of plans. The topographically based 'blueprints' of the 1947 Act embodied a certainty of purpose and a belief in the expertise of the planner which was reflected in their production.

Survey, Analysis and Plan, was the simplified prescription historically ascribed to the legacy of Patrick Geddes which has underlain most British plan production (Breheny and Batey, 1981). Areas were to be extensively surveyed and their key problems or issues identified before the planner could synthesise the collected information in planform. This formula satisfied the need to behave in a rational way, attempting to demonstrate professional expertise and to provide adequate justification for decisions made. The need for rational justification has been a statutory requirement in all recent town and country planning legislation and the collection of copious data prior to decision-making has been seen as serving this rationalist ideal. Critics have emphasised the inevitable disjuncture which still remains between data collection, its analysis, and the link to policy prescription. Data alone can provide no single route to problem solution or policy objective, but require interpretation, selection and evaluation by subjective individuals. The emphasis on rationality, 'scientific' methods and the need to refer to 'evidence' in justification have ensured that the formula (Survey, Analysis and Plan) continues to find support with some professional planners. Even in the 1970s the production of Structure Plans was slowed by the compilation of encyclopedic 'Reports of Survey' for subregions. With greater availability of computerised data storage, retrieval and manipulation, the accumulation of enormous data bases has proved possible, but their complete 'analysis' seems as remote as ever. The 'Geddes' formula has remained a significant influence on statutory planning, reflecting the search for 'scientific' methods in prediction and evaluation, and the need for rational justification of plan prescriptions.

With changes in the social sciences, business management and the context of plan-making in the post-war period, other methods and techniques were introduced in the public sector. Some reflected the availability of quantification and electronic data-processing on a grand scale, others were borrowed from the commercial sector and management theorists. Most of the changes were initiated in the 1960s as the older 'blueprint' approaches seemed less appropriate and legitimate, faced with increasing development pressures and less public or political consensus about objectives. The 1968 Structure Plan changes emphasised socio–economic land use concerns and local authorities introduced revised planning techniques to cope. Some simply computerised the Survey Analysis Plan formula in an attempt to manage the urban system, but others attempted more corporate approaches to all their services, such as PPBS (Planning Programming Budgeting Systems) and detailed Cost-Benefit analysis, a precursor to Environment Impact Analysis.

New methods were introduced in an effort further to rationalise the process of urban management. For some, like McLoughlin, the city was conceptualised as a dynamic system using computer models of key components and interactions to simulate reality. From this base the implications of defined operational objectives could be quantified and analysed and their attainment monitored. The success of this approach depended upon accurate quantified modelling of the urban system and its effective monitoring. For all the expense on vast computer systems and data collection, no reliable model was available in either the US or in Britain to make this a practical reality and system modelling had but limited application to some of the regional studies published in the late 1960s (McLoughlin, 1969; Jackson, 1972).

Other attempts at rationalist methodology included resorting to simple cost-benefit analysis of the desirability of alternative decisions. The problems of evaluation of environmental amenity were highlighted in the adoption of this technique in the inquiry into the location of London's third airport, generating now notorious financial valuations for 'irreplaceable' features, such as the Norman church at Stewkley (Lichfield, Kettle and Whitbread, 1975, p.70). Assessment of value remained a problem with this approach and in the subsequent development of Planning Balance Sheets. All such schemes require the placing of a value on intangibles such as landscape, accessibility, and amenity, and thus for all their apparent objectivity, fail to resolve contentious issues of valuation of public benefits and social costs. Subjective evaluation, weighting and relative costing of objectives, unfortunately remains central to all such attractive 'objective solutions' to decision-making problems.

The later adoption of techniques borrowed from management theory (PPBS, contingency theory, etc.) attempted to cope with strategic choice in uncertain environments and complex organisations. Linked with corporate organisation of local government activity, corporate planning seemed to offer potential for comprehensive planning within authorities, though statutory land use plans had little in common with annual financial cycles and grant allocations. Differing time scales and lack of effective performance indicators limited co-operation, as did the departmental structures of most authorities. Land use planning timescales did not readily fit authority budgeting and investment programmes and corporate approaches were not welcomed by politicians who felt their democratic choice was constrained by elaborate packages of co-ordinated strategies constructed by officers.

Other attempts to systematise decision-making in reality involved the development of 'mixed-scanning' approaches. Here a broad strategic overview, like the Structure Plan itself, was combined with more detailed consideration of selected key aspects. General policy could thus be integrated with more detailed strategies for particular issues (employment, housing, tourism, etc.) in a form like that of more recent Structure Plans. This emphasis on key issues to be 'scanned' was supported by Department of Environment advice as suitable for the land-use policy framework function of structure plans.

Public support was also seen as essential for public sector planning at this time. Paralleling the changes in methodology in the late 1960s came recognition of waning public enthusiasm for modern plans or recent urban development. The old consensus which was believed to have emerged after 1945 had certainly dissipated and there was little agreement about the nature of desirable change or interpretation of the 'public interest' (Ravetz, 1980).

The political response to growing disaffection was to attempt to generate moore public support for land-use decisions by encouraging greater public participation. The 1969 Skeffington Report proposed the inclusion of a series of stages of consultation in future plan design, and public involvement through meetings and inquiry was incorporated into subsequent legislation. Unfortunately, consultation proved time-consuming and the public showed little interest in wider strategic matters removed from direct impact on their own local environments. Participation has had little real impact on policy formulation or plan production since little power was effectively reallocated. Legislation in 1986 circumvented some stages of local consultation and recent debates on Green Belts and development control have seen a reassertion of wider political controversy as the main representation of public interest rather than formal mechanisms of consultation (Fagence, 1977; Boaden *et al.*, 1982).

Within the public sector the emphasis on rational methodology and justification remains. Repeated attempts at quantification show the importance of demonstrable targets and comparative measures as comprehensible data for public and politicians. Construction of combined indicators to represent deprivation or economic disadvantage was attempted in the late 1970s in an effort to show the relative problems of urban areas, and some were specifically adapted to act as surrogate measures of recreation disadvantage, most notably by the Sports Council in defining areas of need for priority funding (Henry and Marriott, 1982).

Similar methods were exemplified by the 'standards' approach to recreation and play spaces. Accepted and definitive measures for space per head of population provided a readily available tool for evaluation of provision and for possible (re)allocation of resources. Quantification offered a comprehensive basis for investment and despite its limitations could readily achieve support of public and politicians (Torkildsen, 1983).

Changes in the 1960s and 1970s marked an attempt to make public sector development planning relevant to urban change within a mixed economy. One lasting consequence of these changes was that, henceforth, planning was to be seen as a cyclical process rather than a finite programme. Above all it was to be seen as 'a process for making rational decisions about future goals' (Faludi, 1973). The danger in striving to achieve rational methods was that planning was taken to be the unproblematic use of professional expertise, as constituted by its administrative and methodological structures. The emphasis on technical expertise demanded by the rational–scientific ideal was such that 'technical' judgements came to dominate to the exclusion of political direction, as supposed 'facts' were elevated relative to value judgements. The enthusiasm for new techniques had its dangers since these models were only as good as the assumptions on which they were based. Problems of forecasting the future remained as great as ever. Calculating provision for the future became more difficult as parameters became less reliable. The 'scientific' methods of planning of the 1960s and 1970s proved wholly inaccurate in the wake of unforeseen energy and economic crises, and with reduced political support such scientific–rational approaches have tended to be abandoned gradually by authorities, as the plans they generated have become outdated or inappropriate.

The search for new methods serves to demonstrate the importance of context for planning, whether within the social sciences, the economy or in politics. The search for scientific rationality in plan-making and processing represented a period of relative certainty and consistent development within urban land-use and in local authority power in urban management. With less interventionist public planning and more market-based decision-making, planning structures have seemed less relevant and hence have attracted far less political and economic support.

The problems of managing change in an uncertain environment can be seen to have overwhelmed most of the vaunted techniques of the 1960s and 1970s, even to the point of undermining the legitimacy of public sector planning, as its relative impotence becomes apparent. The rational ideal has given way to increased recognition of the reality of 'disjointed incrementalism' (Lindblom, 1959) in planning practice. Planning is seen as a more pragmatic response to changing circumstances, in which a limited number of options are available for consideration, and feasibility tends to dominate in the evaluation of means and goals. With this lower-key approach, disjointed incrementalism accepts that problems can be alleviated rather than solved and that symptoms tend to be treated rather than cured. Within this context there has been much greater reliance on non-statutory instruments and on informal local agreements or development briefs.

Contemporary circumstances, economic and political, have seen a reduction in interventionist planning and greater acceptance of market trends in land allocation. This in turn reflects and reinforces recognition of the limited effectiveness of statutory planning given its largely negative powers over development under the development plan system. With uncertainty over ends or means (or both), with limited development pressures in some areas, and the need to promote the very kinds of private development town and country planning was established to control, there is an absence of any clear role for much of the established development plans system. What Eric Reade calls the 'triumph of bureaucratic professionalism' appears to have dominated and much public policy-making has become short-term, incremental and unco-ordinated, faced with increasingly complex problems and pressures (Reade, 1987).

A detailed account and evaluation of individual techniques employed in public sector leisure planning is not possible in this context because of constraints of space. However, a summary of major techniques is provided in Figure 2.11. The list is not exhaustive and a number of variations to these approaches can be added. The selection is indicative of the range of techniques discussed in the literature. As we have noted there has been a general movement in planning theory and practice away from 'rational', professional planner-led techniques, through community participation to market-led approaches to planning. The techniques are therefore generally cited as ranging from those which imply professional expertise in planning, through those which are designed to involve communities (albeit in often tokenistic terms), to a market-led approach. (For further discussion of some of these techniques see Veal, 1982, Henry and Marriott, 1982, or Roberts, 1974.)

Figure 2.11 Leisure planning techniques

Profession-based	Objective Rationalistic Scientific	Survey–Analysis–Plan Playspace standards Catchment Demand Estimates Cost–Benefit–Analysis Planning balance sheets/grid approaches Social indicators Environmental impact Mixed scanning Incrementalism
Public-based	Participatory	Public participation Community development Market research Advocacy planning
Private-based	Market-led	Planning gain Design briefs Private tenders Management contracts

Conclusions: Leisure Planning in the Commercial and Public Sectors – Pressures and Potential

Like all professional activities, public sector planning, particularly the town and country planning dimension, has achieved political support by emphasising its significance and effectiveness in urban management. The reality of development control has meant, however, that public intervention is largely confined to the negative regulation of private sector initiatives. In times, or regions, of economic depression there is little opportunity for decisive action by public agencies and their effectiveness appears marginal. While the exaggeration of influence may have been necessary to gain political support for the profession, it has also meant that public sector planners have been labelled as blameworthy for changes as disparate as high-rise housing, city centre redevelopment, and extensive road schemes. The reality appears that they have been relatively minor partners in each of these changes. The relative powerlessness of public sector planners within a mixed economy is thus a significant issue. Increasingly, market forces and private sector initiatives have determined the nature of urban development in leisure, as in every other aspect of contemporary life. Public sector planning has thus come to have little influence and few resources to amend or modify the broad trends in market-based leisure and styles of living, whatever public opinion may declare to the contrary.

One major concern of public sector agencies has been the implications of leisure inequalities since 1945. Closely linked to income, there appears to have been a marked polarisation of opportunity dependent upon residential base and access to private transport. The gap in opportunities between car-owning suburbanites and inner city residents dependent on a declining public transport service appears as great as ever. Although more people have been able to cross the divide into relative prosperity and mobility, the gulf in leisure opportunities is real and one which public sector planning has been able to do relatively little to combat.

A feature of growing suburbanisation is that it is best served by the private car, since low density living makes nonsense of public transport economics. Fewer bus users ensure higher fares and less frequent services, and this in turn encourages further dependence on private cars. The downward spiral is reinforced and, without extensive subsidy, apparently irreversible. Mobility, linked to accessibility through income, appears the major determinant of leisure opportunity and public sector planners can do little to stem the outward migration of homes, shopping, leisure centres and even jobs, from the less prosperous inner areas to the more affluent peripheral suburbs. The growing importance of market-based provision makes these trends particularly difficult to reverse, especially when restrictions on public spending and the likely imposition of higher charges where leisure facilities are managed privately are taken into consideration. Leisure, like all other aspects of development, reveals the relatively limited power for initiative within the public sector. Protection or management of residual features seems more likely in future, rather than the implementation of plans to widen participation by those disadvantaged through class, race, gender or disability. Relatively little redistribution of opportunity is possible, even if this is still seen as a public sector responsibility, since market trends appear likely to dominate the foreseeable future.

Trends in leisure activity present other problems for the public sector since increased mobility and affluence for the many has led to over-use of particular areas or facilities. National Parks, Areas of Outstanding Natural Beauty, even seaside resorts and theme parks all present problems of management and control. Conservation of historic and natural features, visual appeal, traffic management, etc. assume greater significance with increased pressures from car-borne tourism. Land-use planning has to face up to the conflicts of interests between users, locals, and developers. Resolution of disputes between farmers and ramblers, quarrymen and naturalists, developers and conservationists, trail-riders and walkers, superstore developers and corner shopkeepers, is unlikely to be entirely satisfactory or uncontentious. One of the functions of public sector planners is to take some of the 'heat' from irreconcilable disputes and often assume a share of responsibility for whatever is determined. Given the limited powers and resources of the public sector the opprobrium may well be ill-deserved but a social necessity nonetheless.

A rising tide of affluence for the majority and an important private sector organised to profit from those benefiting from rising living standards, whether purchased on credit or not, presents difficulties for the public sector. Uneven development and inequalities in leisure opportunities become magnified. Most land-use plans give greater emphasis to economic regeneration rather than leisure provision, and more scope for private investment rather than public sector activity. Urban planning legislation based upon negative control of private development has been predicated upon economic growth and has thus been unable to deal with regional or national recession and industrial restructuring. Market forces have come to dominate and coping with major environmental changes using diminished and diminishing resources appears to have been the lot of most public sector planners recently.

Considering its reduced powers and resources the potential of the sector may appear slight. However, the need to cope with market pressures on land presents problems on a scale almost rivalling the Victorian city chaos in which town and country planning had its roots. The problems are real. Not only are there great difficulties in forecasting, despite the range of techniques available, but public sector planning appears to be dealing with an increasingly uncertain environment, whether economic, social or political, which makes long-term decision-making increasingly difficult (Veal, 1987, Chapter 7). Without a clear national plan for leisure or any other activity, it becomes difficult to implement policies either at strategic planning level or in small-scale decision-making at local level. The need for development planning remains, however, since there seems no other effective mechanism for co-ordinating the work of agencies as diverse as the Sports Council, Tourist Boards, Countryside Commission, Arts Council, Water Boards, and the range of government ministries involved in leisure and recreation. Regional Councils for Sport and Recreation may provide opportunities for discussion, but development control, limited though it may be, provides a policy lever for materially influencing practical outcomes.

Reliance on land-use arrangement and organisation as a central feature of public sector planning appears less and less relevant in a market-led context. Many urban problems are not reducible to locational policies and resolution through the production of land-use plans and development control. Attempts to manage change using the development plans system appear doomed to failure given the limited range of powers and resources being applied to achieve a broad range of socio–economic objectives. More local authorities are forced to act in a promotional manner to achieve development of sites. Attempts at 'planning gain' by inducing developers to provide features of public benefit, whether libraries, link-roads, theatres, or public open spaces, are more difficult in a competitive situation. Informal agreements have replaced formal published plans for many large schemes and limited leverage seems possible to foster socially desirable rather than profitable objectives in such circumstances.

Recent experience suggests a continuing diminution of scope for public sector planning. 'Trend planning', or working in conjunction with the market, is seen by many as a contradiction, since planning by its very existence assumes the need to intervene in market relations. Probably the degree of intervention is critical in this relationship. In times of limited development and unequal resources the extent of public sector redistribution, particularly using a tool as indirect as land-use planning, is necessarily limited. The need, however, to attempt some co-ordination and direction seems inevitable if inequalities are not to be further exacerbated or reinforced without any form of conscious check.

The effectiveness of public sector planning will thus ultimately depend on the scope of the public sector itself as a positive force in society. If in a mixed economy the balance of resources for investment and development rest markedly within the market sector then the contribution of the public sector will be proportionately diminished. Only if such an orientation towards profit-making is deemed politically unacceptable will there be prospect of a reversal of relative powers and the public sector encouraged to pursue socially desirable ends more effectively.

There are distinct parallels to be drawn between leisure planning in public and commercial sectors. The rejection of 'rationalist' corporate plans in the public sector is mirrored in the rejection of formal corporate planning in the commercial sector (Peters and Waterman, 1982). Fixed blueprints are equally inappropriate to both sectors, since both are experiencing highly volatile environments. The mixed scanning approach advocated for public sector planning has its parallel in the 'logical incrementalism' advocated by Quinn (1980) which implies that broad strategic goals may be set at corporate company level but that divisional managers should interpret, specify and readjust objectives according to the particular circumstances of their own business unit. For both sectors, therefore, a system of planning is sought which permits flexibility of response to changing market conditions.

If the influence of public sector planning has waned over the late 1970s and 1980s, that of planning in the commercial sector has grown, particularly with the increase in scale of investment and multinational interest in leisure. Clearly commercial planning has been 'successful' in that return on investment has proved increasingly attractive to investors of capital. However, the potential of commercial planning may be gauged by more sensitive criteria than the gross profit position. One should ask questions about the social costs associated with the financial return on leisure investment. We have illustrated elsewhere (Spink, 1989) how market-led investment reduces the availability of space for recreation for inner city residents by ceding land to other uses which attract a higher return. Similarly the gentrification of certain areas – London Docklands, Salford Quays, the Albert Dock in Liverpool – may be partially accomplished through effectively planned cultural attractions, which make areas more desirable in residential terms. However, this may also result in local people being priced out of the housing market. The fruits of economic growth may thus be filtered through the market to consumers via effectively planned market provision, but for the less affluent, less mobile, the disadvantaged inner city resident the potential of commercial sector leisure planning may be viewed negatively. One's judgement of the success or otherwise of commercial sector planning will, in large part, be a function of one's position in the market place.

Further Reading

For a discussion of the impact of recent political and economic change on public sector planning, Reade's (1987) book *British Town and Country Planning* represents a readable introduction. Veal (1982) provides a fairly detailed description of traditional planning methods and their application to the leisure context, but such methods have to some extent become outmoded as market-led planning has grown in significance. A useful source for discussions of more up to date practical planning methods and projects is available in the planning journals aimed at practitioners, such as *Town and Country Planning* and *The Planner*. The application of commercial planning approaches provides the focus for a number of readable texts.

Amongst the best of these are Bowman and Asch's (1987) and Scholes and Klemm's (1987) books, which though aimed at very different markets (MBA and BTEC HND in Business Studies, respectively) together represent a broad overview of the nature of planning techniques and their application in commercial contexts.

References

Ansoff, H.I. (1965) *Corporate Strategy*, Harmondsworth: Penguin.

Boaden, N., Goldsmith, M., Hampton, W. and Stringer, P. (1982) *Public Participation in Local Services*, London: Longman.

Bowman, C. and Asch, D. (1987) *Strategic Management*, London: Macmillan.

Breheny, M.J. and Batey, P.W.J. (1981) 'The History of Planning Methodology; A Preliminary Sketch', *Built Environment*, 7 (2).

Cherry, G.E. (1982) *The Politics of Town Planning*, London: Longman.

Fagence, M. (1977) *Citizen Participation in Planning*, Oxford: Pergamon Press.

Faludi, A. (1973) *Planning Theory*, Oxford: Pergamon Press.

Haywood, L., Kew, F. and Bramham, P. *et al.* (1989) *Understanding Leisure*, London: Hutchinson.

Henry, I. and Marriot, K. (1982) *Professionalisation and Planning in Local Authority Leisure Services*, Centre for Leisure Studies, Salford University.

Hofer, C.W. and Schendel, D. (1978) *Strategy Formulation: Analytical Concepts*, St. Paul/Minnesota: West.

Jackson, J.N. (1972) *The Urban Future*, London: Allen & Unwin.

Kirby, D. and Carrick, R. (1985) *Planning in Britain: An Introductory Framework*, Slough: University Tutorial Press.

Lichfield, N., Kettle, P. and Whitbread, M. (1975) *Evaluation in the Planning Process*, Oxford: Pergamon Press.

Lindblom, C.E. (1959) 'The Science of Muddling Through', reprinted in Pugh, D.S.(ed), *Organization Theory*, Harmondsworth: Penguin.

McLoughlin, J.B. (1969) *Urban and Regional Planning*, London: Faber & Faber.

Mintzberg, H. and Waters, J.A. (1985) 'Of Strategies Deliberate and Emergent', *Strategic Management Journal*, 6.

Peters, T.J. and Waterman, R.H. (1982) *In Search of Excellence*, London: Harper & Row.

Quinn, J.B. (1980) *Strategies for Change: Logical Incrementalism*, Homewood, Ill.:Irwin.

Ravetz, A. (1980) *Remaking Cities*, London: Croom Helm.

Ravetz, A. (1986) *The Government of Space: Town Planning in Modern Society*, London: Faber & Faber.

Reade, E. (1987) *British Town and Country Planning*, Milton Keynes: Open University Press.

Roberts, M. (1974) *An Introduction to Town Planning Techniques*, London: Hutchinson.

Scholes, K. and Klemm, M. (1987) *An Introduction to Business Planning*, London: Macmillan.

Spink, J. (1989) 'Urban Development: Leisure Facilities and the Inner City', in Bramham, P., Henry, I., Mommaas, M. and van der Poel, H. (eds), *Leisure and Urban Processes: Critical Studies of Leisure Policy in West European Cities*, London: Routledge.

Torkildsen, G. (1983) *Leisure and Recreation Management*, London: E. & F.N. Spon.
Veal, A.J. (1982) *Planning for Leisure: Alternative Approaches*, Papers in Leisure Studies, 5, Polytechnic of North London.
Veal, A.J. (1987) *Leisure and the Future*, London: Allen & Unwin.

3 The Management of Human Resources in the Leisure Industries

Robert J. Brown

Introduction

The aims of this chapter are to introduce students to the behavioural science theories and ideas which have shaped the field of human resource management, and to develop a critical approach to both the theory and practice in the field.

To achieve this aim the chapter is divided into two parts. In the first part the theoretical foundations of human resource management are outlined and evaluated from an academic perspective. The second part then deals with the applications of these theories in managerial practices currently in use within the human resources field, and concludes by raising some critical issues on evaluation of these practices.

Theoretical Foundations of Human Resource Management

Taylorism and Scientific Management

From our perspective of present day managerial practices, the most relevant starting point is the work of Frederick Taylor, and the Scientific Management Movement associated with his name. Taylor trained as an engineer and made his first contribution to the field in a paper presented to a meeting of engineers in 1895, entitled 'A piece-rate system, being a step towards partial solution of labor problems'.

In this paper Taylor identified a tendency in employees not to work as hard as they were capable, and labelled this tendency 'systematic soldiering'. He argued that such behaviour was due to managerial inefficiency, since management did not reliably know how much work any employee could produce, and therefore left decisions on the methods of production to the discretion of the employees, who resorted to inefficient rules of thumb.

Taylor argued for the methods of science and the logic of engineering to be applied to management, introducing measurement and planning in an attempt to develop a science of work. Each task was broken down into its elementary operations, and these operations timed meticulously, so that the time to complete any task could be calculated from these elemental operations. He further refined his approach by identifying 'the one best way' of performing each task which minimised the total time taken, yet secured the quality of task performance required. His systematic methodology earned his approach the title 'Scientific Management'.

Taylor extended his 'scientific' methodology to recruitment, recommending the selection of employees based on their fitness for the job rather than the more common criteria of nepotism or patronage. This approach would ensure the selection of the 'first class' man (*sic*), necessary for the success of his scientific approach to management. This first class man, once selected, would be trained to perform each task in the one best way that Taylor had identified, and would be encouraged to adopt this optimal method through a system of differential payments.

Taylor's differential piece-rate system involved two different payment rates for the same job, a higher rate of pay when the work was finished in the shortest possible time and in perfect condition, and a lower rate if the job took longer, or if the work was defective. This motivational system required that production targets be set, and the higher price paid only when these targets were met, thereby establishing an incentive for the workers to work rapidly yet carefully.

Taylor also applied his scientific methodology to the organisation of supervision, recommending that workers report to a different supervisor for each function, thereby introducing his principle of 'functional supervision-ship'. This idea, however, did not increase productivityyyy and did not gain widespread support in factories.

Taylor's approach rested on his belief that the changes he recommended would be accepted because they had been scientifically determined'. He believed that managers would accept responsibility for planning, co-ordination and controlling work, and for fixing production targets by scientific measurement techniques, rather than their formerly arbitrary methods. Workers likewise would accept revised methods of working because of the rewards of higher pay and less fatigue, if they followed his 'one best way'.

Taylor's naive and simplistic expectations of managers and workers revealed his primitive view of human behaviour. His view conceptualised man as a machine responding to purely economic motivation, operating in isolation, with no extraneous influences from his employing organisation, his community, his culture or the multiplicity of other roles upon him.

Scientific Management as a movement was subjected to a scathing critique by Henry Braverman (1974), who traced the application of

Taylor's ideas in the fragmentation of work within factories, and in the deskilling of jobs, a feature characteristic of the major production industries of the 1960s. He criticised Taylor's neglect of, and antipathy towards, trade unions in his analysis of worker behaviour, and his naive assumption that individual workers would pursue their own self-interest without regard to their membership of work groups or union branches. These isolationist assumptions came under empirical scrutiny in the 1920s and early 1930s by a group of sociological researchers, who were subsequently titled the 'Human Relations Movement'.

The Human Relations Movement

The Human Relations Movement had its origins in a series of research investigations within the Western Electric Company in Chicago, known as the 'Hawthorne Experiments', and reported fully by Roethlisberger and Dickson (1964). In the first of four phases of research from 1924 until the 1940s, experiments were set up to investigate the effects of altering various environmental conditions, such as lighting levels, upon the efficiency of electrical component assemblers. No conclusive relationships were found between illumination levels and output, possibly because of poor research design.

In 1927, new experiments were conducted using a group of six women whose work levels had previously been covertly measured. They were installed in a test room, cut off from their former colleagues, and their working conditions were systematically varied. They were successively placed on a group bonus scheme, given rest pauses, free snacks, shorter hours and working week, with most earlier privileges being retained. In the twelfth period all the privileges were removed, and then restored in the subsequent thirteenth research period. These studies showed that in all but one of these periods output per hour increased, including the twelfth period when all privileges had been removed. Relationships between the women were observed to be friendlier, and the small group was aware of their former workmates' envy.

The 'Hawthorne Effect' was proposed to explain the continued improvement in output, particularly during the period when all privileges were withdrawn, whereby the unexpected productivity increases were due to the special attention that the group enjoyed in being singled out for the experiments. Although later authors have highlighted methodological weaknesses which could have explained the improved productivity, the proposed Hawthorne Effect gained the support of many management theorists as an explanation for the unexpected in employee behaviour. Subsequent experiments, using other work groups, tested specific hypotheses on selected variables, and found similar increases in productivity but found correlative and causative factors no easier to determine.

Another phase of structured interviews was initiated to determine employee attitudes on specific issues, such as working conditions and supervision, but were deemed too direct properly to elicit employee attitudes. They were subsequently modified to more open-ended counselling sessions, where employees' dissatisfactions were explored. These interviews revealed differences in orientation between male and female employees, variations in attitude with position in the plant and the employee's function within it, and influences upon the attitude to work from the employee's wider social role and responsibilities. The interviews with the supervisors revealed anxieties arising from their marginal role between workers and management, and the existence of common sentiments within functional groups.

A third phase introduced anthropological methods in setting up the Bank Wiring Room Observation Group. This group continued their former work but were isolated in a special Observation Room, with an observer present throughout. The observer discovered that the group shared a precise notion of a fair day's output, and when this figure was exceeded, they would report a false figure closer to the daily norm and reduce their efforts the following day. The group applied sanctions such as abuse and ridicule to those who either repeatedly over-produced or under-performed. It also emerged that the supervisors colluded with employees in these mechanisms of control over work which optimised their effort and reward bargain. These informal group mechanisms of control became the focus of the observers' subsequent attention, and revealed that the group had an effective system for policing its informal rules. Within the group each employee had particular roles and a group-conferred status often indicated by a nickname.

The final phase of the Hawthorne Experiments institutionalised the personnel counselling, originally to allow employees to 'talk out' their concerns, but this counselling degenerated through the loss of the counsellors' impartiality, to an information gathering and manipulation exercise.

These studies, often associated with Elton Mayo, whose involvement came late in their progress, have been used to support somewhat dubious conclusions. They have been credited with discovering 'Social Man' as the more developed variant on Scientific Management's 'Economic Man', and with revealing the seductive impact of the Hawthorne Effect. The argument that the group being subject to special attention, rather than the actual changes experienced, explains their improved performance, implies that it is a social, not a physical effect, and it is the influence of the 'social' dimension which is the essence of human relations.

In one of the best critiques of the studies, Carey (1967) has pointed out how the conclusions are widely at variance with the evidence presented. There were no correct control procedures in the experiments to show that the observed increases in output were due to the experimental changes alone, and that changes in group composition over the twelve periods of the first phase of experiments seriously undermine the validity of the results.

Despite Carey's methodological criticisms, the Human Relations Movement's achievement of academic respect was due to the publicity efforts of Elton Mayo. He abstracted the 'social' factor from the results and promoted it as the unifying principle for all the studies, pursuing its implications for management in his writings. Good managers, he argued, were those who were socially skilled in counselling and leadership. Conflict between worker and management was symptomatic of poor communications, since the competent manager could, through effective communications, build teamwork by expanding the worker's desire and capacity to co-operate with management.

Although one can be critical of Mayo's propagandist uses of the research and its conclusions, the major contribution of the Human Relations Movement to management was to highlight the importance of the informal organisation within formal work structures, and the complex informal social processes by which work groups were able to exert regulatory control over their work situation. The movement developed awareness of relationships within work groups, and the influence of work groups in setting norms and in policing members' behaviour. But, perhaps most importantly, it seduced managers into believing that paternal benevolence towards one's subordinates would win over the most recalcitrant of workers. That management could be successful by delivering social harmony to the workers was perhaps the most significant contribution of the Human Relations Movement, a managerial ideology which any supervisor would be happy to espouse.

Unfortunately Mayo's panacea of fostering social relationships did not eliminate the traditional workplace conflicts between managements and workers, nor did unions seem interested in managerial attempts to induce social harmony. Eventually the direction of academic development shifted to a new focus on how to motivate employees, and spawned the group which have been loosely characterised as the Motivation Theorists.

Motivation Theorists

Following the Scientific Management and Human Relations contributions, managers had come to expect assistance from the academic world in how to deal with their perennial problems, and one question which focused the attention of managers was 'how do I motivate my employees?' Attempts to answer this question spawned several theories and has given rise to a modern day motivation industry described by Rines (1988).

Maslow's Hierarchy of Needs

The most significant of the early theorists was Abraham Maslow, who proposed that individuals all experienced human needs, the more primitive of which were instinctive. He formulated his 'hierarchy of human needs', where individuals experienced needs in the hierarchical order of physiological needs first, followed by security, social, self-esteem, and finally self-actualisation needs at the top of his triangular hierarchy. He argued that human beings would follow his principle of 'prepotency', whereby they would be motivated to act so that they could first satisfy the lower order needs, and then the needs of the next level, and so on up the hierarchy. Once satisfied, the lower levels of need ceased to be motivating, and the needs of the next level in the hierarchy became the motivator. Individuals would always seek to progress up the hierarchy, according to Maslow, and would be motivated by the continued existence of an unmet need.

Maslow's hierarchy has been a very powerful organising idea in management over the years, as evidenced by its appearance in successive generations of management training courses. Despite its seductive attractiveness, however, the theory has a number of weaknesses. Its analysis of human needs is overly simplistic, treating the experience of need as a unitary phenomenon, whereas psychological evidence would suggest that our needs are diverse and complex, and may not even be consciously acknowledged, even though they are guiding our behaviour. Given the complexity of modern economic and social life, individuals may be on more than one level of the hierarchy at any one time, and may have different needs in differing domains of their life, of which work is but one. Furthermore the hierarchy is uni-directional, asserting that all individuals will progress upwards through the hierarchy as their lower order needs are met, although commonsense evidence would suggest that individuals may move up or down the levels of need, in response to particular economic or social circumstances. Other critics attack Maslow's classification of needs as being at variance with the reality of human experience. Factor analytic studies have found no evidence that human needs fit Maslow's neat classification.

In a subsequent revision of his theory, however, Maslow qualified his general theory to accommodate modifying factors, such as the role of association, habit and conditioning, and the relation between needs and cultural patterns.

Perhaps the most damaging of the criticisms of Maslow's hierarchy is that it has not been validated empirically, and when attempts have been made to do so, the results have not unequivocally demonstrated its utility. In the largest set of studies to test Maslow's theory, Porter (1961 and 1964), and Porter and Mitchell (1967) found little evidence to support the general validity of the hierarchy among American managers.

Alderfer (1969 and 1972) developed Maslow's theory by reducing it to three levels of need, those of Existence (E), which combined Maslow's two lowest levels, Relatedness (R) which mirrored the social level, and Growth (G), encompassing Maslow's two highest levels, to provide the ERG model of motivation. Alderfer's refinement did allow for regression to lower levels of need from higher levels, since his own research demonstrated that the satisfaction of a need level was associated with the importance of the need itself, rather than the importance of the next higher level need. He has also reported factor analytic support for his *ERG* classification.

Despite these refinements, and their initial intuitive appeal, need theories of motivation have not gained general acceptance as an adequate explanation of how or why people behave at work. Despite being standard fare in courses and textbooks for managers, they have tended not to have been incorporated into managerial practices.

McGregor's Theory *X* and Theory *Y*

Another psychologist, often credited with having extended Maslow's theory by linking his needs to reality, is Douglas McGregor. McGregor maintained that people were motivated by needs of their own to a much greater extent than by pressures brought to bear on them by management. He presented his model of motivation in the form of two contrasting 'theories' of humankind to which managers subscribed, and which could be used to characterise their managerial style.

In the first, Theory X, managers held certain assumptions about mankind, and how these influenced the motivation to work hard. These were:

- The average human being is born lazy and will avoid work if he or she can
- Because people dislike work, most of them must be forced, controlled, and threatened with punishment to get them to do a fair day's work
- The average person prefers to be told what to do: they wish to avoid responsibility, have little ambition, and want security above all.

Under Theory X assumptions the manager would feel justified in motivating their employees by instructing them clearly, and then driving them by constant supervision to ensure that instructions were carried out. In such situations the individuals would respond to being told what to do and to being forced to do what they would otherwise avoid.

In contrast to Theory X, McGregor presented an alternative set of assumptions, wherein mankind was seen as eager to take on responsibility in their work, which they considered part of their normal life. These assumptions which he called Theory Y, were:

- Work is as natural as play, if the conditions are favourable
- Control imposed from above, and the threat of punishment, are not the only ways for getting workers to work satisfactorily
- The average person, under proper conditions, not only accepts but even looks for responsibility
- A large proportion of people have the ability to use their imagination, ingenuity and creativity to solve difficult problems that may arise on the job.

Although originally presented as theoretical propositions, Rose (1978) argues that these assumptions constitute more of a programme than a theory, and consequently cannot be critically evaluated using the same criteria as for other psychological theories. Nonetheless, adopting a more pragmatic form of evaluation, Maslow spent some time trying to apply Theory *Y* within a company, and pointed out that demands made by the theory are such that only the tough and the strong can take them, and accused McGregor of inhumanity to those insufficiently strong to take on the responsibilities of Theory *Y*. These difficulties notwithstanding, McGregor's contribution encouraged many managers to adopt the more 'enlightened' practices of Theory *Y* as a panacea for the motivational difficulties with their employees.

Herzberg's Motivator–Hygiene Theory

Maslow's theory argued that a need, once satisfied, ceased to motivate the individual. Herzberg used a research technique known as the critical incident method, where individuals were asked to identify the factors associated with occasions when they felt motivated, and those associated with when they were dissatisfied. Using factor analysis Herzberg concluded that there were two distinct sets of factors that influenced employee motivation. One set of factors, such as increased pay, canteens at work, car-parking, etc. which he labelled 'hygiene factors', merely served to reduce dissatisfaction but did not contribute to motivated performance. Another set of factors, including increased responsibility, greater auto-nomy, enhanced decision-making power, etc. were necessary for employee motivation and effort, and these he labelled 'motivators'. Under this Two-Factor Theory of Motivation (Herzberg, 1966) when managements wished to motivate employees, they would need to provide the motivators, since provision of the hygiene factors alone would not ensure motivated responses from their employees.

Although developed from empirical research, Herzberg's theory has been criticised by Cooper and Makin (1984) because of the ambiguity of some of the data upon which it rests. They also point out that support for his theory has generally come only from studies using similar population samples, and from research designs which have required self-reporting of attitudes and performance. Self-report methodologies are vulnerable to respondents being unable or unwilling to make accurate assessments of their own performance. More critically, however, it is possible that Hertzberg's findings could be explained by the tendency, identified by attribution theory research, for individuals to attribute responsibility for weaknesses or failures to external causes, whereas successes are attributed as due to the individual's own abilities.

Whatever the validity of Hertzberg's research, it did move the field on from Maslovian armchair theorising to empirical research into employee motivation. Its conclusions on the nature of the motivating factors focused attention on attempts to modify the design of jobs so that they would involve more discretion and responsibility. These efforts led organisations to embark on Job Enrichment, Job Enlargement and Job Redesign programmes, now collectively referred to as the Quality of Working Life Approach.

Quality of Working Life Approaches

Hertzberg's research findings – that factors inherent in the job could transform motivation, whereas improving the hygiene factors served only to reduce dissatisfaction – were used as justification for increasing the motivational factors within the job by enriching individual jobs, and making them more interesting, thereby increasing the quality of working life for employees. Such modifications to job content have become known as the Quality of Working Life approach.

Within Quality of Working Life approaches, the term 'job enrichment' is used to refer to changes in job content which increase the range of the tasks 'vertically' – i.e., combine some tasks usually performed by employees at a higher level in the work process. Job enlargement, by contrast, increases the tasks horizontally by adding more tasks of the same level, but such that the total job is wider with less repetition of single tasks.

Both enrichment, whereby more responsibility and authority has been added, and enlargement, where more task variety is provided, have been found to increase the motivational properties of the job (Wall, 1978).

Hackman and Oldham (1976) presented their Job Characteristics Model to predict the effect of any particular job design upon the work-related attitudes and behaviours. Their model presents the relationships between core job dimensions, such as skill variety, task identity, autonomy, etc. and critical psychological states, including experienced meaningfulness or responsibility for the outcomes of the work, and personal and work outcomes such as high quality work performance, low absenteeism and turnover, etc.

The predicted outcomes from the job design, however, are subject to influences from individual differences. Hackman and Oldham suggest that the effects of the job design on personal and work outcomes are moderated by an individual's Growth Needs Strength, (GNS). Consequently an enriched job will have an effect only upon those employees who have a high need for autonomy and responsibility, and may have no effect upon those without such needs.

The Job Characteristics Model, which seeks to predict the outcome of changes in job design, represents an advance on Herzberg's theory since it accommodates individual responses within it. It has received general support from research by Wall, Clegg, and Jackson (1978). One study of the redesign of the work of sales representatives by Paul and Robertson (1970) produced impressive results in both improved attitudes and performance, lending weight to the contribution of job design approaches.

However the Quality of Working Life approaches are not without criticism. First, it can be difficult to identify the gains that come from redesign alone, since many other factors in the situation change at the same time – e.g., payment systems, clocking-in systems, supervisory methods, etc. – so that the claimed improvements may be partially explained by motivating features of these simultaneous or consequential changes. Secondly the ideology guiding job design differs from the dominant ideology of most work organisations, in that personal development and individual involvement are given priority over the more traditional values of profitability and managerial prerogative. This focus upon the individual and individual development has often come under attack by managers, and by trade unions who perceive it as a threat to collective action. One weakness common to many job enrichment and enlargement applications has been a neglect of the concerns and interests of trades unions over such changes. While such developments can offer significant motivating advantages for some individuals, these same changes can alter the demarcation lines which trades unions see as important to job security and the continuation of their workplace power. The failure to understand the pluralistic reality of many workplaces has often caused many job enrichment and enlargement programmes to encounter strong opposition from trades unions at the workplace.

Expectancy Theory

Research in cognitive psychology suggests that an individual's behaviour is considerably influenced by their expectations of what will happen in the future. Vroom (1964) applied this finding in his Expectancy–Valence theory of motivation, which proposes that motivation is a function of two factors, expectancy and valence, according to the following equation:

Force of Motivation (F) = Expectancy of Desired Outcome (E) x Valence of Desired Outcome (V)

Expectancy refers to the individual's perception of the likelihood of a particular event or outcome occurring, while Valence is how attractive that outcome is, and how likely it is to result in satisfaction (see Figure 3.1). Other authors have elaborated Vroom's model to include other variables, such as Instrumentality (*I*), referring to the extent to which the expected outcome can be instrumental in obtaining another desired outcome. Lawler and Porter (1967) enlarged the model to incorporate the fact that effort is not the only determinant of performance, and they accommodated individual differences by including Abilities and Role Perception as intervening variables between Effort and Performance.

Figure 3.1   Expectancy theory

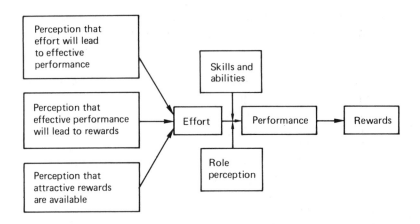

Abilities refers to characteristics such as intelligence, manual skills, and personality traits, while role perception refers to the behaviours the individual feels he should engage in to perform his job successfully, and determines the direction in which effort is applied. Since individuals vary widely in their abilities and how they see their roles, the inclusion of these as intervening variables makes this version of expectancy theory more sensitive to individual differences than Vroom's original model.

A further refinement by Porter and Lawler (1968), which accommodated the importance of feedback in learning, was made by the inclusion of feedback loops linking the Performance as an outcome with Expectancy, and Performance with Valence. This allowed for individuals to learn from their experience, and so to modify their future expectancies or valences.

Given the complexity of the elaborated model of Expectancy Theory, much research has been directed at testing particular hypotheses derived from the model. Dachler and Mobley (1973) tested the model on semi-skilled workers on two manufacturing sites, and found a positive correlation between their index VIE (Valence x Instrumentality x Expectancy) and work performance, so that the higher the index the greater the work performance. Lawler and Suttle (1973) found similar results in their study of 69 retail managers. Results to date indicate that the Expectancy Model has been only partially successful in relating motivation to peformance, but it has helped reveal the complexity and multivariate nature of motivation. Since the model provides empirically testable hypotheses, further research may yet reveal the critical variables in employee motivation, although these are likely to be multifactorial.

The belief that no single motivational change, such as introducing an incentive scheme, could be successful if introduced in isolation, gave support to new approaches which sought organisation-wide changes, and known as Organisation Development approaches.

Organisation Development

Organisation Development Approaches

Organisation Development is normally associated with any approach which seeks to change the organisation as a whole, rather than any specific part or process. In one pioneering study Trist and Bamforth (1951) examined the introduction of mechanisation to coal mining in Britain. The traditional method coal mining by self-selecting teams, who cut and moved the coal, and fixed the roof supports as they progressed into the coal face, was replaced by a semi-automatic mechanised method of cutting and moving the coal. This new method allowed a wider coal face to be worked by larger groups of miners, but the work was paced by the machinery rather than by themselves.

The new method fragmented the formerly close-knit work teams, dispersed them across the coal face, and led to lower morale, with higher levels of absenteeism and increased accident frequencies. It also required much greater levels of supervision than the small team methods. In another mine where the same equipment was introduced, the management installed different organisational arrangement, developing multi-skilled teams, the rotation of tasks within shifts, and rewarding shift teams as a whole, rather than by individual payment as at the other mine. The results of these different organisational arrangements showed in higher production, lower absenteeism and improved morale. This study drew attention to the importance of the technological system and structural factors in influencing people's behaviour at work, and revealed the different effects that could be achieved when social and psychological factors were taken into account.

In 1956 von Bertallanffy produced a seminal book on Systems Theory within biology, which analysed the relationship between the whole and the component parts of biological organisms. The insights and analytical capacities of this new theoretical model were noted and applied to organisations by Fred Emery (1965). The lessons from the classical coal mining study were taken up by other systems theorists within the Tavistock Institute of Human Relations, and gave rise to the 'Socio-technical Systems Theory', which argued for social and psychological factors to be given equal weighting to technological factors in the design of work and work processes. The Tavistock researchers argued that, contrary to Scientific Management's approach, jobs should not be divided into fragmented tasks. Rather, autonomous work groups should be given responsibility for different 'whole tasks', with the leaders of the work groups assuming the role of facilitators and representatives.

Evidence from research by Woodward (1965) lends support to the notion of social systems and technological systems interacting in organisation design. She found particular structural characteristics and modes of social organisation were associated with certain technological systems in her study of British manufacturing organisations. Her arguments for sensitive interaction between the social and the technological found subsequent expression in a major organisational development initiative undertaken by Volvo (Blackler and Brown, 1980). Volvo replaced the traditional moving assembly line method of vehicle construction with an 'assembly island' process whereby cohesive work groups produced one complete vehicle at a time, sharing the responsibilities and the tasks among all the members of the team.

But just as the technology being introduced into an organisation can affect the social system, the structures within organisations show different capacities to cope with changing circumstances. Burns and Stalker (1966) examined the relationship between the structures of different manufacturing companies, and their capacity to cope with changes in their environment, identifying two polar types, Mechanistic and Organismic organisations. Mechanistic organisations are heavily bureaucratic, relying upon hierarchy and rules and upon clear lines of demarcation between tasks and roles of different levels within the organisation. Organismic organisations, on the other hand, are designed to respond rapidly to changing circumstances. They have little task specification and demarcation for their members, with priorities and task allocation being continually reviewed, and emphasis placed upon relevant knowledge and expertise. Authority emerges more as a network than a hierarchy, and rests upon expertise and commitment rather than pre-ordained rank. The communications similarly resemble a network, and are open as opposed to highly structured and formal within the Mechanistic organisation. Organisations, however, do not always conform to these pure Mechanistic and Organismic types.

Modifying attitudes towards the customer has become the focus of the more recent organisation development processes such as Customer Care programmes, Right First Time campaigns, and Total Quality Management. Because of the high level of commonality in delivering services such as catering, transport, etc. many organisations have sought to distinguish their services in the marketplace through distinctive standards of customer service. These organisational change processes, common in many manufacturing organisations also, represent a development from the earlier organisational development approaches which focused mainly on the employees. These newer processes place significant emphasis upon the customer, as well as the employee, and in many cases encourage participants to see their fellow employees as their customers, based on the theoretical premise that perceiving one's customers in a new light is likely to lead to more positive behaviours towards them.

Organisation Culture Approaches

The efficacy of such organisation development processes cannot be directly established in many cases, so the proxy measures of organisation culture and climate have been used in their support. Culture has been defined by Hofstede (1984) as 'the collective programming of the mind', and organisation culture can be thought of as the subtle processes by which employees' behaviour is shaped within an organisation. In a significant descriptive study Deal and Kennedy (1982) examined the processes which many large internationally successful organisations used to ensure the desired behaviour from their employees. They identified that organisations frequently have strong 'corporate cultures' which communicate the dominant values of the organisation, and the knowledge of 'how things are done' to new entrants. These relay the norms and expectations which employees use in their dealings with others, and frequently prescribe the procedures and methods sanctioned by the organisation.

Peters and Waterman (1982) provided empirical support for the influence of corporate cultures in their book *In Search of Excellence*, tracing linkages between strong and distinctive organisational cultures and the success of organisations in the marketplace. Although they used market criteria for success, such as market share of profitability, organisational success was associated with a strong sense of commitment and high levels of organisation loyalty from the employees.

Many practitioners have used this research as adequate justification for the provision of programmes to establish and maintain strong corporate cultures within organisations, each with their own distinctive values and orientations. Although few evaluations of such organisational culture approaches are available, Smith (1986) has demonstrated the contribution of an organisation culture approach in a financial services company.

Another programme which incorporated the organisational culture approach with a marketing-oriented Customer Care campaign, was the 'Putting People First' programme adopted by British Airways. This hybrid programme sought to modify the value system within the airline so that the customer became more clearly valued than before, and to influence all employees' awareness of, and behaviour towards, the customer as a means of gaining future customer loyalty. Since the introduction of the programme, the airline has demonstrated considerable commercial success in increasing market share. However, it is not possible formally to evaluate this programme for its impact upon employee behaviour due to the confounding of key variables by the simultaneous privatisation of the airline.

Cross-cultural Transfers

In Cross-cultural Transfer approaches, a derivative of technology transfer processes, the organisational processes dominant in one national culture are transplanted to another. Hofstede (1984) has conducted the definitive research in this field. Using 40 different nations, he examined patterns of thinking and social action within and between societies, and identified by factor analysis four main dimensions on which country cultures differ – those of Power Distance, Uncertainty Avoidance, Individualism and Masculinity. This allowed him to characterise each national culture on pairs of these dimensions, thereby providing some indication of the degree to which cultural differences might influence the transfer of technological and organisational processes.

The cultural differences between America and Japan have been used as the basis of a novel motivation theory, in William Ouchi's Theory Z. Ouchi's theory rests on Trust, Subtlety and Intimacy. Trust and Subtlety are management techniques, but Intimacy is a state of the environment, and according to Ouchi, all three are necessary for the true benefits of Theory Z to function. Ouchi argues that Theory Z works in Japan because trust is an inherent element of the national business environment. Each level of the organisation hierarchy knows that all others have as their primary goal the success and well-being of the company. Subtlety is the more personal acceptance and respect for the idiosyncracies of others, based on lengthy experience of working with the same individuals, such that the pressures applied are unspoken or unobserved by outsiders. This subtlety is developed through such dimensions of Japanese society as lifetime employment and respect and rewards for seniority, which reduces overt competition. Intimacy derives from the extended influence of the company throughout communities, as in company-sponsored or financed schools, hospitals and housing. Since those who work together often live together within the same company housing, they participate in a 'sense of community' described by Ouchi as 'intimacy'. These three elements of Theory Z are constantly interacting within Japanese society, on and off the job.

The key issues for cross-cultural transfer approaches are how such cultural dimensions might influence organisational success in new countries, or how much modification they might have to undergo to achieve the same effect in other cultures. Analytically acceptable research studies into the influences and adjustments of cross-cultural transfer are likely to appear in the future, but aspects of cross-cultural transfers have been described in a number of publications. Wickens (1988), the Personnel Director of Nissan (UK), has outlined how Japanese organisational processes were utilised or modified to build the high levels of employee commitment which characterises the success of the Nissan operation to date, particularly the efforts to remove the traditional class symbols and barriers which have characterised British industry in the past. Broad (1987) has reviewed the role and contribution of Taiso, or physical exercises in building employee commitment within Japanese companies and recalls that industrial recreation was a common feature of British industry throughout the 1950s and 1960s.

In many of these descriptions of the organisational practices of companies from other nations, the role of the trades unions are frequently ignored, and the existence of conflict neglected. However no review of human resources management theory in Britain is complete without considering the role of industrial relations in shaping employee behaviour.

Industrial Relations

Industrial Relations refers to the wide range of processes and practices which make up the joint regulation of work by management and the trades unions. Fully to understand the influence of industrial relations upon work behaviour, the reader is encouraged to consult one of the standard texts on the subject, but in what follows I have briefly outlined the industrial relations trends and processes which have had an impact upon employee and managerial behaviour into the late 1980s.

Trades unions have existed in Britain for over a century, but were originally organised only in mining and heavy engineering industries where working conditions were very poor. They depended upon members' support for strikes and other forms of industrial action to win concessions from employers. Throughout the growth of the factory as a locale for production their power grew by recruiting members in key jobs, those with the power to halt production and reduce profits. Frequently the organising of workforces by unions was opposed, and recognition of the unions was withheld by employers because they were seen as an infringement upon 'management's right to manage'.

The role of trades unions has continuously been disputed in Britain, and in the late 1980s they have been described by certain politicians as an historical anachronism. Nevertheless they have enjoyed the support of governments in the past so that their present behaviour reflects in part their former roles. During the First World War the notion of employees' rights and employee representation was established initially by government within the munitions industry, and the tradition of joint consultation and employee representation was subsequently extended through the Whitley Council system to the modern civil service. The Second World War brought further governmental recognition of the role and contribution of trades unions. In the post-war recovery, however, the unions revealed their industrial power through strikes in the docks and motor industries. They demonstrated that they could win concessions from managements for their members in periods of labour shortages so that their membership grew throughout the 1960s and 1970s.

During the 1970s the then Labour government accepted trade union involvement in the management of organisations by passing legislation designed to extend collective bargaining to all employees. The EEC requirement for Britain to explore mechanisms for increased employee participation in their employing organisations provided a further boost to trades unions, as they anticipated being identified as the most appropriate channel for employee representation.

The sociologist Alan Fox (1966) has argued that the conflicting beliefs in managerial prerogatives and collective bargaining were reflected in differing frames of reference, which had strong influences upon managers' and workers' behaviour. His 'unitary' frame of reference was characterised by the belief that employees and management were all members of the same team in pursuit of common goals, and that the existence of conflict within the organisation was because of failures by management to communicate these common goals adequately. Under this unitary frame of reference trade unions were an historical anachronism which had outlived their relevance.

Fox's 'pluralist' frame of reference, on the other hand, held the belief that organisations were composed of different interest groups, each with their own objectives and methods, some of which would be incompatible with the objectives of other groups. The existence of conflict, therefore, was to be expected, and trades unions were seen as a legitimate mode of expression of the objectives of their members.

While one could focus upon key industrial relations processes such as collective bargaining, etc. it would seem that the shifting emphasis from pluralist to unitarist frames of reference is the major industrial relations influence upon human resource management today. The unitarist frames of reference of management have been supported by new employment legislation in the 1980s, which has markedly limited the activities of trade unions. The decline in union membership in the decade has mirrored the decline in union power at the workplace, and has allowed the resurgence of managerial prerogatives. Management's right to mange has been asserted most vigorously in the new service industries, such as the leisure industry, where trade unions are either weak or non-existent.

Although industrial relations influences have seldom been evaluated in the field of human resource management, and have been neglected by many of the theories and movements within the field, they have had a profound effect in shaping employee behaviour in Britain in the post-war period. In the review of management practices to follow, these influences must be considered since pluralist frames of reference are still held by some groups of employees, and the absence of overt conflict over innovations in human resource management must not be interpreted as unitarist consensus.

Management Practices in Human Resource Management

In this section of the chapter I have reviewed particular management practices, which draw directly or indirectly upon the theoretical and practical approaches reviewed earlier. Any review of management practices cannot but be selective, and the choice included here has been based on examination of current practices adopted by major leisure providers in the public and the private sectors.

Recruitment and Selection

Taylor identified the importance of selecting the right people for each job in his recommendations on the recruitment of 'first class' men. Despite the sexism of his recommendations the principle of improved selection has been grasped by managements within the leisure industry, through the adoption of psychological testing as one measure to ensure better selection.

Many leisure employers require candidates to undergo psychometric testing for managerial positions. Some organisations favour personality tests, or aptitude tests such as critical reasoning or numerical analysis, while others such as Ladbrokes use Assessment Centres, in which each candidate undergoes extensive testing on a range of psychological variables, on their skills, attitudes, values and competences, and has a series of interviews with different assessors. The objective of such testing is often to identify those candidates whose profile a range of tests matches most closely the profiles of successful managers within the organisation.

However one major criticism levelled at many of the organisations using such selection techniques is that tests have been introduced without giving adequate consideration to the validity of their selection criteria. While their managers can describe the desired profile from such tests, they have not always determined the relationship between the desired profiles and subsequent success in the job. The major contribution of testing and

Assessment Centres is that they can improve selection, provided one can determine an empirical relationship between the characteristics being tested and subsequent effective job performance, a task still in progress in many leisure organisations. Nonetheless, the adoption of testing techniques has introduced more formal and valid methods of selecting the best candidate than the long-favoured but unreliable method of the interview. Tests offer the capable employee the chance to progress on the strength of their abilities rather than on other more prejudicial criteria.

Flexible Employment Practices

One distinguishing feature of the leisure industry is that it is heavily influenced by consumer demand which is not always easy to predict accurately in advance. The advent of hot weather in Britain provides ample evidence of unpredictable demand. Suddenly motorways and roads to the coast become jammed, seaside towns are flooded with visitors and the normally predictable consumer demand for ice-cream, cold drinks, sportswear, etc. becomes an uncontrollable rush. Such vagaries of climate, television coverage of sporting events such as tennis at Wimbledon, etc. all render consumer demand for leisure services highly volatile, and consequently have forced the leisure industry to develop flexible responses to unpredictable demand and unforeseen circumstances. Much of this flexibility is reflected in new employment practices and new conditions of employment.

Some leisure employers now maintain two groups of staff, one group forming the core staff employed full-time, with another group available employed on a fixed part-time or casual basis, to meet the peaks of demand as they arise. These patterns of employment are particularly common in leisure activities where event management plays a large part, since employers need a large number of staff only for the duration of the event, and do not wish any on-going financial commitment outside of the hours required. To meet these peculiar circumstances, many national centres with frequent large events have developed 'casual employees' banks' of people with an interest in leisure, who are happy to make themselves available for the hours required, and who respond to requests as consumer demand dictates. These organisations find this flexible arrangement of 'committed casual staff' allows them to call on additional labour as required, without any financial overheads other than the maintenance of the staff register and the necessary telephone liaison.

Whilst not an example of job redesign acceptable to the academic purist, the development of flexible employment practices, such as casual staff banks, self-employed staff, split-shift working, and mobile relief teams, etc. are evidence of practical responses to the need to cover peaks in consumer demand, or shortfalls in the supply of full time or committed part time staff.

Such practices have proved successful in meeting the short-term needs of leisure employers for staffing coverage. Their longer-term efficacy, however, must be evaluated with respect to prevailing economic and employment conditions, where service industries are growing at a faster rate than ever before while unemployment continues at a level unthinkable in earlier decades. Whether the managerial practices of flexible employment would have emerged, or will continue to exist under conditions closer to full employment is an issue for economists and social planners. Managements, however, must consider for the longer term, whether the maintenance of two different groups of employees, with different conditions of employment and different expectations of job security, will ultimately lead to conflict between groups and with management.

Another managerial practice adopted predominantly in the commercial sector which pursues the goal of flexibility of labour, is that of single status employment. The pursuit of single status – i.e., the removal of the distinctions between white collar and blue collar employment and the equalisation of their non-monetary employment conditions – has been an objective of some British trades unions for some years. A number of leisure organisations have introduced single status employment where all employees are paid a salary and enjoy the traditional benefits of salaried staff, in return for behaviour expected of staff employees, such as working flexibly as and when, and where required by the needs of the service, working additional hours without the payment of overtime, and demonstrating commitment to the goals of the employing organisation through the ignoring of traditional demarcation boundaries.

Whilst such practices can be part of a wider organisational development programme designed to build employee commitment, trade unions often argue that the primary objective of such changes in the contracts of employment is to remove the obligation for paying overtime to employees. In the light of the evidence presented earlier on job design and organisational development, it is possible that such piecemeal changes, not accompanied by genuine efforts at building employee commitment, may have only a short-term ameliorating effect, and may lead to increased employee resistance in the longer term. Where employees perceive the achievement of single status, not as a benefit but as a new means of control, it is likely to lead to conflict in the future.

Measurement of Performance

The Scientific Management practice of better measurement of work capacity and performance has found a resurgence in 1980s Britain. Many areas of public sector service provision have been required to develop performance indicators so that they can provide some better estimate of their efficiency and their effectiveness. Many leisure services managers, therefore, have had to draw up satisfactory measures of their resource use, and to identify measures which could validly evaluate their effectiveness in achieving key objectives. These changes have directly affected the public sector of leisure in particular, through the government imposed requirement for competitive tendering. As a result managerial practices in the public sector are increasingly converging with those in the commercial sector, whereby the efficiency and effectiveness of all managerial activities in the leisure sector will be open to comparison and scrutiny using managerially acceptable performance indicators.

This new emphasis on performance measurement has been incorporated into the longer established managerial practice of performance appraisal, whereby employees' performance over a period of time has been assessed and judged by a superior. In the past such appraisals have been highly subjective and judgmental, with the process being influenced by the nature of the relationship between the superior and the subordinate. Now many leisure organisations have used these performance indicators as targets and objectives in the performance appraisal process, and have replaced the formerly qualitative judgements with quantitative measures of employee performance.

Methods of Rewarding Employees

Many managers in leisure are now combining performance appraisal techniques with remuneration schemes based on performance related pay, such that the best performers receive the highest financial rewards, often at the expense of the poor performers who forfeit rewards under zero-sum budgeting. Clearly the integration of such measurement methodologies with performance appraisal and performance related pay are all managerial practices which owe a debt to Scientific Management, and tend to emphasise financial rewards over other incentives recommended by other theorists. There is increasing evidence of commercial success for the organisation, accompanied by personal financial advancement for the management from such practices, which has acted to silence the criticisms from those arguing that work should provide rewards other than just money. The success of these approaches must be viewed, however, in the overall context of the social and economic support for entrepreneurial activity from the prevailing political climate, and judgement about their efficacy under different political conditions must be deferred.

Despite the focus on financial rewards by many managements, employees may also be experiencing enhanced motivation through the setting of management targets. Locke and Latham (1979) presented the intuitively appealing Goal-Setting theory that people are more motivated to perform when set specific goals, and when feedback is given on performance. Accumulating evidence lends support to this theory, and since the present emphasis upon measurable performance requires the setting of specific goals, there is scope for improved employee motivation, provided they are involved voluntarily in the process.

Training and Development of Staff

Perhaps the one enduring lesson which practitioners have drawn from theory in the human resources management field is that training is necessary both for self-development and for improving organisational effectiveness. As a consequence there has been widespread growth in training activities in the leisure industry, as the industry tries to develop managers for the future, and to shape the behaviour of the employees needed for the present.

Customer Care programmes have been introduced into many leisure organisations to develop both their staff and their organisation. Telephone techniques training has been used to create positive attitudes towards the organisation among potential customers, while service delivery training has ensured that new customers will wish to return. The development and maintenance of positive staff attitudes and behaviours through such programmes have demonstrated their efficacy, if commercial success is used as the evaluation criterion. More diverse proxy measures such as reduced staff turnover, improved co-operation and fewer grievances have also been claimed as evidence of their success in motivating employees.

Some commercial leisure organisations are investing heavily in Leadership training, and many use outdoor pursuits courses for the development of leadership and team working skills. Such courses do contribute to improved self-confidence in participants and as a result claim significant benefits for improved practice at the workplace. In the absence of formal evaluation, and despite the enthusiastic claims from successful participants, the relationship between such training practices and better managerial performance must remain not proven. Meanwhile the more established practices such as external courses, developmental projects and assignments, postings to other divisions, managerial coaching and consultations with a mentor continue as the main source of management development for the industry, given their record of past success.

In a recent change in organisational practice, Mecca Leisure, one of Britain's largest leisure companies, determined that they could not find the skilled staff they needed from higher education or the marketplace, and adopted their own in-house and on-the-job training programme called 'Putting the Pieces Together' as a means of developing their managers of the future. The programme is designed to run over a number of years and to provide each recruit with the training and development he or she needs to achieve managerial goals at each stage. The adoption of this programme represents an advance on past practice in the leisure industry, and can be seen to have significant motivating implications for the managerial participants.

Employee Relations

Perhaps the most significant changes in managerial practices within human resource management have occurred on the issue of industrial relations. 'Industrial relations' has traditionally referred to situations where trade unions have regulated the relationships between employer and employees. Where good industrial relations prevail, the unions have usually been granted legal recognition and its attendant rights to organise the workforce, to represent its members within procedures, and to participate in collective bargaining on their behalf. The existence of industrial relations practices within the leisure services of many public sector organisations has been regarded as evidence of the prevalence of a pluralistic frame of reference (Fox, 1966) within these organisations, and the acceptance of trade unions having a legitimate representational role.

However, since the beginning of the 1980s the political climate has hardened towards trade unions, and their activities have come under greater legal restraint than even before. This change in the political climate has been accompanied by a resurgence in the unitarist philosophy of management's right to manage. Both of these inter-related factors have encouraged employers to rethink their relationships with trades unions and to question the relevance of industrial relations to their organisations. Within the public sector of leisure this rethink has been advanced by the imposition of competitive tendering, and the potential contracting out of leisure services has provided opportunities for undermining trade unions by removing their recognition rights. There are growing indications within the leisure industry that industrial relations strategies are progressively being replaced by new unitarist employee relations strategies, characterised by direct communications between managements and employees, but without the mediation of traditional workplace union channels.

One major commercial sector leisure employer, Ladbrokes, has adopted this employee relations approach by introducing sophisticated new communications strategies, including briefing groups, videotaped awareness campaigns, corporate presentations, and 'open door' management policies. Beneath these influencing campaigns, not dissimilar to the customer care campaigns referred to above, are subtle pressures to persuade employees to forsake trade unionism for commitment to the organisational goals.

Clearly where an organisation is pursuing a policy of replacing pluralist industrial relations strategies with unitarist employee relations strategies, they will wish to maintain confidentiality, and thereby render evaluation difficult or impossible. However the spread of employee relations practices would seem to be on the increase in the commercial sector, and is likely to penetrate those parts of public sector leisure services which wish to win in the competitive tendering exercise, since the threat of impending job losses provides a powerful weapon in removing many of the privileges won by trades unions for their members over the years. Where the likelihood of winning a tender for the provision of leisure services is predicated on the removal of trade union practices such as demarcation, control of overtime, etc. then the removal of trades unions themselves, and their attendant industrial relations processes, becomes more likely.

Cross-cultural Transfers

Among the best examples of cross-cultural transfer is that of Customer Care programmes, which were pioneered in the leisure industry by American organisations such as MacDonalds, and Disneyland. Another transfer is that of the Quality Circle, a practice common in Japanese organisations where a supervisor leads open discussions with employees on how best to achieve quality and production targets. The quality circle meets on a regular basis to review past difficulties, and to pool ideas for future improvements. Implicit in the process is the proposition that quality is a shared responsibility, and that everyone should strive to ensure quality in their individual efforts.

The approach has a long and successful history within Japanese industry, notable for its high levels of cultural consensus and commitment, lifetime employment and respect for seniority and status. Having contributed strongly to Japanese success, it faces a real challenge in delivering similar success in a different cultural environment, particularly one like Britain, marked with a long history of industrial conflict, and where the trades unions perceive them as another facet of the unitarist ideology of team-working. However, there is evidence from Hill (1986) that they can succeed where top management are committed to them, the trades unions indifferent, and the working environment conducive.

Conclusion

In our selective review of current managerial practices, we see that practising managers have adopted certain ideas from the theories and movements which make up human resources management. Often these ideas have been only partially applied, or have been significantly modified in the application from their original theoretical formulation. Where they have been applied the criteria used to determine their success have often been commercial indicators, which at best can be only proxy measures of an individual's responses, and at worst can have been explained by factors completely unrelated to the theoretical ideas being applied. Any conclusions are limited by the lack of acceptable evaluation reports which go beyond the anecdotal, to reveal the variables and relationships critical to the successes claimed for such applications.

In other instances practitioners have adopted theoretical ideas and discarded them because they were either too difficult to apply or were unacceptable to the organisation culture seeking a solution, or the recipients were unable to see the relevance of the ideas to their daily tasks and roles. Such experiments have seldom been written up so we are unable to form a judgement upon the validity of the ideas themselves.

When we review the extensive nature of the theory within the field of human resources management, and the limited range of applications reported in the literature, we cannot fail to conclude that present day managers have not found as much that has proved useful in practice as one would have expected. One possible explanation for this limited conversion of theory into practice must lie in the recognition that all the theoretical ideas were developed in an economic, political and social context unique to their time, and must thereby be influenced by those contexts. As ideas they were not developed in a vacuum, and cannot be treated as having some abstract and universally applicable truth. The application of any of these theoretical ideas, therefore, which fails to take account of these context effects must be considered as having limited validity and effectiveness. Any claims of success in improving human resources management must be considered with scepticism until the influences of the environmental context have been isolated. This has probably never been more true than at present when strong political endorsement of particular managerial practices has influenced managers to adopt certain unitarist practices in preference to other more pluralist approaches. We can only await acceptable empirical evidence of their effectiveness (or otherwise), before incorporating them into the body of human resources management knowledge.

Further Reading

Rose (1988) is a good source of additional information on the ideas outlined in this chapter, with the merit of containing much of the recent research and academic thinking produced in the 1980s.

Ribeaux and Poppleton (1978) is a textbook for those with an understanding of psychology. It is comprehensive in its coverage, and explores the contradictions that arise from research findings in an attempt to develop coherent theory.

Cooper and Makin (1984) was specially written for managers who might not have a background in the behavioural sciences. Consequently it has presented many theoretical ideas and research findings in a way that the lay person can easily understand. Its coverage of topics, however, is limited.

Buchanan and Huczynski (1985) is a good textbook, with extensive coverage of sociological ideas and numerous examples of their application, for those who need to have complete information in the field.

References

Alderfer, C. (1969)'An Empirical Test of a New Theory of Human Needs', *Organisational Behaviour & Human Performance*, 4, pp. 142–75.

Alderfer, C. (1972) *Existence, Relatedness and Growth: Human Needs in Organisational Settings*, New York: Free Press.

Blackler, F. and Brown, C. (1980) 'Job Redesign and Social Change: Case Studies at Volvo', in Duncan, K., Grunekerg, M. and Wallis, D. (eds), *Changes in Working Life*, London: Wiley.

Braverman, H. (1974) *Labor and Monopoly Capital: The Degradation of Work in the Twentieth Century*, New York: Monthly Review Press.

Broad, J. (1987) 'Japanese Management', *Personnel Management* (August).

Buchanan, D. and Huczynski, A. (1985) *Organisational Behaviour, An Introductory Text*, London: Prentice-Hall.

Burns, R. and Stalker, G. (1966) *The Management of Innovation*, London: Tavistock.

Carey, J. (1967) 'The Hawthorne Studies: A Radical Criticism', *American Sociological Review*, 32, pp. 403–16.

Cooper, C. and Makin, P. (1984) *Psychology for Managers*, London: Macmillan/ BPS.

Dachler, H. and Mobley, W. (1973) 'Construct Validation of an Instrumentality–Expectancy–Task–Goal Model of Work Motivation: some theoretical boundary conditions', *Journal of Applied Psychology*, 58, pp. 397–418.

Deal, T. and Kennedy, A. (1982) *Corporate Cultures*, Harmondsworth: Penguin.

Emery, F. (1965) *Systems Thinking*, Harmondsworth: Penguin.

Fox, A. (1966) *Industrial Sociology and Industrial Relations*, Royal Commission on Trades Unions and Employers' Associations, Research Paper, 3, London: HMSO.

Hackman, J. and Oldham, G. (1976) 'Motivation through design of work: test of a theory', *Organisational Behaviour and Human Performance*, Vol. 16, pp. 250–79.

Hackman, J. and Porter, L. (1968) 'Expectancy Theory Predictions of Work Effectiveness', *Organisational Behaviour and Human Performance*, 3, pp. 417–26.

Herzberg, F. (1966) *Work and the Nature of Man*, New York: World Publishing Co.

Hill, (1986) *Towards a New Philosophy of Management*, London, Tavistock.

Hofstede, G. (1984) *Culture's Consequences*, New York: Sage.

Lawler, E. and Porter, L. (1967) 'Antecedent Attitudes of Effective Managerial Performance', *Organisational Behaviour & Human Performance*, 2, pp. 122–42.

Lawler, E. and Suttle, J. (1973) 'Expectancy Theory and Job Behaviour', *Organisational Behaviour & Human Performance*, 9, pp. 482–503.

Locke, E. (1968) 'Toward a Theory of Task Motivation and Incentives', *Organisational Behaviour & Human Performance*, 3, pp. 157–89.

Locke, E. and Latham, G. (1979) 'Assigned versus participative goal setting', *Journal of Applied Psychology*, vol. 60, pp. 299–302.

Ouchi, W. (1981) *Theory Z*, New York: Addison-Wesley.

Paul, W. and Robertson, K. (1970) *Job Enrichment and Employee Motivation*, London: Gower.

Peters, T. and Waterman, R. (1982) *In Search of Excellence*, New York: Harper & Row.

Porter, L. (1961) 'A Study of Perceived Satisfaction in Bottom and Middle Management Jobs', *Journal of Applied Psychology*, 45, pp. 1–10.

Porter, L. (1964) *Organizational Patterns of Managerial Job Attitudes*, New York: American Foundation for Management Research.

Porter, L. and Lawler, E. (1968) *Managerial Attitudes and Performance*, Homewood, Ill.: Dorsey.

Porter, L. and Mitchell, V. (1967) 'Comparative Study of Needs Satisfactions in Military and Business Hierarchies', *Journal of Applied Psychology*, 51, pp. 139–44.

Ribeaux, P. and Poppleton, S. (1978) *Psychology and Work*, London: Macmillan.

Rines, M. (1988) 'The Business of Motivation', *Management Today* (February).

Roethlisberger, F. and Dickson, W. (1964) *Management and the Worker*, New York: Wiley.

Rose, M. (1978) *Industrial Behaviour*, Harmondsworth: Penguin (2nd edn, 1988).

Smith, G. (1986) 'The Motivation of Sales Executives', *Ashridge Papers in Management Studies* (Autumn) Ashridge Management College, Berkhamsted, England.

Taylor, F. (1947) *The Principles of Scientific Management*, New York: Harper & Row.

Trist, E. and Bamforth, D. (1951) 'Some Social and Psychological Consequences of the Longwall Method of Coal-Getting', *Human Relations*, 4, pp. 3–38.

Vroom, V. (1964) *Work and Motivation*, New York: Wiley.

Wall, T. (1978) 'Job Redesign and Employee Motivation', in Warr, P.B. (ed.), *Psychology at Work*, Harmondsworth: Penguin.

Wall, T., Clegg, C. and Jackson, P. (1978) 'An Evaluation of the Job Characteristics Model', *Journal of Occupational Psychology*, 51, pp. 189–96.

Wickens, P. (1988) *The Road to Nissan*, London: Gower.

Woodward, J. (1965) *Industrial Organization: Theory and Practice*, Oxford: Oxford University Press.

4 Financial Management and Leisure Provision

Mike Stabler

Introduction

This chapter is concerned with financial management in the voluntary, commercial and public leisure sectors. The aim of the chapter is to give an insight into the nature and purpose of financial management and to demonstrate its contribution to the assessment of the efficiency and effectiveness with which resources are employed. Inevitably this is done in an introductory and selective manner because the subject is so extensive. The topics of most relevance to leisure which are examined include: the meaning, scope and structure of financial management; information and accounting systems covering the role and interpretation of final accounts; ratio analysis and performance measures; financial management methods; cash flow and budgetary analysis; capital appraisal; and sources and methods of finance.

Almost without exception any form of leisure provision will necessitate financial management. At its most simple level it might be managing a small club formed to allow members of a community to participate in their chosen activity. At the other end of the spectrum it might be the management of a multinational and conglomerate company such as Thomsons, the holiday tour operator, marketing all manner of leisure activities. Set rather apart from these two extremes is the operation of leisure facilities by the public sector, largely through local authorities.

Whatever the form of provision there is a need to establish the aims and objectives of the organisation; and the means to achieve those objectives. The main forms of leisure provision have widely differing objectives. The voluntary sector generally seeks to maximise benefits for its members, whereas commercial organisations primarily pursue profits, thus defining their objectives in financial terms. The public sector is more concerned with wider social objectives at a national and local level such as the promotion of participation, good health and community spirit. Whatever the primary objective of an organisation it has responsibilities with respect to its employees, clients or members, shareholders, creditors and the community at large. To an extent both the form of provision and objectives govern the necessary financial management.

Definitions and Scope of Financial Management

What exactly, then, is financial management, and what is its relationship with accountancy and other discipines? Most attempts to define financial management accept that it involves the formulation of aims and objectives, policies, planning and control systems, and that it embraces most aspects of the operation of an organisation whether profit-seeking or not. It may be defined as: the estimation of the financial resources needed and their provision at the appropriate time for specified purposes at minimum cost, including the identification and appraisal of investment opportunities, and the planning and control of financial matters to facilitate the attainment of the objectives of the enterprise.

Financial management has developed from the three traditional divisions of accountancy, financial, cost and management accounting. It is an essentially pragmatic subject which has tended in the past to be isolated from other disciplines. Originally the subject was concerned only with sources and methods of finance but it is now an integrated and composite area of study and practice incorporating elements of economics, mathematics, statistics, systems analysis, and behavioural science.

A recent publication by Sizer (1985) on management accounting sets out its foundations and the text by Watts (1984) provides an overview of its nature and scope. In the current context a thorough review of material in this field is not appropriate for two principal reasons. First, the majority of texts reflect its use in commercial manufacturing enterprises. Secondly, in considering its application to leisure provision, only certain aspects need be examined.

The principal areas of interest are summarised in Figure 4.1 which attempts to show, irrespective of the sector of provision, the most important interrelationships between the components of financial management and their linkages to external factors.

Figure 4.1 gives a very much simplified picture of management in order to bring out the distinctions between Monitoring/Control and Planning, and between tactical and strategic aspects of management, and to give an idea of the decision sequence. In reality, the interconnections between control and planning would be more complex and the sequence would be subject to numerous feedbacks.

After a brief consideration of the external environment influencing the operation of leisure organisations, the impact of economic factors is outlined, including reference to the contribution the discipline of econo-

Figure 4.1 Diagrammatic representation of the elements of financial management

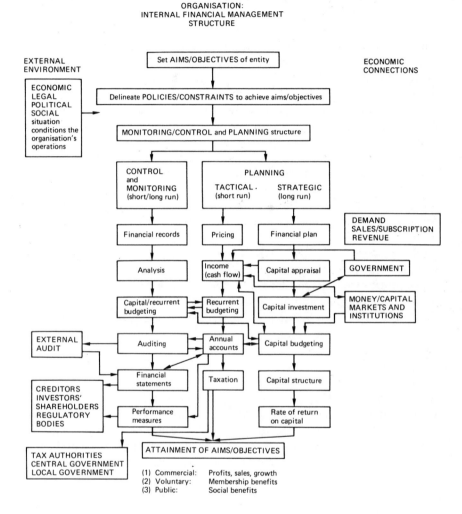

mics makes to the financial management of such organisations. The remainder of the chapter examines their internal financial management structure and functions, largely following the steps shown in Figure 4.1, and endeavouring to explain, as fully as space permits, not only financial management techniques but their relationship to other disciplines.

The External Environment

The recent economic and political climate has given a sharper focus to the management of financial resources in both the private and public sector. In the public sector, in common with other services, leisure provision has been subjected to close scrutiny concerning value for money, account-ability and economy. Allied to this is the introduction, where possible, of competitive tendering as well as outright 'privatisation'. In the private sector, in an increasingly competitive and technological world, the main concern has been to improve efficiency both by enhancing sales revenue and controlling costs, including the introduction of labour saving equip-ment, and thus increase profits. In such circumstances there are consider-able implications for the financial management of leisure organisations.

Local authorities have sought to develop their financial management in order to adapt to the current stringent expenditure situation. Some authorities have decided on strategies which give priority to certain services, others have pursued policies to improve efficiency and some have adopted 'creative accounting'. Private companies have tended to make greater use of monitoring and control systems relying much more on accountancy specialists. The voluntary sector has also recognised the need for a more professional approach, adopting commercial accounting me-thods.

With respect to the legal environment, this is largely concerned with the need to comply with requirements on reporting the financial state of the organisation. Commercial leisure providers have to make final accounts available for auditing and taxation purposes. If they are limited companies they have to fulfil obligations to shareholders and will come under the provisions of the Companies Acts. Most texts on financial accounting make some reference to legal requirements: see, for example, Holmes and Sugden (1985).

Government bodies are also required to make financial information available and are subject to external auditing, as are local authorities, whose operations are regulated by the Local Government Acts. These requirements are covered in public sector accounting texts, for instance Henley *et al*. (1983). Voluntary leisure organisations, unless the bodies are registered charities, are subject to virtually no legal requirements but there is a moral obligation to give periodic financial reports to members.

Economic Connections

Of the other disciplines associated with accounting in general, and financial management in particular, the closest links are with economics, for three reasons. First, the subject is concerned with the external environment of financial management involving such factors as demand, prices, market competitive structure, the use of resources and the macroeconomic situa-tion, including government policy. Secondly, economics itself, in its analytical and methodological development, has drawn on elements of mathematics, statistics and systems analysis which are also relevant to accountancy. Thirdly, it has made a significant contribution to accounting techniques and practice, as well as continuing to perform an interpretative and commentatory role. These links are acknowledged by those in the profession since, in the education of accountants, economics is considered an essential ingredient.

There are texts which consider the relationship of the two subjects in a general way, such as Mathews (1962). Once the relevant economic concepts have been identified, their application in accounting can be located in the accountancy literature, most readily as one would expect, in texts on management accounting and financial management. Sizer (1985) gives a comprehensive coverage of the former and Pitt Francis (1973) of the latter. Notable examples of adoption and adaptation of economic concepts are: break-even analyis; pricing; particularly marginal cost pricing; capital appraisal, investment analysis/capital rationing; valuation of assets/inflation accounting; costing and internal pricing. These reflect the emphasis economics places on issues concerning: efficiency; distribution (demand, pricing and market conditions); the allocation of resources (human, capital and land). These concerns will be highlighted at appropriate points in tracing the management of financial resources with respect to leisure provision.

Financial Management Structure

Aims, Objectives and Policies

Referring to Figure 4.1, the aims and objectives of an organisation and their relationship to the three forms of leisure provision have already been outlined. 'Policies' and 'constraints' are also clearly a function of the form of provision. Both aims and objectives and policies and constraints will be referred to in the ensuing discussion of the control and planning process.

Monitoring, Control and Planning

As the presentation in Figure 4.1 suggests, monitoring, control and planning are determined more or less concurrently. In reality long- and short-term plans are formulated prior to setting up monitoring and control systems whose purpose is to assist in the achievement of aims and objectives contained in those plans. 'Planning' concerns the predetermination of courses of action on such matters as pricing, marketing, profits, growth and investment which arise from the main aim of provision and the resources available to the organisation. There are a number of stages in the compilation of plans which will vary with the nature of the provision and whether strategic or tactical plans are being considered.

Strategic financial planning, as illustrated in Figure 4.1, involves mostly decisions on capital. Tactical financial planning is more concerned with day to day operations regarding the short-term cycle of income and recurrent costs. The stages in the financial planning process, which require little explanation, are given in Figure 4.2. Figure 4.2 does not differentiate between long- and short-term planning, as the process is essentially similar.

The left-hand side of Figure 4.2 demonstrates the relationship between the planning and control process. The solid arrow which feeds back to the derivation of potential plans suggests the stage at which reformulation of plans is necessary, should there be a marked variance in the projected and actual outcomes of the selected plans. It is of course conceivable that a more fundamental reformulation is necessary if the aims and objectives of

Figure 4.2   The financial planning process

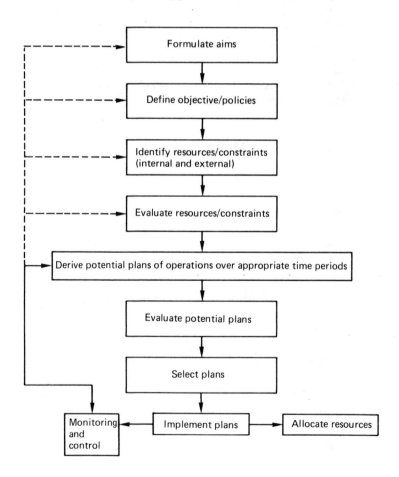

the organisation are not being attained, or there is a change in the resources available, or in constraints. The broken line therefore indicate feedback to one or more stages prior to the derivation of potential plans.

Financial Management Information and Systems

The whole internal structure of the management of financial resources and its appropriate accounting stems from the basic concept of the continuous flow of funds. This flow concept is best appreciated by briefly considering the initiation of a leisure project. Funds have to be acquired either through borrowing, or from the organisation's or individual's own resources, or possibly by grants or donations. Capital expenditure is required to secure land, premises and equipment and recurrent costs such as staff, materials, energy, etc. for running the facility. The 'product' has to be priced and marketed. Assuming that appropriate decisions have been made and implemented, revenue will accrue and will need to be allocated to meet capital and recurrent costs. The principal components of revenue and expenditure, which should be self-evident, are presented in Figure 4.3. Any surplus of revenue over expenditure is either retained or distributed. In the case of commercial concerns profits will be allocated to reserves or paid to the owners or shareholders.

Public sector facilities are likely to differ from private and voluntary sector entities not only in operating at a loss, thus receiving substantial grants or subsidies, but also in being subject to transfer charges. For example, a local authority leisure centre may pay for services from other departments such as environmental services, personnel and treasurers.

The notions represented in Figure 4.3, together with Figure 4.1, illustrate to an extent both the nature of the information and the necessary accounting systems required to facilitate management of an organisation.

The examination of the information requirements and aspects of accounting systems which have been selected as currently most pertinent to the management of leisure provision financial resources are considered under the headings of Accounting Data and Management and Methods.

1. Accounting Data

- Record keeping and financial accounting
- Interpretation of accounts and performance assessment.

2. Management and Methods

- Cash flow analysis and pricing
- Capital investment appraisal
- Sources and methods of finance.

Figure 4.3 Flow of funds: principal items of income and expenditure

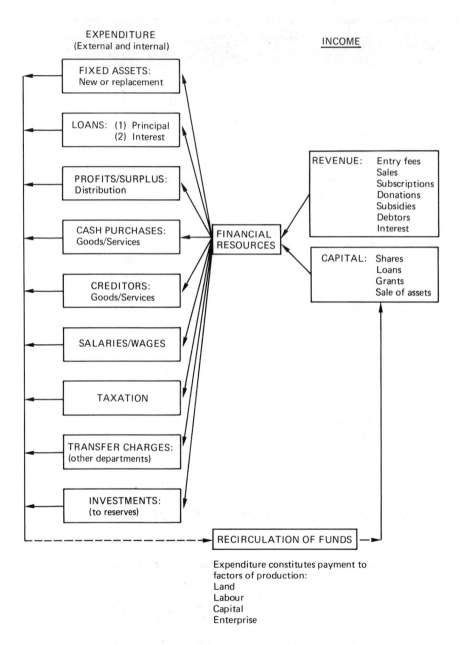

EXPENDITURE
(External and internal)

INCOME

FIXED ASSETS:
New or replacement

LOANS: (1) Principal
            (2) Interest

PROFITS/SURPLUS:
Distribution

CASH PURCHASES:
Goods/Services

CREDITORS:
Goods/Services

SALARIES/WAGES

TAXATION

TRANSFER CHARGES:
(other departments)

INVESTMENTS:
(to reserves)

FINANCIAL
RESOURCES

REVENUE: Entry fees
                    Sales
                    Subscriptions
                    Donations
                    Subsidies
                    Debtors
                    Interest

CAPITAL: Shares
                    Loans
                    Grants
                    Sale of assets

RECIRCULATION OF FUNDS

Expenditure constitutes payment to
factors of production:
Land
Labour
Capital
Enterprise

Accounting Data

Record Keeping and Financial Accounting

Accounting Records

Accounts using a double entry bookkeeping system are the very foundation of financial, cost and management accounting, and consequently financial management. The double entry system enables an accurate and complete record to be kept of each transaction and, as the information in the accounts covers all areas of the day to day running of the organisation, control can be maintained. However, the most important feature of the system within the context of financial accounting is that it facilitates the summary of records and the construction of integrated statements to indicate the financial position of the organisation for both internal and external analysis and interpretation.

It is not possible to undertake a detailed examination here of bookkeeping. Normally its principles are explained in the introductory chapters of books on financial accounting (see the basic references given in the further reading at the end of this chapter), but it should be noted that practice in the United States differs slightly from United Kingdom conventions.

An appreciation of the basic bookkeeping process can be gained by considering financial transactions, their classification and their purpose. The three main leisure provision sectors referred to earlier are likely to conduct five main groups of transactions:

* Revenue (entry charges, sales, subscriptions, etc.)
* Cost of sales (cost of acquiring trading stock, e.g. bar, catering)
* Expenses (incurred in course of earning revenue)
* Acquisition of funds (financial capital):

– Ownership funds (internal funding)
– Borrowed (external funding)

* Accumulation of assets (fixed and current).

Every transaction is recorded twice, as a debit entry in one account and a credit in another.

A distinction is normally drawn between capital and revenue accounts. The capital account which relates to the finance put into the entity by the owner, shareholders, public body or members is normally divided into fixed and working capital. In effect, funds are allocated to the acquisition of fixed assets; the amount remaining is the working capital which is used in the running of the business entity.

Accounting conventions usually classify records into cash or ledger. Cash accounts deal with movements of cash in hand and bank accounts, all other records being termed ledger accounts.

The double entry system and its associated accounts provides essentially a record of:

- Profits/surplus and losses
- Assets and liabilities.

This facet of accounting is examined below in considering the functions of the profit and loss account and balance sheet.

The Final Accounts Introduced

The notions of profits and changes in assets and/or liabilities are the vital ingredient of all financial statements which are of benefit to those both within and outside the organisation. The final accounts, drawn from financial records, which are normally presented in the annual reports of commercial entities, are the:

- profit and loss account or income statement
- balance sheet
- sources and application of funds
- statement of value added
- directors' report
- auditors' report
- notes to the accounts.

These summary accounts are sometimes given on both an historic and current cost basis. Accounts on an historic basis are prepared at prices prevailing in the year they were compiled, whereas those at current cost reflect changing prices in times of inflation. It is a requirement to show the results of the previous year. For comparative purposes, to identify trends, it is desirable to present reports and results for the previous 5 to 10 years.

Understanding final accounts is not unduly difficult: their meaning is almost self-evident once the principles of their construction have been grasped. Though the sources suggested as suitable for financial accounting deal with those accounts, their interpretation is covered more clearly and comprehensively in texts specifically on the subject. Bird (1983) has written a seminal work on the subject, but an extremely concise and well presented introduction is given in Brett (1987) while Holmes and Sugden (1985) give a more detailed exposition.

Since these summary accounts are such a fundamental concept, underlying most aspects of financial management, an illustrative example is given in Figure 4.4 based on a commercial concern.

Figure 4.4 Typical business profit and loss account and balance sheet: possible adaptation to the public and voluntary sectors

(1) Profit and loss account	£	£
Turnover (sales)		x
Less cost of sales	x	—
Gross profit		x
Less : direct costs: staff	x	
running expenses	x	
depreciation, etc.	x	
	x	
overhead costs: staff	x	
running expenses	x	
rates/rents	x	
administrative recharges:		
R & A Dept	x	
Other departments	x	—
Net operating profit (loss)		x
Less : interest (debt charges)	x	—
Net profit (loss) on ordinary activities		x
Less : extraordinary items	x	—
Net profit (loss) for year		x

	£
Net assets	x
Percentage return (loss)	x
Capital employed	x
Percentage return (loss)	x

(2) Balance Sheet	£	£
Fixed assets: Premises		x
Equipment		x
Current assets: Stocks	x	
Debtors	x	
Cash in hand/in bank	x	
Creditors (short-term)	x	
Net current assets		x
Total assets *less* current liabilities	—	x
Creditors (long-term)	x	—
Net assets		X
Capital and reserves		
Loans/grants	x	
Profit and loss account	x	x

Notes: In a business enterprise:

(1) Taxation would be included in the profit and loss account after deduction of interest charges, and likely to be shown as provision for taxation in the balance sheet under capital and reserves
(2) Dividends would be shown after net profit (loss) in the profit and loss accounts
(3) Share capital would be included as an item under capital and reserves in the balance sheet

Other items peculiar to specific businesses may be found in both the profit and loss account and balance sheet

The Final Accounts Defined

1. **Profit and loss account or income statement**: this summarises the results, gains or losses of the organisation's operations for a given period, identifying the main sources of income and costs of achieving them.
2. **Balance sheet**: the balance sheet lists the assets, liabilities and owners' equity of an enterprise at a given point in time. It also distinguishes between short- and long-term assets to establish whether there are sufficient of the former to cover short-term liabilities.
3. **Sources and application of funds**: this statement identifies the resources obtained (financing operations) whether from the enterprise's operational revenue or reserves or outside agencies, and indicates how these funds have been spent (investing activities). It draws on information given in the balance sheet and profit and loss accounts, distinguishing between capital and recurrent transactions which increase or decrease the funds available.
4. **Statement of value added**: the statement shows the difference between what the enterprise paid for its inputs and what it sold the product for. In a sense it is an expansion of the revenue and cost of sales section of the profit and loss accounts. From it can be identified how the total revenue has been contributed by, and distributed among, the providers of resources both internally and externally.
5. **Directors' report**: it is a requirement for limited companies and is a statement of the enterprise's activities over the accounting period.
6. **Auditors' report**: validation of the entity's records and final accounts by an independent accountant is normally a legal requirement.
7. **Notes to the accounts**: these are included to explain the method of calculation and composition of major items, covering such matters as depreciation, taxation, investments, interest received and paid, directors' emoluments, capital structure, etc. Annual reports for limited companies must contain items (1), (3), (5) and (6) and are a valuable source of information. They have both a reporting and interpretative function. Externally, the functions and uses of final accounts are for: professional and regulatory organisations, legal requirements (e.g., Companies Acts), auditing, taxation, creditors, the Stock Market, potential investors (personal and corporate), public relations and national statistics. Internally they serve proprietors and shareholders, management, employees and audit accountants.

External Relevance of Final Accounts (see Figure 4.5)

With respect to the external reference, at this point it is necessary only to mention the significance of final accounts in relation to the attempts by the professional or regulatory bodies to standardise accounting practice. The

Figure 4.5 The functions and users of final accounts

EXTERNAL		
	1.	Professional/regulatory organisations
	2.	Legal requirements (e.g. Companies Acts)
	3.	Auditing
	4.	Taxation
	5.	Creditors
	6.	Stock Market
	7.	Potential investors: (1) personal sector
		(2) corporate sector
	8.	Public relations
	9.	National statistics
INTERNAL	1.	Proprietors/shareholders
	2.	Management: planning, monitoring and control
	3.	Employees
	4.	Auditing

Accounting Standards Committee (ASC), has pursued this by a process of consultation through the medium of what are known as Exposure Draft (EDs) and proposals for Statements of Standard Accounting Practice (SSAPs). Once SSAPs have been agreed and published they place on management and auditors an obligation to adhere to them as far as possible; in effect they constitute self-regulation by the professional bodies. The adoption of SSAPs, as far as is possible for non-profit-making institutions, has been advocated by the Chartered Institute of Public Finance and Accountancy (CIFPA), the professional association devoted to the interests of public bodies.

Though SSAPs are essentially concerned with external appraisal, they do assist in the internal management of the organisation. As their designation suggests, their purpose is to standardise procedures which is of use in cost and management accounting as well as financial reporting, especially to facilitate the making of comparisons. Ashton (1983) has comprehensively described and analysed SSAPs, but reference is also made to them in texts on all branches of accounting.

Internal Application of Final Accounts

Within the context of financial management, it is clearly the analysis and interpretation of final accounts which is of vital interest, notwithstanding that an organisation's fortunes are determined by external assessment of its performance. The most important statements, to which attention will be largely confined, are the profit and loss account and balance sheet.

Though public and voluntary sector leisure organisations have different objectives from commercial concerns, there is still a requirement for, and advantage to management to produce, final reports. These two sectors produce expenditure and income statements which is their equivalent of the profit and loss account. In practice, certainly at local club level, voluntary sector accounting is apt to be rudimentary, very often being little more than a single entry record of cash receipts and disbursements. Where receipts exceed expenditure a surplus is transferred to the organisation's reserves. In the case of local authority provision, which in the majority of cases does not cover its operating costs, deficits are incurred which have to be met from other sources. Balance sheets in the commercial sense are rarely constructed in the public sector specifically for leisure facilities, though they are produced for the whole organisation. They are seldom compiled in the voluntary sector, notwithstanding that some organisations hold substantial assets and incur liabilities (Ravenscroft and Stabler, 1986).

An important feature which distinguishes the two sectors from the commercial sector is that accounting is on a cash basis as opposed to the accruals approach. The former enters into the accounts transactions as they occur, while the latter 'matches' revenue with the costs associated with earning it, for the same period, even though the cash transactions have not actually occurred. Under a cash basis it is more difficult to establish the financial position of the entity, and therefore to derive measures of performance. Local authorities, encouraged by CIPFA as part of the issue of accounting standards referred to above, are moving towards an accrual system. Stabler (1984) has argued, with an appropriate illustration relating to local authority leisure centres, that it would be of benefit for the public and voluntary sectors to adopt methods employed in business and that it is possible to do so with some adaption.

Interpretation of Accounts and Performance Assessment

It is possible here only to outline in a selective manner the interpretation of the two main final accounts, the profit and loss account and balance sheet, which is carried out under the following heads:

- The structural relationship between the profit and loss account and balance sheet
- Comparisons of results over time
- Comparisons of results with other similar entities
- Calculation of ratios
- Derivation of performance measures.

The Structural Relationship Between the Profit and Loss Account and Balance Sheet

This is essentially the impact of profit and surpluses or losses, recorded in the profit and loss account, or the assets and liabilities and owners' and shareholders' equity shown in the balance sheet:

- In the profit and loss account: Sales minus Cost of sales equals Gross profit/loss; Gross profit minus Expenses equals Net profit/loss

- In the balance sheet: Assets minus Liabilities equals Ownership funds.

Thus, through what can be termed the 'accounting equation', changes in net profits or losses (P/L) will change assets (A) or liabilities (L), thus leading to a change in ownership/shareholders funds (S), that is;

$$\triangle P/L = \triangle A - \triangle L = \triangle S \text{ (where} \triangle = \text{change in } \ldots)$$

In sole proprietorship or partnerships the net profit, or a proportion of it, will be drawn as the return on the investment in the enterprise. In limited companies it will be distributed as dividends. Only that profit retained and allocated to reserves will increase net assets and the value of a company, which should be reflected in an increase in the price of the company's shares. The linkage of profits or losses and assets and liabilities will be considered again in examining ratios and performance measures.

Comparisons of Results Over Time

In commercial concerns, under favourable trading conditions, profit will be expected to grow in real terms – that is, after adjusting for the rate of inflation. In line with this growth should be a corresponding growth in the value of the assets of the entity and distribution of profits to the owners or shareholders. In effect, ownership yield should be sustained either in the form of capital growth and/or income.

Normally the progress of the enterprise is expressed by showing the percentage change from year to year in key variables such as sales revenue, gross and net profits, earnings per share, dividends (in both financial and percentage yield terms), net assets and net worth. These terms are explained in Brett (1987).

Comparisons of Results With Other Similar Entities

Assessing the performance of the entity with other similar organisations is an invaluable external reference check. It is of particular relevance where financial targets are inappropriate, such as in public and voluntary sector provision. Indeed, external comparisons are facilitated for local authorities in the UK by the CIPFA Statistical Information Series, such as Leisure and Recreation Statistics and Leisure Charges (produced annually). The first endeavours to cover all local authorities in England and Wales and the second is on a sample basis.

Where there are facilities run on commercial lines in the public sector then there is no reason why they should not be compared with enterprises in the private sector; Stabler (1984) has advocated this for certain services such as bars and catering within leisure centres.

Calculation of Ratios

Ratio analysis in some respects is the nub of the interpretation of annual reports, with considerable implications for planning and control internally as well as constituting an effective external means of assessment. To an extent ratios are a measure of performance in themselves, having a distinct advantage over absolute monetary measures. Most ratios currently used are derived from items appearing in the profit and loss account and balance sheet, being based on four fundamental variables   sales, cash, stocks and debtors – and their relationship to capital.

As ratio analysis was developed for application in manufacturing and retail businesses, a number of financial ratios are not really relevant to service activities, particularly leisure. Moreover, when applied to non-profit-seeking entities in the public and voluntary sectors, it may be necessary to obtain other information from within or outside the organisation. Examples of this are given below. However, if suitably adapted, ratio analysis can be a useful tool in leisure enterprises.

In the commercial world there are two main groups of ratios, profitability ratios, and liquidity and solvency ratios.

- Profitability ratios: the commercial measure of success is profit, and a number of ratios link it to the fundamental variables already referred to. A key relationship is:

$$\frac{\text{Profit}}{\text{Capital}} = \frac{\text{Profit}}{\text{Sales}} \times \frac{\text{Sales}}{\text{Capital}}$$

However, there are different definitions of both profit and capital which create many variants of this key equation. Which definitions are adopted is very much a function of the purpose of the analysis. Profit can be gross, or net, which might be taken before or after interest payable and taxation. Capital may be the total assets of the business, that contributed by long-term investors or by ordinary stockholders or by working capital. Bird (1983), Morley (1983) and Holmes and Sugden (1985) deal with these questions of definitions and ratios. Other profitability measures which might be derived are:

$$\frac{\text{Value added}}{\text{Sales}} \; ; \; \frac{\text{Value added}}{\text{Wages and salaries}} \; ; \; \frac{\text{Sales}}{\text{Stocks}} \; ; \; \frac{\text{Sales}}{\text{Debtors}}$$

All these ratios are interrelated and attention to the four fundamental variables would be called for by management if profits did not meet expectations. For instance, profits would decrease if (sales remaining constant) costs increased, or a higher level of stocks was held, or debtors took longer to settle their accounts. Increases in stocks or debtors would increase the amount of financial capital tied up in the business and reduce the rate of return on it. Changes in the variables would also hold implications for the cash flow of the business and its ability to raise finance, a point taken up later.

What might be termed the 'bottom line' ratio is the profit/capital ratio which enables the rate of return on capital, as a percentage, to be established. In economic terms this should at least reflect the opportunity cost of funds invested in the business, perhaps the prevailing market rate of interest being the datum.

- Solvency and liquidity ratios: profitability does not ensure solvency or liquidity; it is often possible for businesses, especially new ones, to overtrade – i.e., attempt to conduct the business at a level the current capital resources are unable to sustain.

External assessment of solvency and liquidity, using ratios, tends to concentrate on the structural relationship between assets and liabilities. Solvency means that short-term liabilities can be met by income. Solvency ratios therefore indicate the extent to which current liabilities are covered by the current assets held, whereas liquidity ratios consider the assets and the ease and speed with which they can be turned into cash. These are essentially short-run concerns, but in the long run the whole financial structure of the enterprise needs to be considered – i.e., from what sources and how it has funded its operations. It is an old maxim in accounting that financing long-term assets from short-term borrowing is a recipe for disaster. This aptly illustrates the need for a sound structuring of the financing of both long and short-term assets and liabilities.

The two most common measures of solvency and liquidity are the Current and Liquidity ratio:

$$\text{Current ratio:} \quad \frac{\text{Current assets (CA)}}{\text{Current liabilities (CL)}}$$

$$\text{Liquidity ratio:} \quad \frac{\text{Current assets minus stocks (CA-S)}}{\text{Current liabilities}}$$

The meaning and composition of current assets and current liabilities can be established by reference to texts which explain final accounts. It is also of value to calculate the ratios discussed above using examples given in those texts but it is of greater benefit to derive them from a set of business final accounts (see Figure 4.4).

It should be apparent that in service enterprises such as leisure provision, except where stocks of goods are kept for certain operations, there is no distinction between the current and liquidity ratio. Furthermore, other short-run ratios of solvency and liquidity – for example, those which relate sales to creditors, debtors and stocks – are hardly relevant to leisure provision which tends to operate on a cash basis.

The ratios used in the long run to measure solvency and liquidity concern the financial structure of an enterprise. An important one is the gearing or leverage of the enterprise (i.e., the loan to equity or share ratio); another is 'interest cover', of especial significance in a highly geared company. A company is said to be 'highly geared' if most of its capital is financed by means of loans rather than shares. The company should ensure that it has sufficient funds to pay the interest on the loans it has contracted, hence the term 'interest cover'.

There is now a considerable body of knowledge on the values that ratios should take for specific types of business, as well as on ratio analysis in general. For example, mark ups, stock turns, ratios of return on capital, and profit/earnings ratios will vary not only within a particular industry but also between different sectors such as manufacturing, services and retailing. However, certain ratios, with some exceptions, are viewed as being universal. It is generally accepted that the current ratio should be 2 and the liquidity ratio 1. Statistics on ratios can be found in the annual publication *Industrial Performance Analysis*, compiled by Intercompany Comparisons. Much research has also been conducted on the prediction of business failure using liquidity and solvency ratios; for example that done by Altman (1968) in the US and by Taffler and Tisshaw (1984) in the UK.

As already suggested, many ratios are not applicable to leisure service enterprises. However, even in the public and voluntary sector there are profit centre activities (e.g., bars, catering and sports equipment sales) even if they are not treated as such by those who control them. Many ratios used in the retail trade would thus be relevant, except perhaps for those concerning debtors.

In terms of the overall objectives of non-profit leisure provision, profitability ratios can be adapted to meet their needs. For instance, if the maximisation of participation is the principal objective, revenue (sales) and/or costs, both operating or capital, can be expressed as a ratio per user. Other ratios might relate hours open, floor area, staff numbers and hours to revenue and costs; Department of the Environment; Audit Commission (1983), Coopers & Lybrand Associates (1979), Stabler (1984), have indicated the application of profitability ratios to non-profit-seeking leisure facilities. Miles (1986) has given representative figures for stately homes and the Scottish Sports Council (1979) has done so for leisure centres.

Though ratios are very useful management tools to effect comparisions from year to year or with other similar enterprises, there are dangers in placing too much reliance on them. It must always be borne in mind in the leisure field that there are differences between commercial and public sector provision. Cognisance should also be taken of differing accounting policies, technical differences in the calculation of variables and the peculiarities of the trade and locality.

Derivation of Performance Measures

Performance measures may be distinguished from accounting ratios in being largely non-financial in nature. This makes them ideally suitable for non profit-seeking leisure enterprises, particularly when assessing the attainment of objectives. In a sense performance measurement is a wider concept, concerning effectiveness, whereas ratio analysis deals more with efficiency. In the literature, reference is often made to effectiveness, efficiency and economy. 'Effectiveness' indicators are qualitative statements which indicate how well an organisation is operating and that it is achieving its objectives. 'Efficiency' is a more difficult concept to define. In economics, in a narrow definition, it is production at minimum average cost or, if redefined more in accounting terms, maximising output with given costs or minimising costs for a given level of output. In its widest meaning efficiency is the maximisation of social welfare. 'Economy' in the accounting sense is essentially the same as the narrow definition of efficiency as economists understand it.

Within the last decade what is known as 'social accounting' has been developed. This consists of statements, normally included in the annual report of a commercial enterprise, which indicate its contribution to the economy and society. The statements cover aspects of operations such as money exchange with the government, foreign currency transactions, employment, and corporate objectives. To an extent this kind of accounting is associated with a social welfare audit – that is, the enterprise can be judged on the social costs and benefits it generates. For discussion of the more non-financial aspects of accounting see Carsberg and Hope (1984).

These ideas of social accounting concentrating on effectiveness are very relevant to the performance assessment of public sector activities such as education, health, housing, transport and environmental services. Currently the debate about value for money and the allocation of resources to education and health concern the problem of measuring performance.

In the public sector leisure field performance measures are very much concerned with relating the objectives of provision to costs. Often, however, the objectives, especially at local authority level, are diffuse and perhaps unspecified, simply because it is difficult to quantify them. Measures of performance have consequently tended to focus on the short run, what might be termed 'process measures' (Stabler, 1984) such as participation, frequency and duration rates, expressed as a percentage of the population. In built facilities, entrants per hour, per day, and per head of staff have been used. Some measures have related participation to financial ratios, such as provision costs or subsidies per participant or for specified activities. The Department of the Environment: Audit Commission (1983), Coopers & Lybrand Associates (1979), Scottish Sports Council (1979), and Stabler (1984) have all suggested the kinds of measures which might be used in non-profit-seeking organisations.

Overall, in devising leisure performance 'measures' some obvious but nevertheless important factors should be remembered: by who, for whom, for what use? It may also be of value to consider their categorisation into high level indicators concerning objectives and lower level ones to be applied for routine management planning and control.

Questions of performance measurement and the attainment of objectives, effectiveness and efficiency have to be viewed within the context of recurrent and capital cash flows and budgets which form the basis of cost and management accounting, and to which attention is now turned.

Management and Methods

Some Preliminary Observations

So far, the examination of the management of financial resources has concentrated on the use of accounting information drawn from the statements employed in financial accounting to report the results and position of the enterprise. The focus now changes to consider the management of the flow of funds to achieve the objectives of the enterprise. An appreciation of the continual cycle of the flow of funds can be gained from Figure 4.3, and the associated commentary above.

Financial management procedures regarding this flow owe their origins to management and cost accounting. The main purpose of management accounting is the provision of information needed for decision-making and the control and planning of the enterprise. In essence, it is the internal use of accounting data as opposed to its external use in financial accounting. Cost accounting is a specific aspect of management accounting which is concerned with ascertaining and allocating the direct production and overhead costs of an organisation. It normally attempts to establish standard costs and budgets with which the variance of actual or outturn costs can be compared. It is thus largely a control system but can perform a planning function by the use of forecast budgets.

By analysing and interpreting information in the planning and budgeting process on costs, the volume of production, price, sales revenue, profit margins, capital investment, sources and methods of financing investment and so on – i.e., the flow of funds and financing of the operations of the organisation – management accounting becomes financial management.

Cash Flow Analysis, Pricing, and Budgeting

Cash Flow Analysis

It has already been shown that a leisure enterprise's income is generated in two major forms: a recurrent flow from charges or subscriptions, sales, revenue subsidies, and a capital flow from ownership funds, borrowing and/or share issues, capital grants and donations. Financial management is certainly about the planning and monitoring of this, but it is also concerned with the cash flow as opposed to income flow. It is clearly in an enterprise's interest to generate as much income as possible, but if this merely increases stock holding, outstanding debtors' balances and the liabilities to creditors, it is at the expense of liquidity. By 'liquidity' is meant the ease with which assets such as stocks and debts can be converted into cash, as explained earlier when examining accounting ratios. As shown above, this is characteristic of overtrading and may create insolvency.

In commercial leisure provision in the absence of stocks, debtors and creditors, the cash flow problem is more likely to be related to too low a level of revenue in relation to the capital investment. This may be a function of a number of variables, the most signficant being the level of demand, prices charged and trading sales on the revenue side and the investment and financial capital required on the cost side. In the public domain, both the problem and the variables will be very much the same.

Cash flow statements are a key element in short-run and long-run financial management. Clearly, particularly in setting up a new leisure enterprise, the planning – or perhaps more correctly the forecast estimate – of cash inflows and outflows is crucial and may need to be for a relatively long time period if the business needs to recoup initial capital costs and build up 'trade'. In contrast in an existing business, operating in a stable market, the cash flow statement may not need to cover a long period if no marked increase in capital expenditure is envisaged.

For an established business past and present records have two uses, first they assist in the monitoring and control of cash flow. Secondly, they form the data base for the forecast of future cash flows with suitable adjustments for such factors as inflation, fluctuations in the assets and liabilities of the enterprises and changes in taxation. A traditional method of forecasting this flow is through trend analysis, using moving averages but other, computer based, models are increasingly applied. These matters are explained in texts on management accounting of which Sizer (1985) is a fairly comprehensive example.

Returning to the question of cash flow statements over fairly long periods, these should be on a discounted (DCF) basis in order to give an accurate estimate of their present value, a sounder basis on which to make management judgements than undiscounted statements. Discounting is a process whereby future monetary returns and costs are divided by a suitable factor, based on the rate of interest which could be earned on investment funds, to ascertain what the present value of a future sum really is. What discount rate should be applied is a matter of dispute which cannot be pursued here. However, some issues surrounding DCF are considered below in examining investment appraisal.

Pricing

Entry charges and the prices of ancillary services and commodities are a crucial determinant of the level of use of leisure facilities. What the charges and prices should be are a function of a number of variables such as the quality of the experience, the time of year, week and day, the socio–economic characteristics of the catchment area, the competition, marketing and management style. In economics the issue is encapsulated in the concept of elasticity of demand which considers the relationship between changes in prices and the responsiveness of demand to those changes. If leisure providers can establish participants' elasticity of demand it greatly assists them in determining their pricing policy and consequently the revenue which will be generated. For example, if demand is elastic (i.e., responsive to changes in the price charged for a commodity or service) then a policy of raising prices to increase total revenue will be misguided for in fact revenue will fall. Bovaird *et al.* (1984) have done extensive work in this area of financial management in a study of the impact on demand at public sector countryside sites of changes in charging policy. The concept of elasticity can also explain the relationship between price and mark up (gross profit) that entrepreneurs might obtain. The more elastic is demand, reflecting a more competitive market, the smaller the mark up and conversely the less elastic is demand, the larger the mark up is likely to be. Economic theory suggests that this is consistent with profit maximisation. However, in practice even commercial leisure enterprises may not necessarily be profit maximisers; they might wish to maximise sales or growth. Most commonly businesses work on a cost plus basis but nevertheless will be unconsciously acknowledging the elasticity concept if they are obliged to vary prices to ascertain those which the market will bear. This is demonstrated in lower off-peak prices in order to spread demand and fill spare capacity.

Without entering the realms of consumer behaviour theory and marketing, the importance of establishing the appropriate price in leisure provision lies in the impact it has on the cash flow as a result of changes in revenue. In turn this holds implications for the long-term value of the enterprise.

Cash flow statements will also be affected by capital receipts, from share issue or loans, and by expenditure as a result of capital investment. Calculation of the optimum cash flow – i.e., that which maintains a balance between inflows and outflows, allowing the enterprise to achieve its objectives – involves the compilation of budgets which can be differentiated into capital and revenue or recurrent. Budgets are predictions of expenditure and income and thus have a policy-making and planning function as well as being a control and monitoring device in that, in due course, the predictions are compared with outturns. They also assist in setting standards for evaluating performance.

Budgeting and Management Systems

Budgets take a number of forms ranging from those largely comprised of standard costs to ascertain total expenditure to those more concerned with management and planning. The form of budget also reflects the planning horizon. Revenue budgeting covers relatively short-run operations, usually a year, whereas capital budgeting concerns the long-run conduct of the enterprise and may be for 50 years or more for the amortisation (i.e., provision for the repayment of a debt) of buildings.

In the case of public sector leisure provision, particularly through local authorities, where a number of facilities are run, individual budgets would be devised for each section or facility. These are amalgamated with the overall budget for the authority in order to determine the revenue which will need to be generated through user changes and, ultimately, the rates where provision is subsidised. Large commercial leisure entrepreneurs may also calculate budgets on a divisional or profit/cost centre basis.

The preparation of budgets by the public sector was originally connected with central government control and economic policy but in recent years has been seen much more as a management tool. Local authorities in the UK are encouraged by their accounting body CIPFA (1979), to standardise budgets either by the nature of expenditure and income, known as line item budgeting, or by the purpose of expenditure, referred to as programme budgeting. For leisure provision, the latter is more appropriate because it enables management to identify the resources used for specific services or facilities. What normally occurs is for authorities to control budgets for broad categories of services such as education, housing and recreation and then to break these down into individual service or facility units. For each unit expenditure and income is shown on a line item basis: entry fees, sales grants, etc. for income and employees, running expenses, debt charges, rates, etc. for expenditure.

- **Incremental budgeting (IB)** is the simplest kind of annual budget, whereby a budget for the forthcoming period is based on the magnitude of the current one – that is, projections are based on current expenditure and income, with adjustment being made for foreseen changes. This method is appropriate for routine, or continuing, operations in which there is a strong mandatory element. However, the approach tends to create its own unquestioning inertia which may be undesirable where value for money is a paramount consideration.
- **Zero base budgeting (ZBB)** developed by the US Department of Agriculture, assumes that all expenditure has to be justified at the beginning of each budget period. Thus it is as if the budget is for a completely new service or facility each time the planning process is initiated. It is a suitable method when financial stringency needs to prevail. However, it can be costly in terms of time and resources and is probably not valid for leisure provisions for which large capital investment has been carried out in the past.
- **Planning, programming and budgeting system (PPBS)** is very much a method which meets the needs of decision-makers rather than central government control. It is a system which considers how the resources available to an enterprise should be used to achieve its objectives by identifying and evaluating possible programmes, at the same time employing procedures for the control and review of their implementation.

The system concentrates on the purpose of expenditure and consequently cuts across departmental, divisional or committee boundaries. In some respects it is a kind of cost-benefit-analysis (CBA), examined in the next section, but is concerned with continuing programmes of provision as opposed to the once and for all appraisal of a leisure capital project.

At first seen as an ideal planning, control and management system PPBS has now fallen somewhat into disrepute. Apart from the problems of cutting across traditional organisational boundaries, it has been alleged that the identification of objectives and the problem of establishing the meaning and measurement of output has undermined its practical application. Nevertheless, it is potentially a valuable budgeting method for leisure provision because it makes management aware of the need to keep objectives in mind in decisions on the allocation of resources.

There are other budgeting and management systems which are in essence variants of those outlined here, some of which embody wider social and environmental issues. However, it is not possible to pursue their examination here. For a more detailed analysis of the IB, ZBB and PPBS systems as applied in the public sector, consult Henley *et al.* (1983), and Jones and Pendlebury (1983).

What should have emerged in this outline of budgeting is that in the more sophisticated systems like PPBS, any distinction between revenue and capital budgeting begins to disappear. However, capital budgeting has retained a separate identity simply because it deals specifically with the financial management of capital programmes or projects. This aspect is now considered in conjunction with capital appraisal.

Capital Appraisal

The identification and evaluation of individual investment opportunities is termed capital appraisal, which normally includes consideration of the method of appraisal such as payback or discounted cash flow (DCF). Capital budgeting is the system for, and process of, deciding currently on the allocation of financial resources over time in the expectation of earning returns or benefits. The basic problem is that there is an almost infinite number of investment opportunities, but limited funds for undertaking them.

In a sense, capital budgeting embraces capital appraisal for it is concerned with the:

- Evaluation of each project
- Method of financing each project
- Total capital expenditure.

Capital budgeting is inextricably linked with revenue budgeting because the initiation of projects eventually appears as an item termed debt charges, constituting the repayment of principal and interest, in the revenue accounts. In leisure enterprises, particularly in the public sector, the original capital costs and any subsequent investment expenditure are a considerable financial burden often representing the whole of any loss suffered and necessitating a subsidy in one form or another. Indeed some local authorities recast accounts to exclude debt charges, sometimes with rates and recharges from other departments, to leave only those items of significance in assessing management and over which it can exercise control. Texts on accounting normally include a brief examination of capital budgeting (see Sizer 1985, for example), though there are also specialist texts dealing specifically with this area (see Bromwich 1976).

Capital appraisal with its associated capital budgeting, is the establishment of systematic decision rules in order to optimise investment and to minimise the risk of making expensive mistakes, especially in a growing economy subject to rapid technical change and the need for large scale investment. To an extent the philosophy underlying the Standard Approach to Sports Halls (SASH) project (Ecotech Research and Consulting, 1988) acknowledges the need for flexibility in both the construction and management of built facilities to meet changing needs and to reduce costs through standardisation. Similarly, Ravenscroft (1984) has argued that the whole life costs, both running and capital, should be considered at the initiation stage of the leisure projects.

Given that leisure provision involves substantial capital programmes over long time periods it is essential that discounted cash flow (DCF) methods are employed. It is not possible to explain DCF analysis here. The reader is referred to the monograph by Hawkins and Pearce (1971), but sound introductions are included in accounting texts (such as Sizer, 1985).

There are certainly differences between private and public sector approaches to capital appraisal, reflecting their respective aims. However, in general they both should follow the same procedure:

- Define the objectives of the organisation
- Identify projects
- Identify the costs and returns/benefits
- Evaluate the costs and returns in monetary terms
- Discount the costs and returns at an appropriate discount rate
- Apply the adopted decision criteria for ranking and selecting projects.

In the private sector the objectives will be profit related whereas in the public sector they should be concerned with welfare, though financial targets like loss minimisation might be set. These objectives give rise to the other distinctions in capital appraisal in the two sectors. In terms of the costs and benefits identified in a public sector appraisal these may include social costs such as noise, congestion, delinquent behaviour on the one hand, and the socio–economic benefits on the other. The inclusion of such items, together with non-monetary objectives, is the core of cost-benefit-analysis (CBA) and marks it off as a separate method of capital appraisal. Notwithstanding its suitability as an approach in the public sector, particularly if embodied in PPBS, it has been advocated as applicable to commercial entities as they become more conscious of their social responsibilities.

There are many technical factors associated with CBA which make it appear a complex procedure. The major concerns are:

- whether market prices are appropriate for evaluating costs and benefits
- the problem of ascertaining the value of non-market, known as intangible items
- the method of discounting
- the choice of discount rate
- the treatment of risk and uncertainty
- the question of the redistributive effects on the welfare of groups in society.

In addition, public sector projects tend to have longer lives, involving larger capital outlays and longer lead times before benefits start to accrue, thus making comparison with private sector methods more difficult. These are issues which have been extensively researched in theory and make CBA a useful framework in which to assess leisure projects, despite some of the practical difficulties associated with it which have tended to undermine decision-makers' confidence in it.

Useful introductions to CBA have been written by Mishan (1971) and Pearce (1971). More advanced treatment can be found in Dasgupta and Pearce (1972). Applications to leisure are mostly concerned with site specific informal countryside recreation pioneered by Clawson and Knetsch (1966) though more recently Coopers & Lybrand Associates (1979) have considered it in relation to sports centres. It remains a potentially valuable appraisal tool with especial relevance to projects with major welfare objectives designed to meet the demand and needs of particular social sectors.

Sources and Methods of Finance

This area of financial management is related to revenue and capital budgeting and capital appraisal. It also links back to financial statements, namely the balance sheet and profit and loss account. It concerns the financial resources needed to maintain day to day operations, especially in the period after the setting up of an enterprise, and the funding of capital programmes.

Sources can be categorised as internal or external. Internal sources are those which enable the enterprise to finance its operations from resources which it holds or generates. These sources can be identified by inspection of the balance sheet and, to a lesser extent, the profit and loss account.

Fixed assets can be realised and invested in the business, reserves and cash and liquidity holdings can be run down, contingencies for tax can be drawn on and even payments to creditors deferred. Here again the pricing of the product plays a part in determining the magnitude of internal sources; this can be ascertained from the profit and loss account.

In the public sector, given that CIPFA has advocated adoption of business methods, internal sources and methods of finance are an equally vital area to consider, particularly in times of financial stringency and control over access to external sources such as rates, government grants and loans.

External sources of finance in the private sector are important in the setting up of a business. The money market institutions deal in short-term loans, usually up to one or two years, to finance variable costs such as employees' wages and salaries, materials and fuel. The capital market is a source of funds for the acquisition of fixed assets: land, buildings, equipment. The two most common methods of financing fixed assets are by the issue of shares for limited companies and the contracting of loans. There are variants of these two methods which do not need to be examined here. The main point of interest is their respective impact on the enterprise. The repayment of principal and interest are a first charge on the assets of the business in the event of it being wound up and can be a substantial burden. However, they are a legitimate expense so can be offset against taxation. Ordinary shares, the vast majority of those issued, carry no obligation for the enterprise to pay dividends, but nevertheless, if none are paid the share price of the company may be depressed and its ability to issue more shares be impaired. It has already been shown in the section on ratio analysis and performance measurement how a company's health with respect to its solvency and capital structure is judged. Brett (1987) deals with these aspects of external funding at some length.

In the public sector though the sources and methods of external funding are very different, the principles of and need for a sound financial structure still apply. This has been demonstrated with regard to loan charges as a significant fixed cost element of local authority leisure provision. Henley *et al*. (1983) give a clear outline of the circumstances prevailing with respect to external funding in the public sector.

Other methods of securing funds for fixed assets of relevance to both commercial and non-profit leisure organisations are: sale and leaseback of land and property which is owned, venture capital for specific projects, and leasing or hire purchase for the acquisition of equipment. These methods, which do not increase the ownership equity, are covered in texts such as Holmes and Sugden (1985) and Sizer (1985).

It is worth reiterating the point that both sources and methods should be sought which match the appropriate short-, medium-, and long-term financial needs of the enterprise. This should be borne in mind in examining this area of financial management in the texts.

Some Concluding Observations

Financial management is a broad subject, with a strong theoretical base strongly influenced by economic concepts, giving rise to quite complex techniques. As should be apparent from this survey, it is of most relevance to commercial operations where profit-seeking and competition make it imperative for financial planning, control and monitoring to be efficient and effective. Moreover, it should be clear that the examination has been in terms of general business activity. This simply reflects that it is only recently that leisure has been of significance commercially, and that in non-profit leisure provision sectors, sound financial structures and practices are seen as being of vital importance.

An attempt has been made to offer a critical review but of necessity this brief excursion into the subject has been selective, being guided by both current issues and the existence of references to illustrate its application to leisure provision.

Further Reading

This chapter has made reference to a number of texts of general relevance, or of value in connection with specific aspect of financial management. These are cited in the references for the chapter. Listed below is some further source material of a more introductory nature: Dyson (1987); Hartley (1987); Livesey (1983); Mott (1987); Robb and Wallis (1988); Watts (1984).

References

Altman, E.I. (1968) 'Financial Ratios, Discrimination and the Prediction of Corporate Bankruptcy', *Journal of Finance*, 23 (4) (September) pp. 589–609.

Ashton, R.K. (1983) *UK Financial Accounting Standards*, Cambridge: Woodhead-Faulkner.

Bird, P. (1983) *Understanding Company Accounts*, London: Pitman (2nd edn).

Bovaird, A.G., Tricker, M.J. and Stoakes, R. (1984) *Recreation Management and Pricing: The Effect of Changing Policy on Demand at Countryside Recreation Sites*, Aldershot: Gower.

Brett, M. (1987) *How to Read the Financial Pages*, London: Hutchinson Business Books.

Bromwich, M. (1976) *The Economics of Capital Budgeting*, Harmondsworth Penguin.

Carsberg, B. and Hope, A. (1984) *Current Issues in Accounting*, Oxford: Philip Allan.

Chartered Institute of Public Finance and Accountancy (1979) *The Standardisation of Accounts: General Principles*, London: CIPFA.

Chartered Institute of Public Finance and Accountancy (annually) *Leisure and Recreation Estimates*, London: Statistical Information Series.

Chartered Institute of Public Finance and Accountancy (annually) *Leisure Charges*, London: Statistical Information Series.

Clawson, M. and Knetsch, J.L. (1966) *The Economics of Outdoor Recreation*, Baltimore: Johns Hopkins.

Coopers & Lybrand Associates (1979) *Sharing Does Work: The Economic and Social Benefits of Joint and Direct Sports Provision*, Study 22, London: Sports Council.

Dasgupta, A.K. and Pearce, D.W. (1972) *Cost-Benefit Analysis: Theory and Practice*, London: Macmillan.

Department of the Environment Audit Commission (1979).

Department of the Environment: Audit Inspectorate (1983) *Development and Operation of Leisure Centres: Selected Case Studies*, London: HMSO.

Dyson, J. (1987) *Accounting for Non-Accounting Students*, London: Pitman.

Ecotech Research and Consulting (1988) *SASH Centres in Use II: Management and Design Performance*, London: Sports Council.

Hartley, W.C.F. (1987) *An Introduction to Business Accounting for Managers*, Oxford: Pergamon (4th edn).

Hawkins, C.J. and Pearce, D.W. (1971) *Capital Investment Appraisal*, London: Macmillan.

Henley, D., Holtham, C., Likierman, A. and Perrin, J. (1983) *Public Sector Accounting and Financial Control* (sponsored by Chartered Institute of Public Finance and Accounting), Wokingham: Van Nostrand Reinhold.

Holmes, C. and Sugden, A. (1985) *Interpreting Company Reports and Accounts*, Cambridge: Woodhead-Faulkner (3rd edn).

Jones, R. and Pendlebury, M. (1983) *Public Sector Accounting*, London: Pitman.

Livesey, F. (1983) *Economics for Business Decisions*, London: Pitman.

Mathews, R. (1962) *Accounting for Economists*, Melbourne: Cheshire.

Miles, C.W.N. (1986) *Running an Open House: A Guide to the Public Opening of Houses*, London: Surveyors Publications.

Mishan, E.J. (1971) *Cost-Benefit Analysis*, London: Allen & Unwin.

Morley, M.F. (1983) *Ratio Analysis*, Published for the Institute of Chartered Accountants of Scotland, Edinburgh: Gee.

Mott, M.A. (1987) *A Guide to Costing and Management Accounting Techniques*, London: Pan.

Pearce, D.W. (1971) *Cost-Benefit Analysis*, London: Macmillan.

Pitt Francis, D. (1973) *The Foundations of Financial Management*, London: Pitman.

Ravenscroft, N. (1984) 'The Leisure Facility Investment Decision: Consideration of Whole-Life Costs', Leisure Studies Association, Conference Paper, 27, in Wilkinson, J. (ed.), *Leisure: Politics, Planning and People*, 6, *Policy and Planning*.

Ravenscroft, N. and Stabler, M. (1986) *The Finance of Sport in a Rural District, Voluntary Sector Case Studies: Report of Survey*, Department of Economics, University of Reading.

Robb, A.J. and Wallis, R.W. (1988) *Accounting Terms Dictionary*, London: Pitman.

Scottish Sports Council (1979) *A Question of Balance: a Study of Sports Centres and Swimming Pools*, Edinburgh: The Scottish Sports Council.

Sizer, J. (1985) *An Insight into Management Accounting*, Harmondsworth: Penguin.

Stabler, M.J. (1984) *The Assessment of Performance of Non-Profit Organisations: The Operation of Sports Centres*, discussion paper in urban and regional

economics, Series C., Department of Economics, University of Reading.
Taffler, R. and Tisshaw, H.J. (1984) 'A New Tool to Aid the Auditor in the Going Concern Decision', *Accountancy*, 89.
Watts, B.K.R. (1984) *Business and Financial Management*, London: Pitman (5th edn).

5 Leisure Management and the Law

Valerie Collins

Introduction

Providers of recreational facilities and organisers of recreational activities attract legal duties relating to their responsibilities. This chapter will consider those duties under the following four main headings: duties owed to participants, spectators and other visitors; duties owed to neighbours; duties owed to employees and the duty to comply with the law.

Duties Owed to Participants, Spectators and Other Visitors

The Duty Not to be Negligent

All participants in and spectators of recreational activities run the risk of injury, and the problem facing lawyers when someone is injured is deciding which injuries are 'occupational hazards' and which should be the subject of a claim for financial compensation from the person responsible. The person responsible may be either a fellow participant, the organiser of the activity or the occupier of the premises used.

A person who has been injured may seek financial compensation at civil law if that person can show that someone has been negligent and that that negligence was the cause of the injury. To establish that there has been negligence the following elements must exist:

- A duty of care must be owed
- There must be a breach of that duty
- Actual damage must have resulted from that breach.

To decide whether or not a duty of care exists in a particular situation the test formulated in the case of *Donoghue* v. *Stevenson*[1] will be applied.

According to this test:

> You must take reasonable care to avoid acts or omissions which you can reasonably foresee would be likely to injure your neighbour. Who, then, in law, is my neighbour? The answer seems to be – persons who are so closely and directly affected by my act that I ought to have them in contemplation as being so directly affected when I am directing my mind to the acts or omissions which are called into question.

The application of this test to recreational activities makes it clear that anyone involved in such activities owes a duty of care to anyone connected with that activity.

In deciding exactly what comprises this duty of care, the law is not, and cannot be, precise. It can only establish general principles to be applied in each particular situation. The following matters will be considered when assessing the duty of care that exists in a particular situation:

1. The age of the persons concerned. Where children are involved a stricter duty of care is imposed. In *Affuto Nartoy* v. *Clarke and L.L.E.A.*[2] a teacher forgot he was playing rugby with young schoolboys who were smaller and weaker than himself and he injured a fifteen-year-old boy when he tackled him. The teacher was found to be negligent.
2. The expertise of the persons concerned or any other relevant characteristics. For example, more care would be expected to be exercised when taking a group of beginners for athletics than in supervising a training session for Olympic athletes.
3. How dangerous the particular activity is. The more dangerous the activity, the higher the degree of care that should be exercised.
4. The risks of injury occurring and the cost of taking precautions. Both these aspects are illustrated by the case of *Bolton* v. *Stone*[3]. During a cricket match a ball was driven out of the ground and it hit and injured a pedestrian walking past. The ball went over a protective fence which was 17 feet high and 78 yards from the batsman. A ball had been hit out of the ground only six times in the previous 30 years. The court decided there had been no negligence as the risk of injury was small and the cost of guarding against it prohibitive.
5. The foreseeability of the particular accident occurring. In *Clarke* v. *Bethnal Green Borough Council*[4] a child was preparing to dive off a springboard when another child holding onto the underside of it let go. The child on the board was thrown onto the edge of the pool and injured. The court decided there had been no negligence as this type of accident had not occurred before and was not foreseeable. But, once a particular type of accident has occurred, it may be deemed to be foreseeable in the future.

6. Suitability of the particular premises or equipment for the activity concerned. In *Gillmore* v. *London County Council*,[5] Gillmore had joined a class in physical training organised by the council for which he paid a fee. The class was held in a hall with a highly polished floor and Gillmore slipped and was injured. The council were found to be negligent because they had failed to provide a reasonably safe floor for the class.

In relation to suitability and safety of premises, the Occupiers' Liability Act 1957 imposes a similar duty of care on occupiers to all persons entitled to be on their premises. This duty is a duty to take such care, which in all the circumstances of the case is reasonable, to ensure that a visitor will be reasonably safe while using the premises for the purpose for which he was invited or allowed by the occupier to be there. This duty extends to the selection of persons to put up structures on the land, and the occupier will be liable if an incompetent person has been employed.

This duty has been further extended by the Occupiers' Liability Act 1984 to trespassers when an occupier is aware of their presence or likely presence. This duty is to protect trespassers from any 'danger' where:

1. He is aware of the danger or has reasonable grounds to believe it exists,
2. He knows, or has reasonable grounds to believe, that the entrant is in the vicinity of the danger or that he may come into the vicinity of the danger, and
3. The risk is one against which, in all the circumstances of the case, he may reasonably be expected to offer the entrant some protection.

Having decided what the duty of care comprises in a particular situation, the court will then decide whether in the circumstances there has been a breach of duty. As the duty is only to take reasonable care precautions need not be taken against every possible risk. Provided the activity has been conducted as safely as could reasonably be expected there will be no negligence. In *Jones* v. *London County Council*,[6] Jones was doing a course of physical exercises which was supervised by an experienced instructor. Jones was injured but the court decided there was no evidence of negligence and that an activity did not become dangerous just because an accident might happen.

Where the injury or damage has been caused by faulty equipment the breach of duty may be either by the user, the supplier or the manufacturer. The user – that is, the organiser of the activity – will be in breach of his duty if the fault could have been discovered through a simple maintenance check. Where the equipment is complex it should be regularly serviced by the manufacturer. A duty is thus imposed on the user to organise regular servicing, and on the manufacturer to perform an efficient service. The Consumer Protection Act 1987 provides that there will be strict liability for damage caused by defective products supplied after the Act came into force (March 1987).

Once it has been established that there has been a breach of duty then it must be decided who should pay any damages subsequently awarded by the court. The person actually responsible will be liable, but as that person may not be able to settle the total amount by one payment the employer of that person may be sued through the operation of the principle of vicarious liability. Employers are usually insured against the public liability of their employees but will be liable only where the employee is negligent during the course of his employment. An employer may also be liable if he employs a person who is not competent to do the job he was employed to do. Where an employee has been negligent and the employer is found to be liable the employer may in turn sue the employee, although in practice this rarely happens.

To escape liability one of the following four defences may be pleaded:

1. That the particular accident was not foreseeable.
2. *Volenti*. This defence, which is given the Latin tag, *volenti non fit injuria*, meaning 'no harm is done to he who consents', is available where the person injured has freely consented to the particular risk resulting in the injury.

   Volenti cannot be claimed if the injury is caused recklessly or deliberately, or is not a risk associated with the particular activity concerned – for example, injuries caused by faulty equipment.

   To establish *volenti* it must be proved that the plaintiff consented to the act complained of with full knowledge of the risks involved and that the consent was voluntary. A person whose job involves compulsory participation in sport cannot be said to consent freely to the risks involved. *Volenti* was pleaded successfully in the case of *Murray* v. *Harringey Arena Ltd*[7] where a six-year-old spectator was hit in the eye by the puck. There was no evidence of such an incident occurring before and the court decided the owners of the rink had not been negligent. Such a danger was incidental to the game and could reasonably have been foreseen by any spectator, thus he had accepted the risk, whatever his age. But the age of the spectator may now be taken into account (following the introduction of the Occupiers' Liability Act 1957).
3. Contributory negligence is another defence or partial defence. Should a participant suffer injury partly due to his own fault and only partly due to the conduct of the occupier or organiser then the Law Reform (Contributory Negligence) Act 1954 provides that the amount of damages recoverable for injuries suffered may be reduced by an amount adjudged by the court to cover the participant's share of responsibility. Anyone pleading this defence must prove that the participant was negligent and that that negligence contributed to the injuries suffered.

4. A break in the chain of causation. Liability may be avoided where another event occurs which breaks the chain of events started by the defendant's conduct. In such a case the defendant is liable only for the loss occurring before the intervention, and not for the whole loss. In *Hosie* v. *Arbroath Football Club Ltd*[8] a man was seriously injured when a football crowd surged towards a gate on the ground and it gave way because it had not been properly maintained. The club were found to be liable as occupiers of the ground because they knew, or should have known, that the gate would give way under pressure and someone could be injured. The court decided the behaviour of the crowd did not break the chain of causation and relieve the occupiers of liability.

A participant bringing an action in negligence will be claiming damages for injuries suffered, and although the aim of an award of damages is compensation not all injuries are compensatable as some may be considered to be too remote. It would be unfair to make a person liable for all the consequences of his actions. A person will always be responsible for all injuries arising from intentional conduct, but he will be liable only for reasonably foreseeable injuries resulting from unintentional conduct. Once it has been established that the kind of injury that occurred was foreseeable the person responsible will be liable for that injury, even though it was more extensive than could have been anticipated – for example, because the victim had an unusually fragile skull.

Although it may be tempting to try to limit or avoid liability by the display of notices to that effect it is not possible to exclude all liability for injury, loss or damage because the Unfair Contract Terms Act 1977 provides that where premises are used for business purposes liability cannot be excluded or restricted for death or personal injury resulting from negligence. In other cases of loss or damage liability for negligence can be excluded only where this is 'reasonable' within the terms of the Act.

The Duty to Take Care of the Property of Participants and Visitors

In most recreational facilities an area is usually made available where those participating may change and leave their clothing and other belongings. The question often arises concerning who is responsible for the loss of any personal items left in changing rooms. Generally, it will depend on the circumstances of each case. If there is some expression of liability for such items – for example, the provision of attended changing rooms, with no reference to the fact that liability is not accepted – the organiser or occupier will be liable for loss of, or damage to, property. This liability arises because users of the facility can assume that the provision of an attendant guarantees the safety of their property. The absence of an attendant does not necessarily mean that no liability is being accepted – for example, the provision of lockers and keys may lead to an assumption that property is being looked after.

Liability is not dependent on there being a contract between the user and the management, although usually there will be one as the user generally pays to use the facilities. In such cases it may be argued that safe storage for belongings is part of the service for which the user is paying. Even where there is not a contract the law may still say there is a contract of bailment. This is a form of agreement by which one person agrees to look after the property of another and there is no need to prove that payment was made in return. Under the terms of a contract of bailment a duty is imposed on the person taking care of the property to look after that property as if it were his own.

Management may try to exclude or limit liability by means of an exemption clause, either expressed in the contract or imposed by implication on the user by means of notices prominently displayed on the premises. To be effective, such a clause must be communicated to the user before he leaves his belongings. Even then, as a result of the Unfair Contract Terms Act 1977, such an exemption clause, even if validly communicated, cannot be effective unless it may be regarded by the courts as being 'reasonable' in the circumstances. This will obviously vary from situation to situation but, for example, while it might be reasonable for the management to exclude liability for loss of property in an unattended changing room in which every user is given a locker and key without extra charge, it will be an entirely different matter if every user is required to put their clothing and belongings in a basket which is handed to an attendant. The courts will also take into account what payment, if any, was made by the user for the general facilities, the relative 'bargaining strengths' of the parties and the frequency with which the user in question used the facilities. Someone who uses a facility regularly may be deemed to have accepted the particular arrangements there.

The Duty to Comply With Any Contracts Made

Not all agreements are legally enforceable contracts. To establish that a contract exists at law it must be possible to identify an offer, an acceptance matching that offer, consideration (which is usually payment or a promise to pay), and an intention to create legal relations. Purely social agreements – for example, an arrangement to play squash – are not contracts, as there is no intention to create legal relations. However, where an agreement may have all the attributes of a contract the courts may still not recognise it because one of the parties may have declared itself to be 'bound in honour only'. In *Jones* v. *Vernon Football Pools*[9] the court decided that such a clause on a football coupon declared an intention not to create legal relations, and that there was therefore no legal obligation to pay the winnings on the coupon.

Any adult in full possession of his or her faculties who has signed a contract will normally be bound by it, whatever it says. This is because everyone is expected to take good care of their own business interests, and everyone is therefore advised to 'read the small print'. Only where there has been a misrepresentation by one of the parties will the courts normally step in and either set it aside or award damages by way of compensation to the injured party.

A contract may not include all the terms which govern the relationship between the parties, so it may be necessary for the courts to imply certain terms to make commercial sense of the agreement. Terms are implied by the courts to cover situations which the parties themselves have not covered, or they are terms implied in particular types of contract by an Act of Parliament – for example, the Sale of Goods Act 1979. In the former case the courts will impose terms they would have expected the parties to have agreed to had they considered the matter. The assumption of additional terms ensures that the contract is workable, which is presumed to have been the original intention of the parties.

The law of contract governs not only the more obvious commercial contracts which exist in sport, but also the many and various arrangements under which people participate in recreational activities. In some cases it is obvious that there must be some form of contract – for example, when a football fan pays his money to get into the football ground. Whenever someone pays money to spectate, one would expect the law to regard the situation as a contractual one. However, often some sort of legal relationship is created even when the user or spectator is allowed in free of charge; in such situations, a person either enters under an implied contract or is allowed in as a 'licensee'. In either situation, the person concerned is owed certain legal duties and the user or spectator must at least be taken to have agreed to behave himself. The difficulty lawyers face in such situations is that very little of such an agreement has been put down in writing and therefore the terms of such an agreement must be found by implication. It is easy to imply an undertaking by the organiser that the premises are safe and the event well organised (duties imposed by law anyway) and an agreement by the user or spectator to behave but, in relation to the spectator, is there a right to dictate what seat should be occupied or to change the programme without warning?

There are no standard rules in these areas. The courts must examine any written evidence available – for example, tickets and advance publicity – or 'imply' a reasonable understanding into the relationship (for example, the obvious need to separate rival fans). Some organisers may try to resolve possible uncertainty by printing conditions of entry on the ticket, or making reference to conditions and where these conditions may be found. They may also try to include exemption clauses absolving them from liability in the event of loss or injury which again are either printed on the ticket itself or contained in conditions to which the purchaser is referred. Conditions printed on tickets will not be effective unless the purchaser was aware that he was being given something which referred to conditions, and not just a receipt, and that the nature of the conditions in question was 'reasonably' communicated to him. Even then, it is no longer possible, thanks to the Unfair Contract Terms Act 1977, for an organiser to exempt himself from liability either to a user or spectator, for physical injury or death caused through negligence. Any other purported exemption – for example, loss of property – will be judged according to whether or not it is 'reasonable'. This does not mean that an organiser is always liable for injury or loss to a participant, simply that should the organiser be found to be liable that liability cannot be evaded simply by pointing to an exemption clause referred to in the wording on a ticket, or a notice displayed on the premises.

The Duty Not to Discriminate

Recreational activities have posed certain delicate problems concerning the implementation of statutes designed to eliminate both racial and sexual discrimination in all walks of life. Discrimination on the grounds of colour alone is generally unlawful in sport, but as it is the basis of both national and international sport that the teams fielded should be 'home grown' a special section was included in the Race Relations Act 1976 which makes it lawful to discriminate, in team selection, against anyone who is not of the required nationality or origins, or who does not satisfy a particular residential qualification.

Legislation concerning sexual discrimination has thrown into doubt the legality of all-male preserves in recreational activities. The Sex Discrimination Act 1975 makes it unlawful to discriminate on grounds of sex either by refusing facilities for one sex, or providing them on less favourable grounds. Sexes may, however, be separated on grounds of 'decency'. As far as sport itself is concerned, section 44 of the Act provides:

> Nothing shall, in relation to any sport, game or other activity of a competitive nature where the physical strength, stamina or physique of the average woman puts her at a disadvantage to the average man, render unlawful any act related to the participation of a person as a competitor in events involving that activity which are confined to competitors of one sex.

Thus if cricket is a game at which the average woman would be at a disadvantage, she cannot insist on playing in a team of men.

Duties Owed to Neighbours

The Duty Not to be Negligent

Occupiers of recreational facilities and organisers of recreational activities also owe a duty to persons outside their premises not to be negligent. The extent of this duty will depend on the foreseeability of the accident that occurred and the cost of taking precautions. In *Hilder* v. *Associated Portland Cement Manufacturers Ltd*[10] the defendants allowed children to play football on their land, knowing that the ball often went onto the adjoining highway. In an action following an accident caused by a straying football the defendants were found liable as the accident was foreseeable and the risk should not have been ignored. However the opposite decision was reached in the case of *Bolton* v. *Stone*, which was discussed earlier in this chapter when the principles of negligence were considered (see p.128).

The Duty Not to Create a Nuisance

However much the provider of recreational facilities may feel the facilities add to the amenity of the area, there may be neighbours who think otherwise. The law protects such neighbours by providing legal restraints against the commission of a nuisance either public or private.

A public nuisance is a crime of strict liability. This means that the offender may be convicted even though he is not at fault himself, but simply created a situation in which others caused the nuisance. In law this is anything interfering with the public's right to use a public place – for example, large crowds gathered on a highway making it impossible for anyone to use that highway. Public nuisance may also occur where an activity makes the use of a public highway dangerous – for example, because golf balls are regularly hit over that road. Usually the 'public' is deemed to mean that a substantial number of people are affected, and not just one or two.

An example of this offence occurred in the case of *Moore*[11] where the accused was found to be guilty of a public nuisance when he organised pigeon shooting on his land, and in consequence a large crowd collected on the highway to shoot at pigeons as they escaped, causing an obstruction of the highway. Obstruction of the highway is now an offence under the Highways Act 1980. Many other instances that have in the past been judged to amount to a public nuisance, including polluting rivers, causing excessive noise and dust, are now the subject of special legislation. Proceedings are not likely to be brought at common law if a statute covers the situation, but it remains available. In *Castle* v. *St Augustine's Links*

Ltd[12] it was decided there was a public nuisance where golf balls were often hit onto or over a public highway from a nearby golf course, endangering users of that highway.

Although public nuisance is primarily a crime, it can also give rise to a civil action for damages by anyone who has suffered more loss or damage than simply the general inconvenience to the public. However if a neighbour is the victim of loss or damage in relation to private property then it is more appropriate to sue for private nuisance. A successful action in private nuisance relies on the existence of five elements in the action complained of:

1. Interference with the plaintiff's enjoyment of his land
2. A continuing interference, not one isolated incident
3. The interference must be unreasonable
4. The interference must have either been created by the defendant, caused by his neglect of duty, or continued by him
5. Generally the plaintiff must suffer actual damage.

In order to bring an action the plaintiff must have an interest in the land affected by the action complained of. In every case of nuisance there must be an element of continuity – for example, a series of explosions or continuous noisy activities. The interference may take the form of a threat of danger or discomfort to the plaintiff as well as actual danger, discomfort or damage. Actions in nuisance may be brought against organisers and occupiers. In *Miller* v. *Jackson*[13] the action brought concerned the playing of cricket on a village green. Cricket had been played there since 1905, long before the plaintiff's house had been built. The plaintiff sued the cricket club for damages in negligence and nuisance because cricket balls were frequently hit into his garden. The court decided that there was negligence on the part of the cricket club as the risk of injury was foreseeable and that the playing of cricket did constitute an unreasonable interference with the plaintiff's enjoyment of his land and was a nuisance. However, the court went on to say that there were special circumstances, namely that the plaintiff knew when he bought the house that cricket was played on the green and also that the village as a whole had an interest in the existence of a cricket ground. Therefore the plaintiff was only awarded damages, and was not granted an injunction to stop cricket being played on the green.

However, in *Kennaway* v. *Thompson*[14] an appeal was allowed against a decision to award damages in lieu of an injunction, because of the public interest in the club concerned. Here the plaintiff had built a house next to a man-made lake on which a motor-boat racing club was already organising motor-boat racing and water ski-ing. During the first five years of the plaintiff's occupation of the house there was a considerable increase in the activities of the club and race meetings were being held most weekends in the summer. An injunction was granted on the grounds that in a case of a continuing actionable nuisance the option to award damages should be exercised only under very exceptional circumstances and in this case the public interest in continuing the activity did not prevail over the private interest in obtaining an injunction. An injunction was granted to reduce the noise and number of race meetings.

There is no exact definition of what is an 'unreasonable interference', but the test seems to be what is reasonable according to the ordinary habits of people living in the particular area. The court balances the interests of the various occupiers, weighing up competing interests and taking into account the extent and duration of the interference and the encroachment on the ordinary use of the plaintiff's property. Should the interference be due to the fact that the plaintiff uses his property for a special purpose which makes it unusually sensitive to interference then there will be no nuisance.

If the interference affects only the plaintiff's convenience and enjoyment but there is no actual damage to property then the interference must be substantial and one of which a man or woman with ordinary feelings would complain. The nature of the locality will always be taken into consideration when deciding whether or not a particular activity is a nuisance. Finally it should be noted that, where a defendant is found to be acting maliciously, what might normally constitute a reasonable interference may be found to be unreasonable.

To escape liability in an action for nuisance the defendant may be able to prove one of the following defences: *volenti*, contributory negligence, statutory authority, or that a prescriptive right has been acquired because the nuisance has existed openly and continuously for at least twenty years.

Remedies available for nuisance are damages, an injunction (an order by the court to stop that particular activity), or abatement of the nuisance. Abatement is the removal of the nuisance by the person affected by it – for example, lopping off the branches of an overhanging tree. Abatement is subject to three conditions: that an injunction would have been granted anyway, that no unnecessary damage was done, and that where it involved entry onto another person's land prior consent was obtained unless it was an emergency. However the courts do not favour abatement because of the possible consequences!

Private nuisance actions have been brought successfully in several cases concerning recreational activities. In *Stretch* v. *Romford Football Club Ltd*[15] speedway racing had been introduced at the defendant's football stadium and a resident nearby, in what was essentially a quiet residential area, claimed this constituted a nuisance due to the substantial noise increase over and above that caused by football matches which disturbed his family. Witnesses claimed they found the noise disturbing. The defendants were unsuccessful in their attempt to establish that the family were unusually sensitive to noise, an actionable nuisance was established and a perpetual injunction was granted.

Duties Owed to Employees

Managers of recreational facilities and organisers of recreational activities will have to employ staff, and will therefore have to comply with the law concerning employment. This is a complex area of the law and to some extent it is an extension of the law of contract as it centres around the contract of employment. There are two types of contract of employment. One is between an employer and an employee, which is a contract of service – for example, a sports centre manager employing a full-time receptionist. The other is that between an employer and an independent contractor, which is a contract for service – for example, a manager employing a company to relay the floor in the sports hall. It is necessary to distinguish between these two types of contract due to the differing rights and responsibilities that arise from them. For example, an employer is vicariously liable for the negligent actions of his employees but not for those of independent contractors. The law has evolved tests to decide into which category a particular contract falls, and these centre on considerations such as the amount of control exercised over the person concerned, the importance of that person's work to the employer's business, who pays the wages and how, the payment of income tax and the form in which the contract is drawn up. This section is concerned with the contract of service and the rights and responsibilities that arise from it.

The Contract of Employment

This is governed by the general law of contract and legislation requiring that certain provisions should appear in a contract of employment. The Employment Protection (Consolidation) Act 1978, as amended by the Employment Act 1980, provides that every employee is entitled to a written statement from his employer containing basic information specified in the Act. Such a statement must be provided within thirteen weeks of the start of employment and must give the information specified – for example, names of employer and employee, date employment started, rate or scale of pay, hours of work, etc.

This statement is not the contract of employment, as usually the contract will have been made before the employee starts work. This statement is a record of the terms of the contract, binding on both parties, and applicable from the first day of employment. If an employee has been provided with a formal written contract containing all the conditions the employee should be aware of, then a written statement of the terms is not necessary. The terms of the contract may be varied only with the consent of both parties.

Payment of Wages

Employers must pay for work done; if a wage has not been specified in the contract of employment it is implied that a reasonable amount will be paid for the work done. There is no duty on the employer to provide work, but there may be a duty to pay the employee when no work is available. Entitlement to holiday pay and sick pay depends on the terms of the contract, although an employer is now under a statutory duty to pay sick pay imposed by the Social Security and Housing Benefits Act 1982.

A duty may arise to pay an employee who is not actually working – for example, where an employee with at least four weeks' service has been suspended because the place of work has become a health hazard. Where an employee has been put on short time or been 'laid-off' temporarily there is a duty to pay that employee during suspension from work for all or part of the normal working hours, provided the contract has not been terminated. There are two exceptions to this duty; first if such a term was deliberately excluded from the contract, and secondly where the failure to provide work is due to circumstances beyond the employer's control – for example, a secondary strike. Where the contract does not provide for pay on workless days there may be a right to a statutory guaranteed payment under the Employment Protection (Consolidation) Act 1978. In some circumstances an employee may have time off during working hours with pay, for example, to pursue public duties or carry out trade union duties.

A female employee who is expecting a baby is entitled to maternity leave with pay provided she has been continuously employed for at least two years by the eleventh week before the expected confinement. The actual entitlement depends both on the terms of the contract and the provisions of relevant statutes such as the Employment Protection (Consolidation) Act 1978.

It is lawful for an employer to make a deduction from an employee's payment at the request of that employee for payment to a third party, provided such an arrangement forms part of the contract of employment. An employer must now also deduct certain sums decreed by law from wages and these include income tax, national insurance and attachment orders. Under the Attachment of Earnings Act 1971 the courts have the power to issue attachment of earnings orders. These mainly relate to maintenance awards, judgement debts and fines.

There is also a duty imposed on employers by the Sex Discrimination Act 1975 to ensure that where men and women are employed in like work or work rated as equivalent neither sex should be treated less favourably than the other unless the employer can show a material difference in the work undertaken which justifies a difference in pay. 'Pay' includes any benefit which the employee receives either directly or indirectly as a result of his employment.

Membership of Trade Unions

According to employment legislation every employee has the right not to have any action taken against him by his employer to stop or deter him from joining a trade union or taking part in trade union activities. An employee also has the right not to join a trade union and cannot be compelled by his employer to join one.

Discrimination

Two Acts of Parliament which relate to discrimination must be observed in the recruitment of staff and the framing of the terms of employment. The Race Relations Act 1976 provides that it is unlawful for an employer to discriminate against a potential employee on racial grounds. Discrimination may be the unfavourable treatment of an applicant for a job, offering less favourable terms of employment, or simply refusing his application. Discrimination may also occur once a person is actually in employment through lack of opportunities for promotion, transfer, training, refusal of benefits normally available to employees or unreasonable dismissal. Any action taken for a genuine reason unconnected with racial grounds will not be discrimination – for example, a refusal to employ someone who does not have the necessary qualifications.

Sexual discrimination is unlawful under the Sex Discrimination Act 1975, and includes treating a person less favourably than members of the opposite sex, or making a job unnecessarily difficult for a person of the opposite sex. These provisions make it unlawful specifically to advertise for a male or female and an employer in breach of this provision may be summonsed by the Equal Opportunities Commission and heavily fined, as may the newspaper publishing such an advertisement. All applicants for a job should receive application forms and all applications should be treated equally.

Safety at Work

An employer has always been under a duty at common law to provide a safe system of work, safe equipment and safe premises. Breach of that duty will give rise to a claim for compensation. There is also a statutory duty to provide safety at work which is now embodied in the Health and Safety at Work, etc. Act 1974 (HASAWA). The intention of this Act was to replace all existing legislation with a system of regulations and codes of practice to maintain and improve existing standards of health and safety, applicable to all places of employment. The Act established the Health and Safety

Executive and Health and Safety Inspectors. The Executive operates under the Health and Safety Commission which has the duty of achieving the general purposes of the Act, which are to ensure the health and safety of people at work, and also users of and visitors to such places.

Certain duties relating to particular people are defined in the 1974 Act. Employers must now safeguard, as far as is reasonably practicable, the health, safety and welfare of the people who work for them. This applies in particular to the provision and maintenance of safe plant and systems of work, and covers all machinery, equipment and appliances used. There is a statutory requirement for an employer of five or more people to prepare a written statement of general policy, organisation and arrangements for health and safety at work, to keep it up to date, and to bring it to the notice of all employees. It is also the duty of employers to provide any necessary information and training in safe practices, including information on legal requirements. Employers must consider the specific training needs of their organisations with particular reference to any special hazards. Designers, manufacturers, importers or suppliers of articles or substances for use at work must also ensure, as far as reasonably practicable, that they are safe when used. This duty extends to anyone responsible for articles installed or erected for use at work.

Employees have a duty under the Act to take reasonable care to avoid injury to themselves or to others by their work activities, and to co-operate with employers and others in meeting statutory requirements. The Act also requires employees not to interfere with or misuse anything that has been provided to protect their health, safety or welfare in compliance with the Act.

The Health and Safety Commission and the Health and Safety Executive, as well as publicising the need for health and safety at work, may also instigate prosecutions for breaches of the Act. They can conduct inquiries into accidents that have occurred at places of employment. Enforcement of the Act is primarily a matter for Inspectorates set up under the Act and controlled by the Health and Safety Executive. The Inspectors have wide powers to enter work places and examine records and people to ensure that the Act is being complied with.

One particular effect of the 1974 Act is that it brings nearly all places of work within the Fire Precautions Act 1971, which means that anyone employing staff has to comply with regulations concerning lighting, heating, means of escape and precautions in case of fire. Regulation and enforcement of these provisions is by Inspectors in conjunction with the local fire authority.

Under the Employers' Liability (Compulsory Insurance) Act 1969 certain employers must take out an approved insurance policy to cover disease or personal injury suffered by any of the firm's employees in the course of their employment. Penalties imposed by the Act may be incurred if this is not done, because the aim is to protect an employee who has a claim against his employer.

Dismissal of Employees

The introduction of the concept of 'unfair dismissal' is one of several dramatic changes that have occurred in employment law since the 1960s. By law an employee who is to be dismissed must be given notice of dismissal, this period depending on the terms of the employment, although there are minimum requirements imposed by the law. Merely giving the correct period of notice does not relieve an employer from further liability regarding a dismissal. The grounds for a dismissal and the method of the dismissal must be acceptable in law. According to the Employment Protection (Consolidation) Act 1978 only certain reasons for dismissal will normally be regarded as 'fair'. It has become normal practice for an employer to bring the grounds for dismissal within one of these reasons, or the employer may be found to have dismissed an employee unfairly. Fair grounds for dismissal include: inability to carry out the work, misconduct of the employee, redundancy, breach of a legal duty, or some other substantial reason. Unfair dismissal is not only dismissal for inadequate reasons, but could also be dismissal by the wrong method. Various Codes of Practice have been issued by the government giving guidance concerning the correct method of dismissing an employee, although failure to comply with the current Code of Conduct does not automatically imply there has been an unfair dismissal.

References

Usually an employee looking for another job will want a reference from his present employer. Where an employee has not been satisfactory a difficult situation arises as the employer owes him a legal duty not to say anything condemning about him but at the same time he owes a legal duty to prospective employers to be honest. It may be wise in such circumstances to refuse to give a reference altogether as there is no legal duty to provide a reference unless it is a term of the contract of employment.

Duty to Comply With the Law

Several activities which managers may wish to pursue are covered by specific laws. It is not possible to consider in detail all the areas of the law that must be complied with, but the main areas will be considered briefly below.

Building or Altering Facilities

Generally, any development of land requires a formal application for planning permission which must be made to the local planning authority, and development may not be carried out unless permission is granted.

Sale of Food and Alcohol

Both these activities are covered by extensive and comprehensive legislation. The law relating to the sale of food has been consolidated in the Food Act 1984. Under this Act, which has retained existing regulations, new regulations may be introduced concerning the sale of food. These Food and Hygiene Regulations apply to all premises where food is sold. As food includes drink this means that the Regulations cover activities both in the kitchen and behind the bar. The Regulations lay great emphasis on cleanliness and sanitation and are enforced by local authority Inspectors who have wide powers of entry to premises.

Anyone wishing to sell alcohol must have a licence to do so. Licensing law is mainly contained in the Licensing Act 1964 although there are other important Acts – for example, the Licensing (Occasional Permissions) Act 1983 which empowers justices to grant permission to sell alcohol at certain functions. There are several different types of licence available, for example, the 'Full On Licence' which is held by licensees of public houses or other public bars and the 'Residential Licence' which is held by hoteliers. The procedure for applying for a licence is set out in the 1964 Act and applications are dealt with by licensing justices in the Magistrates' courts. An application for a new licence, or the renewal of an existing one, may be opposed by the police, local authority, fire authority or any other person directly affected (for example, immediate neighbours).

The Licensing Act 1964, and subsequent amending Acts, specify the hours during which alcohol may be sold and the circumstances in which extensions to those hours may be applied for. The Act also specifies certain offences in relation to the sale of alcohol – for example, it is an offence to allow a child under the age of fourteen to be in a bar during permitted hours and no person under eighteen may be served with intoxicating liquor on licensed premises. The Act also makes it clear that the licensee has a special responsibility in respect of the sale of alcohol as no-one may sell alcohol without a licence. A licensee's staff sell on his behalf, and he cannot delegate his authority.

Organising Entertainments

The Local Government (Miscellaneous Provisions) Act 1982 and the London Government Act 1963 provide that it is illegal to provide in any place public music or dancing or public entertainment of a like kind unless an entertainments licence has been granted by the district council or, in London, a London borough or the Common Council. There are exceptions to this requirement which are: music in a place of religious worship or performed as part of a religious meeting, entertainments held at a pleasure fair or entertainments held wholly or mainly in the open air (for which the Act makes special provision). Further provisions of the 1982 and 1963 Acts concern the requirement of a licence for any public contest, exhibition or display of boxing, wrestling, judo, karate or similar sport except at a pleasure fair or wholly or mainly in the open air.

Where the entertainment includes either live or recorded music managers should ensure that they are not breaching the copyright laws.

Fire Precautions

The aims of fire precautions are: to take all practicable steps to avoid an outbreak of fire, to ensure as far as reasonably practicable that should a fire break out it will be contained and prevented from spreading and that it will be tackled without undue delay, and to ensure that in the event of fire all persons who may be within the premises can if necessary be evacuated speedily and safely from the premises to a place of safety. The requirements for fire precautions are contained in a multiplicity of enactments, and standards for fire protection are prescribed in a variety of sets of regulations and codes of practice. For example the Fire Precautions Act 1971 empowers the Secretary of State to designate, as premises needing a fire certificate under the Act, any premises which are being used for a designated purpose within the classes prescribed in the Act; one such class is 'use for purposes of entertainment, recreation or instruction or for purposes of any club, society or association'.

Sunday Observance

Finally, it must not be forgotten that, subject to certain exemptions, mainly cinemas and theatres, the Sunday Observance Act 1780 is still in force. Under the Act any house, room or place which is opened or used on Sunday for public entertainment or amusement and to which persons are admitted by payment of money or by tickets sold for money, is deemed to be a disorderly house and nearly everyone, from the owner to the door-keeper, is liable to penalties. However, ways of avoiding liability have been found. In *Williams* v. *Wright*[16] tickets for a concert held on a Sunday evening stated that admission was free but that reserved seats cost one shilling. The court decided that charging for a reserved seat was not incompatible with admission being free and therefore no offence had been committed. Another example is the practice of making spectators temporary members of an organisation for a day, a device employed regularly by cricket clubs for Sunday League matches.

Conclusion

This chapter has highlighted the major legal duties placed on leisure managers. The level of knowledge intended is that which managers may reasonably be expected to acquire for the purposes of day to day decision-making. However this does not constitute the specialist knowledge of the legal profession and one of the skills of management will be in deciding when and where to seek specialist advice.

Further Reading

There are a number of texts which cover basic principles of the law which relate to issues raised in this chapter. Among the most useful are the following: Baker (1986); Bowers (1986); Davies (1981); Heap (1987).

However there are relatively few texts which address leisure management and the law specifically. Two exceptions are: Collins (1984); Scott (1986).

Case Notes

1. *Law Reports*, Appeal Cases, 562 (1932).
2. *The Times*, 9 December 1984.
3. *Law Reports*, Appeal Cases, 850 (1951).
4. *Times Law Review*, 55, 519 (1939).
5. *All England Law Reports*, 4, 331 (1951).
6. *Justice of the Peace Reports*, 96, 371 (1932).
7. *All England Law Reports*, 2, 320 (1951).
8. *Scots Law Times*, 122 (1978).
9. *All England Law Reports*, 3, 709 (1961).
10. *All England Law Reports*, 3, 709 (1961).
11. *Barnewell and Adolphus's Reports*, 3, 184 (1832).
12. *Times Law Review*, 38, 615 (1922).
13. *All England Law Reports*, 3, 338 (1977).

14. *All England Law Reports*, 3, 361 (1980).
15. *Solicitors' Journal*, 115, 741 (1971).
16. *Times Law Review*, 13, 551 (1897).

References

Baker, C.D. (1986) *Tort*, London: Sweet & Maxwell, Concise College Texts (4th edn).

Bowers, J. (1986) *A Practical Approach to Employment Law*, London: Financial Training Publications.

Collins, V. (1984) *Recreation and the Law*, London: E. & F.N. spon.

Davies, F.R. (1981) *Contract*, London: Sweet & Maxwell, Concise College Texts (4th edn).

Heap, D. (1987) *An Outline of Planning Law*, London: Sweet & Maxwell (9th edn).

Scott, M. (1986) *The Law of Public Leisure Services*, London: Sweet & Maxwell.

Part II
The Contribution of Social Theory to an Understanding of Leisure Policy, and Leisure Management and Planning

6 Analysing Leisure Policy

Fred Coalter

Introduction

In this chapter we will be concerned to identify the nature of the values implicit in the development of leisure policy, and their implications for the role of the leisure professional. The setting of management goals and the choice of means for their attainment are rarely purely technical issues. Such decisions take place within, and are often directly influenced by, the context of political values, attitudes and decisions. Political debates concerning the most appropriate division of responsibility between the public, voluntary and commercial sectors in leisure, the most effective role for local government (i.e., direct provision, subsidy, regulation, contract management) and the proper balance between income maximisation and catering for disadvantaged groups, all serve to emphasise the political dimensions of management decisions.

Such issues are not confined to leisure. They reflect fundamental debates common to all areas of social policy, about 'ends' and 'means'. These debates include the relationship between catering for demand and meeting need; the balance between efficient use of resources and achievement of equity in opportunities; and the balance between maximising individual 'freedom' and achieving equal 'rights of citizenship'.

Debates concerning the nature of choices to be made tend to be polarised – catering for demand versus meeting need; maximisation of income versus maximisation of welfare; public provision versus 'leaving it to the market'. However, we need to recognise that the issues involved are often more complex than such simple contrasts might imply.

The most popular conception of the role of the public sector is that of direct provider – of facilities such as swimming pools, sports and leisure centres, public parks, playing fields, libraries and so on. However, the public sector pursues social policy goals through a much broader range of methods. For example it can provide subsidies (rate rebates, provision of facilities at less than full cost, grants, etc.), or use its regulatory powers either to provide or to constrain particular types of leisure activity (planning controls, licensing powers) to ensure particular levels and quality of leisure opportunities.

In all service areas broad social policy objectives are pursued by varying mixtures of direct provision, subsidy and regulation. In leisure, the relationship between public policy and consumption of goods and services is made even more complex by the variety and heterogeneity of the activities, behaviours, goods and services which constitute 'leisure' (Roberts, 1978). This can be illustrated using Dunleavy's typology (1980) which suggests that there are at least four types of 'consumption processes', each of which has differing implications for the role of the public sector.

Dunleavy proposes that various types of consumption can be identified by examining:

1. the method of organisation (public or private),
2. the criteria for access (non-market or market pricing), and
3. whether or not provision receives a public subsidy (see Figure 6.1).

By using these three dimensions he produces a continuum of 'consumption processes' ranging from the direct provision of wholly collective services (e.g., swimming pools, parks) to wholly individualised consumption (e.g., commercial cinemas, public houses). The implication of this typology is that there is a wide range of possible types of provision or management which can be adopted in pursuit of broad social policy goals.

The significance of such a typology is twofold:

1. It identifies a potentially wide range of contexts within which local government planners, administrators and managers may have to operate.
2. It emphasises choice in relationships between the public, voluntary and commercial sectors.

Such relationships are not simply convenient administrative divisions but reflect values, attitudes and ideologies concerning what is and is not desirable. This emphasises that both the ends of social policy and the various institutional means reflect particular values and attitudes. Consequently both the ends and means of social policy reflect systems of belief about the desirable role of national and local government. The rest of this chapter will therefore identify the various values which underlie public policy decision-making and their implications for leisure policy.

Values and Social Policy

There are a number of possible typologies of values and attitudes regarding social policy and the role of the public sector. For example, Bramham and Henry (1985) adopt a political science approach using the categories of

Figure 6.1 Typology of consumption processes

Type of consumption	Organisation Public	Organisation Private	Criteria for Access Non-Market	Criteria for Access Market	Provision Subsidised	Provision Non-Subsidised	Example
Collective	×		×		×		Urban parks
	×			×	×		Public leisure centres
Quasi-collective		×	×		×		Voluntary groups
		×		×	×		Arts
		×	×		×		National Trust land
Quasi-individualised		×		×	×		
Individualised		×		×		×	Commercial leisure provision

Source: P. Dunleavy, 1984.

Liberal, Conservative, Social Democratic and Socialist as a means for explaining actual or potential social policies for leisure. However, as this typology largely refers to values and attitudes expressed in the party political sphere it may neglect the values and attitudes of professional and managerial interests in the policy-making process. Although such ideologies may bear a close resemblance to particular political positions, Bramham and Henry warn that it may be misleading to characterise such ideal types as specifically 'party-political'.

Therefore, although our analysis will draw on this typology, it will adopt a slightly more abstract organising framework. This is provided by George and Wilding (1976) who propose that attitudes to social policy are best understood as a continuum stretching from 'anti-collectivism' to 'utopian-socialism' (see Figure 6.2).

In varying mixtures the ideological positions in Figure 6.2 offer differing perspectives on the nature of civil society and individual responsibility, the allocative efficiency of the market, the nature and extent of public provision, and the balance to be achieved between the freedom of the individual and equality of opportunity. It must be emphasised that such positions are ideal types, and that rather than distinct positions they represent a continuum of possible perspectives. In the real world we may expect to find that there are no distinct, identifiable boundaries between adjacent points on the continuum.

Ideological debates are central to any discussion of public policy for leisure. Many of these issues and lines of demarcation between various ideological positions concern the extent to which we can speak of leisure 'needs'.

In theory, all social provision is based on the presumed existence of 'needs'. Whereas the market caters for wants, demands and 'desires', the role of public policy is to cater for particular 'needs' which are regarded as appropriate for collective provision, and for which the profit-oriented market would not cater adequately. We are not concerned here to examine the methodogical and theoretical complexities of determining the nature and extent of leisure needs (see Mercer, 1979; Mennell, 1979). Here it is useful to distinguish between 'levels of need'. Low level needs – basic

Figure 6.2   Ideological positions, market implications and core values

Ideological position	Mechanism	Core value
Anti-collectivist	Market + Minimal state	Freedom/demand
Reluctant collectivist	Market + Residual state	Social integration
Fabian Socialism	State + Market	Altruism
Marxism	Non-market	Equality/need

needs for physiological survival and shelter – are likely to be characterised by a general consensus that they should be met, often by public provision and/or subsidy (Hill and Bramley, 1986). However, as we move to 'higher' level needs – e.g., esteem or self-actualisation (Maslow, 1954) – there is likely to be a decline in social and political consensus regarding their definition as a need.

Bramley (1985) suggests that the ambiguous position of leisure services – do they cater for 'needs' or 'wants'? – means that there is little agreement regarding their welfare status. Is leisure an essentially private sphere in which individuals exercise freedom and choice by taking responsibility for catering for their own *wants* and desires? Or is it an area of consumption where collective provision should be made to ensure the achievement of citizenship rights by catering for *need*? These dilemmas are neatly summarised by Parry and Johnson (1974), who suggest that:

> There is a contradiction, not to say a conflict, in our kind of society between the standpoint that leisure ought to be an area in which people should be left to make their own arrangements, or at least in which private enterprise should be left to make whatever provision is profitable, and the belief that leisure policy should be actively developed by local and central government with a view to improving the availability of leisure opportunities.

The rest of this chapter will examine a range of approaches to social policies for leisure which adopt distinct perspectives on this so-called 'contradiction'.

Anti-collectivism and the Primacy of the Market

An anti-collectivist perspective is a mixture of political ideology and economic analysis. Its politics concern the appropriate balance between the individual and the public sector in providing for individual welfare. Its economics highlight the relative efficiencies of the public sector and the market in the allocation of goods and services.

The politics of anti-collectivism are those of 'neo-liberalism' (Bramham and Henry, 1985). Its basic tenets stress both the rights and responsibilities associated with individual freedom. It stresses the importance of freedom of the individual and the right to be free from state interference and control in allocating personal resources and decisions on the goods and services they wish to consume. However, individuals also have a responsibility for their own (and their families') welfare. Further, individuals are seen as the best judges of their own wants and desires – the 'common good' is to be arrived at by individuals seeking to maximise their own interests without interference from government. Consequently, the proper role of public provision is minimal, residual and non-directive.

From such a standpoint the public sector should intervene only where the market would not provide the necessary opportunities and such provision should occur only where it is deemed necessary for the greater freedom of individuals. This might occur, for example, in the case of urban parks. Here it is impracticable to identify and charge all who, directly or indirectly, benefit from the existence of the park and therefore commercial provision is unlikely (Friedman, 1962). However, a fundamental belief that state involvement represents a threat to individual freedom means that there will be a reluctance to extend public provision.

Such a social and political ideology bears a close resemblance to particular ideologies of leisure. For many, leisure is viewed as a private sphere in which self-motivation, self-direction, individual freedom and choice are essential components. In such circumstances not only is a minimalist role for public provision seen as politically desirable but too much intervention might serve to undermine the elements of self-motivation central to leisure (Coalter *et al.*, 1986). Although the argument about generating dependency and undermining initiative is directed at all forms of public welfare provision, leisure services are perhaps more vulnerable than most.

Although the 1975 White Paper, *Sport and Recreation* refers to recreation as 'part of the general fabric of the social services' and part of 'the community's everyday needs', the political legitimacy of the non-market, welfare status of leisure services has not been established. As we have noted, the welfare status of services usually depends on a broad social consensus that they provide for a 'need' for which collective provision is regarded as legitimate or necessary. However, leisure services occupy an uneasy place between ideologies of the market and ideologies of welfare. From this perspective, leisure is viewed as a form of private consumption for which individuals should accept personal responsibility. It is argued that it is not possible to separate 'need' from 'want' (Roberts, 1978); also leisure is not regarded as part of the 'core' concept of needs around which there is a vague (if changing) social consensus (Hill and Bramley, 1986).

The second basis for opposition to public provision (collective consumption) relates to the economics of anti-collectivism. Leisure opportunities provided at below market cost will generate inflated levels of demand among groups who place a high personal value on the activities (Gratton and Taylor, 1985). Because such groups could pay the market price for the facilities this represents an irrational use of public subsidies and makes it impossible to differentiate between those in real need and those whose demands (wants and desires) do not justify public subsidy. It can be seen that in an area regarded as being characterised by choices, wants and desires, this is a fundamental arguement against direct public leisure provision.

To summarise, this position is thus characterised by the following components:

- an ideological concern to avoid dependency and thereby the undermining of individual responsibility and motivation
- an economic concern to avoid the subsidised stimulation of artificially high levels of demand
- a scepticism about the ability to distinguish between 'needs' and 'wants' in pluralist areas of personal consumption, such as leisure.

This is a specific example of a more general belief that consumers are the best judges of their own requirements and that attempts by professional groups (for example, leisure planners and managers) to define needs are misguided. In so far as it is possible, services should be demand-led and consumer-oriented.

Such general ideas lead to three broad types of policies. First, there is an emphasis on 'voluntarism'. The importance of the voluntary sector and 'quasi-individualised' forms of organisation derives from anti-collectivist emphasis on minimal state involvement and the importance of self-organisation and personal responsibility. More specifically, the voluntary sector in leisure is encouraged to promote the self-organisation seen as central to leisure, because people are the best judges of their own interests and in order to reduce local government's direct revenue costs.

Secondly, local authorities should provide directly only essential services, where 'need' is most firmly established and where the market would not provide a sufficient level of provision. As we have already noted, 'leisure' is often regarded as a higher order need and therefore characterised by little social and political consensus. Thirdly, there should be concerted attempts to increase the economic efficiency of services – to reduce levels of public subsidies and maximise income from collectively provided services.

Henry (1986) suggests that the major policy initiative emerging from such a perspective is 'contract management' – the contracting out of responsibility for leisure facilities to commercial management with the role of local authorities being reduced to the specification of standards and the monitoring of performance.

This policy is outlined in the Green Paper *Competition in the Managment of Local Authority Sport and Leisure Facilities* (DoE, 1987). It extends to leisure services the principles set out in the Local Government Bill (1987), which opened various local authority services to competition (refuse collection, catering, ground maintenance, cleaning of buildings). This policy is based on belief that the absence of direct and equivalent competition inevitably leads to inefficiencies in monopolistic public services. The stimulus of competition for the right to provide and manage services will therefore lead to greater efficiency in use of resources and an increased consumer orientation. This process, Compulsory Competitive

Tendering (CCT), is not the same as so-called 'privatisation', in which public assets are sold in order to transfer them directly to the commercial sector (oil; gas; British Telecom; British Airways). Rather it means that local authorities are forced to compete to retain their own services delivery against commercial bidders. The implication is, of course, that they will retain direct responsibility for services in circumstances either where the facilities in question are not attractive to commercial bidders, or where they produce the most competitive, cost efficient and market-oriented bid.

It is probable that major facilities – especially older swimming pools, playing fields, sports halls, libraries, museums – will remain under direct public sector control. However, the processes and ideologies of CCT imply permanent changes in the philosophies and practices of management. In particular, much greater emphasis will be placed on financial management skills and marketing, monitoring and evaluation of usage. Increased emphasis on performance measurement (Sports Council, Greater London and South East, 1988) and increased economic efficiency would mean that leisure facilities would be collectively provided but with market-oriented management and adminsitrative policies. This new 'managerialism' (Dunleavy, 1980; Coalter *et al.*, 1986) would stress increased income from facility charges and reduction of public subsidies.

Such policies would reduce the welfare components of leisure policy, with less emphasis on the need for positive discrimination in favour of disadvantaged groups, through provision at below market price or free. This approach would be essentially demand-led with individuals allowed to express, and pay for, their own leisure wants and desires through the operation of market or quasi-market mechanisms (see Figure 6.1).

Such policies have a number of implications for leisure managers:

- The skills required will be general management skills (finance; accounting; personnel; marketing) rather than specifically 'leisure management' skills. Emphasis will be placed on policies of economic efficiency rather than social welfare – 'facility-oriented' rather than 'people oriented'.
- Where services are 'contracted out', the function of local government officers will be to establish standards, charges for certain sectors of the community (e.g., unemployed, elderly, school groups) and to monitor performance over defined contract periods.
- The function and numbers of local government leisure professionals (especially those with facility-based management experience) may be greatly reduced.

This position therefore implies a redefinition of the role and a reduction in responsibility of local government leisure personnel. This is partly in line with the anti-collectivist general suspicion of professional interest groups who claim a monopoly of expertise in defining and catering for the needs of the community. Such groups are seen to be motivated by self-interest, lacking accountability and being unresponsive to consumer demands.

Reluctant Collectivism and 'Recreational Welfare'

This perspective is much less coherent and integrated than anti-collectivism. George and Wilding (1976) suggest that it is an 'ill-defined collection of political values' whose main characteristic can be regarded as 'pragmatism' – i.e., practical solutions to specific problems. Consequently the criteria for deciding whether commercial provision, voluntary provision, or various forms of public intervention (provision, subsidy, regulation) is appropriate are not always clear. In fact, these vary from service area to service area and even between activities within a service area. It may produce forms of direct public provision within which management policies and criteria for access are market-based. The dominant concern, therefore, is within a 'proper balance' within a 'mixed economy of leisure'.

Like anti-collectivism this perspective stresses the importance of individual freedom and liberty. However, it takes a more fundamental view of the social, cultural and economic constraints on many individuals' freedom and choice. A recognition that a profit-conscious market would not supply leisure opportunities at a 'socially just' level underpins acceptance of some role for public provision and subsidy. Whereas anti-collectivists view inequalities as an inevitable (and acceptable) outcome of the operation of a free market, reluctant collectivists regard inequality in access to certain resources and opportunities as reducing real freedoms.

However, despite a concern to reduce inequalities, the main focus of this perspective could be regarded as economic rather than social. Obstacles to participation are seen as practical issues such as financial cost, lack of transport or lack of personal interest, rather than social barriers such as gender, class and race. This approach compensates for inefficiencies in the market, providing particular goods, services or opportunities where the free market would fail to do so. In this perspective there is an implicit distinction between 'want' and 'need', based largely on ability to pay. The object is to provide, on the basis of non-market criteria, for those in need while those who can afford to pay the market price to fulfil their wants. Although based on an ideological commitment to a residual (and hopefully temporary) role for the public sector, it also draws on economics to support this position.

Often leisure opportunities are regarded as 'merit goods'. That is, the public sector wishes to encourage people to participate in particular activities or pastimes, because not only does the individual benefit but society or the community also (e.g., through improved standards of health). Because specific individuals may not recognise the social or individual value of a particular good it is necessary to provide it at less than market price to encourage participation or consumption. However, one effect of this is to generate inflated levels of demand among participants who place a high value on the service or activity and would pay a market price for the good. This is regarded as an irrational use of public subsidies as it fails to concentrate on those groups or individuals least likely to consume without financial encouragement.

Its pragmatic, issue-specific nature makes it difficult to outline a definitive 'reluctant collectivist' view of leisure. As its focus varies from service sector to service sector, it is possible to maintain several reluctant collectivist positions regarding appropriate social policies for leisure. However, it is worth outlining two broad positions which seem to fall within this category – one pragmatic and one political.

Roberts (1978) proposes a largely residual role for public leisure provision because of the heterogeneous and pluralistic nature of leisure. For Roberts there can be no more than a residual commitment to the distribution of resources in accordance with some criterion of 'need':

> A commitment to service the public's recreation interests is too open-ended to be practical . . . recreation interests are too diverse to make their satisfaction into rights of citizenship. (Roberts, 1978)

Roberts goes on to argue that,

> Despite its imperfections, the market remains one of the most effective participatory mechanisms devised for modern society. Leaving consumers with money in their pockets is an excellent recipe for participation.

Roberts outlines three criteria as a basis for deciding on the appropriateness of public provision. Interestingly the first two are similar to the arguments of anti-collectivists who favour a minimalist role for the public sector.

1. When the supply of resources is finite beyond the short term, the state can defend the public interest against the alternative of, say, commercial monopoly (e.g., land, broadcasting wavelengths).
2. When recreation is an expedient means to a non-recreational objective – e.g., national prestige or public health. (This is similar to the economist's notion of 'externalities' or associated benefits of investment and provision. That is, leisure opportunities are provided not solely because of their inherent value but because they are regarded as a means to an end – e.g., the reduction of vandalism, the improvement of the nation's health and so on.)
3. Robert's third criterion – the pursuit of distributive justice – however, differs substantially from an anti-collectivist position and concerns the issue of 'recreational welfare'. Opportunities for recreation are among the goods and services that public authorities can distribute to enhance the standards and quality of life among otherwise disadvantaged groups.

Accordingly, steps should be taken to identify the 'recreationally disadvantaged' (or even the more generally socially and economically disadvantaged) and selective policies of positive discrimination adopted (e.g., price concessions; special provision; outreach work).

However, it is desirable that such selective policies should apply only to traditional areas of local government sport and recreation provision rather than being based on a more fundamental concept of 'need'. This is because Roberts suggests that the diversity of recreational interests means that their satisfaction should not be turned into rights of citizenship.

The pragmatic refusal to accept access to recreational opportunities as a civil right, guaranteed by public investment and provision, would seem to go to the heart of the issue for reluctant collectivists.

For many the 'right' to leisure opportunities is of a lower order than those which constitute basic elements of social welfare – education, housing, or health services. Access to leisure opportunities may be regarded as a 'social' rather than a 'civil' right. Broad acceptance of a right to leisure opportunities, a recognition of 'recreational disadvantage', does not necessarily imply that the role of the public sector should be that of direct provider. 'Rights' to participate are best guaranteed via a 'mixed economy' of leisure with the 'mix' – of public provision, subsidy, regulation, commercial provision, partnership, voluntary sector, etc. – a matter of pragmatic judgement or ideological preference. It should be stressed that this thinking is not confined to leisure policy. The sectors referred to above – education, housing and health – are all characterised by a varying mixture of public, commercial and voluntary providers.

Roberts's second and third criteria – leisure as a means to non-leisure ends and a concern to ameliorate recreational disadvantage – underpin a particular ideological position which accepts (albeit reluctantly) some role for public provision. Bramham and Henry (1985) refer to this as 'one nation Conservatism'.

For this position the major concern is with social integration and encouragement of a commitment to current social, economic and political arrangements. A recognition that the workings of an unregulated free market could generate socially destabilising divisions leads to acceptance of the necessity for some public subsidy and provision. Welfare services are one method of expressing the social responsibilities of the socially and economically advantaged and ensuring the allegiance of the disadvantaged. There is a sense in which this perspective views non-participating citizens as a threat to social order, while the participating citizen is presumed to be a responsible adult, committed to the social order.

Bramham and Henry (1985) suggest that in cultural policy this perspective emphasises tradition and the 'nation's heritage'. Concerns with social integration and 'one-nation' lead to an emphasis on the 'democratisation of culture' – i.e., the education of certain sectors of the population to appreciate the 'nation's heritage'. More generally, policies will be supported which encourage identification with traditional institutions and the promotion of national pride. In the field of sport, policies will seek to promote identification with the nation through international sporting success.

Because the reluctant collectivist position is broad and heterogeneous, there are inevitable differences concerning the nature and degree of public sector involvement. This 'natural reluctance' is often reinforced by particular views about the nature of leisure itself. Some share the anti-collectivists' view that leisure is a private sphere and that 'the state cannot invade the institutions of leisure without perverting them to its uses' (Scruton, quoted by Bramham and Henry, 1985).

Nevertheless, given the concern for social integration and reduction of some types of inequality, this perspective proposes a more proactive role for the public sector. There is a tendency to accept the historically established legitimacy of current patterns of provision and policies, while seeking to minimise direct costs to local government. This in part derives from political pragmatism and what Dunleavy (1980) calls 'the ratepayer ideology'. A tendency to evaluate all local government expenditure in terms of its consequences for the domestic rate tends to limit the level of subsidy and investment in 'non-essential' services. The Conservative government's introduction of the Community Charge, levied on all individuals rather than residences, can be regarded as an attempt to strengthen this politico–economic restraint on local government expenditure. Interestingly, Dunleavy suggests that within local government 'ratepayers' are perceived in terms of male wage-earners or retired people. Such a conception implicitly excludes the interests of women, young people and the unemployed: groups often defined as 'recreationally disadvantaged'.

The central tension in this perspective is between 'efficiency' and 'effectiveness'. There is concern with the 'efficient' use of economic resources, and with the eradication of waste and overstaffing. Although similar to the economic concerns of anti-collectivists, lack of an ideological objection to public provision per se means that the reluctant collectivist response to these issues is more pragmatic. Where cost benefits might accrue, such a perspective could support selective contracting-out of services (for example, catering). However, the concern with economic efficiency is modified by a parallel concern with 'effectiveness'. This refers to the extent to which services increase the general degree of social welfare, and the extent to which resources and opportunities benefit the 'disadvantaged', for whom provision is made.

This parallels the anti-collectivists' concern that it is not possible to distinguish between 'wants' and 'needs' and to ensure that resources are not given to those who do not need them. Reluctant collectivists will therefore favour selective policies and attempts to 'target' subsidised resources on those most in need, with the charging of full market prices for those who can afford to pay.

As Gratton and Taylor (1985) point out effectiveness, or 'allocative efficiency', requires specific rather than general subsidies, varying from consumer to consumer. However, they suggest that policies which seek to allocate different levels of subsidies to different types of consumers are so complex as to make them administratively unworkable. Certain approaches have been tried – concessions; special sessions; leisure passes – with limited success. The usual pattern has tended to be the crude approach of differentially pricing activities or facilities. Certain activities (e.g., squash), regarded as either having a high price elasticity or being dominated by higher income groups, are priced at or near market level. However, such policies risk reinforcing existing social differences in participation or inequalities in opportunities by effectively excluding those unable to pay higher prices.

One response to these dilemmas has been to suggest that the traditional approach to service delivery is misconceived. Traditionally, much leisure provision has been based on a supply-side approach – i.e., public facilities provided on a universal basis and priced at below true market cost. However, the logic of the reluctant collectivist position, with its acceptance of public provision and its concern to use resources effectively and efficiently, may propose demand-side subsidies. One example of this is in education where parents could be provided with vouchers to admit their children to the school of their choice.

Such a policy combines two core aspects of the reluctant collectivist position. It neatly links a desire to increase individual choice and responsibility with recognition that some form of collective provision is necessary to ensure opportunities at a socially and politically acceptable level. It therefore combines the market ethos, that individuals are the best judges of their own wants and desires, with a view that the state has some responsibility for providing a range of opportunities. Rather than the purpose and content of public policy and provision being defined by professionals, public services become more 'consumer-oriented'. Within such demand-led strategies 'want' is a more important notion than 'need'.

A second response – the encouragement of the voluntary sector and self-organisation in leisure – has both ideological and economic components. Support for the voluntary sector in 'helping those who help themselves' is regarded as ideologically correct because:

- it encourages initiative and self-help
- it encourages (in fact depends on) participation in public organisations
- it encourages acceptance of responsibility for one's own consumption
- it responds to groups of individuals who have defined their own needs.

From an economic perspective, encouragement of the voluntary sector reduces administrative and management costs associated with direct provision. The proper role of the public sector should be as a provider of infrastructure (playing fields, facilities), support (grants, subsidies) and encouragement, to enable the voluntary, self-help sector to flourish. A strong and vibrant voluntary sector in leisure ensures a wide range of leisure opportunities while reducing revenue (and hopefully capital) commitments.

Support for the voluntary sector occurs within the broad belief that the public sector should adopt an enabling role by providing infrastructure (playing fields, facilities) within which groups of individuals take responsibility for organising their own leisure and sporting activities (i.e., a policy of 'helping those who help themselves'). Such policies also frequently have a 'managerial' concern to reduce the financial commitments of the local authority. Self-provision by the voluntary sector can reduce the need for local government capital investment, or voluntary sector management can reduce current expenditure commitments.

The potential problem with such policies is that they fail to cater for the whole community because of the almost inevitable unrepresentative nature of voluntary groups. Mennell (1979) suggests that the organised voluntary sector is doubly unrepresentative. First, all leisure activities are minority activities and therefore there will be competing demands and choices which still have to be made which benefit one sector and penalise another. Secondly, even in total, voluntary organisations are not representative of the whole community. Those who join tend to be middle class and already economically and culturally privileged (see Limb, 1986). The interests of those most likely to be recreationally disadvantaged may not be represented.

Other critics of this approach suggest that the funding of unrepresentative, middle class organisations represents a displacement of local government responsibility to provide for the needs of the whole community. Like the 'contracting-out' tendencies of the anti-collectivists, the definition of local government as a catalyst, and 'pump-primer' of the voluntary sector implies a changing role for traditional facility-oriented leisure managers.

In this regard Hoggett and Bishop (1985) warn that unless care is taken in the nature of the relationships between the public sector and voluntary groups, what they refer to as the 'fragile pluralism' of the voluntary sector may be undermined. They warn against the professional tendency to 'control and order' voluntary groups, and impose a role in tackling 'problems' and 'deficiencies' defined by the council and its officers (like, for example, seeking to direct funded voluntary organisations to cater for groups other than their immediate membership, such as the unemployed). Hoggett and Bishop (1985) argue that one has to accept groups' own definitions of their role and functions, and provide help and assistance without interference. Such a position is a difficult one for leisure personnel who not only are responsible for seeking the optimal use of physical and financial resources but who, according to Hoggett and Bishop, also have an 'evangelical' and 'developmental' attitude, seeking to extend their influence throughout various leisure sectors.

More generally, because the reluctant collectivist position contains a broad range of opinions, it is difficult to outline precise implications for public sector leisure managers. The broad objective of improving social integration via the provision of certain legitimate leisure opportunities is pursued through the 'mixed economy of leisure'. There is no necessary commitment to direct public provision. However, where such provision is made, the manager may be faced with potentially conflicting object-ives – the economically efficient use of resources (i.e. income maximisa-tion and the lowering of subsidies) and the effective allocation of resources to reduce recreational disadvantage (price concessions, increased subsidy). The balance between these two objectives will of course vary widely, although continuing fiscal constraints on local government and pressures associated with CCT will tend to emphasise the importance of economic efficiency.

Where economic efficiency is the key priority, emphasis will be placed on financial management skills and the need to control costs, generate reserves, increase sponsorship and conduct various fund raising exercises. Where appropriate, selective contracting-out of loss-making services (cat-ering, cleaning) will be considered. In addition to this, market research, marketing and promotional skills will be important managerial attributes. Such skills can be exploited in a number of ways – as when, for example, use can be monitored (by user surveys) to identify the social composition of users. This information can be used to increase revenue by concentrating on current users and catchment areas to increase regularity of participation and expand the user base among already participating groups.

However the concentration on current user groups, while increasing revenue, may not address the recreational welfare issue of providing opportunities for disadvantaged groups. From this perspective research, marketing and promotional skills will be used to identify and provide for low or non-participating groups.

Both these perspectives concede a degree of professional autonomy to leisure managers. Such managers may be presumed to have expertise and knowledge which enables them to identify markets, determine need and provide for various groups in the community. As catering for such groups will almost inevitably require price concessions there will be a tendency to cater for them within the context of 'managerialist' definitions. In other words, opportunities for such groups will be programmed into off-peak periods, to fill less popular times of day. Such programming clearly reflects income maximisation rather than a systematic attempt to cater for the needs of the recreationally disadvantaged.

The balance between efficiency and effectiveness lies at the heart of the next perspective, but here the concern is more with effectiveness.

Fabian Socialism and 'Recreational Welfare'

This perspective is less 'leisure-specific' and adopts a more thoroughgoing social analysis of the roots of inequality. Recreational disadvantage is regarded as a product of more fundamental sociostructural inequalities based on social class, gender relations and ethnic disadvantage and discrimination. Consideration of causes and cures for recreational disadvantage is set within broader social, economic and cultural parameters, as leisure inequalities reflect broader patterns of inequality.

Both anti-collectivist and reluctant collectivist positions are concerned to preserve 'freedom' by reducing or restricting state involvement in areas regarded as essentially private. Although they vary in degree, they both perceive the redistributive pursuit of equality as containing a threat to freedom.

The Fabian Socialist perspective suggests that meaningful freedom is not possible without equality. The profit-oriented market is socially inefficient in that it directs goods and services to areas of highest demand rather than greatest need, so that those without economic resources are not able to exercise real choices. The role of the state is to maximise social welfare via collective action and provision, and to correct for inequalities produced and perpetuated by the capitalist market. Such a perspective in leisure provision is similar to that outlined in the 1975 White Paper, *Sport and Recreation* which referred to recreation provision as 'part of the general fabric of the social services . . . one of the community's everyday needs'.

This position is an amalgam of ideas broadly critical of capitalism and committed to the promotion of greater equality. It contains a critique of the inequitable and inefficient nature of the market, with a commitment to social welfare and provision on the basis of need. It is based on a belief in 'rights of citizenship' (see Mishra, 1977).

Social rights involve equality of status in effective participation as a full member of society: 'the right to share in the social heritage and life of a civilised being according to the standards prevailing in society' (Mishra, 1977). Such a position not only stands in opposition to the laissez-faire individualism of both the anti-collectivist and reluctant collectivist positions, but also takes a much less individualistic view of the idea of 'need'. The role of public services should be to provide opportunities for all citizens to have access to whatever goods and services deemed essential to full participation in society.

From this perspective, public provision is not only desirable, to provide non-market opportunities and services, but also essential. It is regarded as morally superior to the market because it promotes social and collective purposes rather than individual self-interest. George and Wilding (1976) suggest that Fabian Socialism entails a commitment to five inter-related core values: equality, freedom, fellowship, democratic participation and humanitarianism. The potential of democratic collective forms of provision for achieving such goals is seen as greater than the increasingly monopolistic and profit-oriented commercial sector. Further, provision should be on a universalist, non-market basis as the selective targeting of the reluctant collectivist position serves to stigmatise and to act as a deterrent, thereby restricting demand.

However, like the reluctant collectivist position, this perspective contains a broad spectrum of opinion, based on variations in emphases among the core values. In order to examine the implications for leisure policy and management, we will look at two positions within Fabian Socialism which we can refer to as 'institutional provision' and 'community recreation'.

The institutional approach to public services is based on belief that a broad range of collectively provided services – like housing, education, health, and leisure – is necessary to compensate for inequalities generated by the market. In certain circumstances, the public sector should go beyond merely compensating for market failures and enter areas previously regarded as the monopoly of the commercial sector (e.g., cinemas, discos). This may be done for a number of reasons, for example:

- To act as 'market leader' and as an example of good practice.
- A refusal to concede all profitable areas to the commercial sector. Profitable areas can then be used to cross-subsidise non-profitable provision and/or to subsidise disadvantaged groups.
- Traditional areas of local government provision are too limited (sport, recreation, arts) to cater adequately for changing leisure needs.

Historically, the institutional approach has placed 'leisure professionals' (planners, administrators, managers) in a privileged position. Central to this is the presumption that professionals have expert knowledge enabling them to identify need and to formulate appropriate policies and provision for particular 'client groups'. From this perspective, leisure professionals require more than facility-oriented, generic financial management skills to achieve economic efficiency. Here the concern is with effectiveness: to ensure that all groups in the community are being adequately catered for and, in particular, that resources are being fairly allocated to the recreationally disadvantaged. Such managers will require sociological and research skills to enable them to define, identify and cater for the range of groups within their communities.

Within this perspective there has been growing concern about the failure of leisure services to cater for a range of disadvantaged groups (women, unemployed, certain ethnic minorities) and social classes (semi- and unskilled groups). This has led to questioning of the professionally dominated 'top down' style of service delivery, in which experts define need and determine the nature and content of leisure provision (what is provided for whom). Like the reluctant collectivists there has been increasing concern that inflexible, bureaucratic and facility-oriented forms of management are inappropriate models for leisure provision (Coalter, 1986; Henry and Bramham, 1986; Murphy, 1986). This critique of traditional 'facility-oriented' models of service-delivery has led to a number of responses:

- encouragement and protection of the voluntary sector. Rather than merely funding existing (and possibly unrepresentative) voluntary groups, this position promotes the development of a broader and more representative range of organisations. This approach was characteristic of the Greater London Council which used grants and subsidies to promote a range of minority interest groups.

- Devolution of management responsibilities to enable leisure centre managers to be more responsive to the needs of the local community, rather than merely implementing centrally determined strategic policies.
- Decentralisation of policy-making which involves members of the local community in the management committees of local leisure centres.

Many of these approaches are referred to by the generic term of 'community recreation' (Haywood and Henry, 1986; Bennington and White, 1986). The term 'community recreation' tends to refer to a vague philosophy rather than to imply precise administrative and management arrangements. This 'people-oriented' approach was given support by the Department of the Environment's Recreation Management Training Committee (DoE 1984) which proposed that 'the recreation manager must increasingly assume the role of helper, counsellor and advocate on behalf of people wishing to enjoy their leisure'. Such an approach has a number of implications for management styles and skills, including:

- The proactive approach, requiring the identification of and catering for the 'needs' of under-participating groups, implies the need for skills to enable the manager to carry out research and consultation within the community. Simply improving the promotion of existing activities will not be sufficient.
- A broader knowledge of social and cultural processes, to enable the understanding of social problems, needs and aspirations of various groups in the community.

Marxism and 'Recreation as Welfare'

Marxism provides not so much a theory of social policy as a critique of current policies and practices and a stress on the limitations of welfare-type policies within the context of a capitalist society. For Marxists, the understanding of social policies must take place within the context of society as a whole.

Capitalism is viewed as an economic system based on the exploitation of one class (the proletariat) by another (the capitalist). The capitalist class owns the means of production (land, capital, technology) and the proletariat are forced to sell their labour for a basic wage, with the surplus they produce being appropriated by the capitalist class. Within the context of an exploitative system, social policies (and all state activities) are not regarded as neutral attempts to increase the general level of welfare and cater for the needs of individuals. Rather the main purpose of the policies of the state is to contribute to the safeguarding of the interests of the capitalist class and to ensure the continuation of an exploitative economic system.

Within this perspective, social policies are regarded as contributing to economic efficiency and profitability and to the reproduction of labour, social integration and stability, and ensuring workers' acceptance of current social and economic institutions. Marxists, therefore, tend to view public leisure policies in terms of 'social control' and 'legitimation'. Leisure provision is regarded as attempting to:

1. reduce social tensions and conflicts
2. disguise social and economic divisions and create an artificial sense of communal or national unity
3. impose ruling-class values on the working-class (for example, arts policies based on the notion of 'democratisation of culture' which seek to provide greater access to traditional art forms in order to inculcate a broader audience with ruling class values and to 'civilise' the working class).

Marxists therefore emphasise the instrumental use of leisure policy. Leisure facilities are provided not only (if at all) because they are inherently worthwhile but as a means to an end. In other words, rather than a concern with recreational welfare – providing for recreationally disadvantaged groups – we have 'recreation as welfare' (Coalter *et al.*, 1986). Such policies are not simply concerned with the 'needs' of particular groups or individuals, but with the broader needs of social integration in a period of deteriorating social and economic conditions (unemployment, inner city decline). There is an emphasis on what economists refer to as 'externalities', the associated benefits of provision. Leisure facilities are provided because they are presumed to contribute to the solution of wider social problems such as vandalism, delinquency, unemployment and inner city deprivation.

A classic statement of these aspects of social policy is provided by the 1975 White Paper, *Sport and Recreation* (DoE, 1975) which contended that:

> By reducing boredom and urban frustration, participation in active recreation contributes to the reduction of hooliganism and delinquency among young people . . . the social stresses on many young people today are enormous . . . if we delay too long in tackling the causes of these stresses constructively, the problems which arise from them will be magnified, and the cost of dealing with their results greatly increased. The need to provide for people to make the best of their leisure must be seen in this context.

In addition, Marxists point to the increasingly prominent role of leisure provision in urban policy. Financing for leisure provision is now an important component of the Urban Programme, and in the wake of the

1981 urban riots the Sports Council established the Action Sports scheme, aimed at involving previously under-participating groups in sporting activities by going beyond the formal facility-based approach and placing sports leaders and outreach workers in the community (Rigg, 1986). Although many of the 'targeted' groups may be regarded as recreationally disadvantaged, critics suggest that the concern is also to ameliorate wider social and economic disadvantage and thereby to defuse protest and ensure social stability (Carrington and Leaman, 1983).

The fine balance between the definition of the 'needs' of groups and individuals (opportunity, choice, self-fulfilment) and the broader 'needs' of society (integration, stability) indicates the dual nature of social policies and is certainly present in policies for leisure.

Some Marxists acknowledge that leisure policies do contain genuine attempts to extend social welfare and recreational opportunities. Further, rather than being a simple imposition, provision is often made in response to public demand and contributes positively to the quality of life of otherwise disadvantaged groups. However, for most Marxist-influenced thinkers the positive, liberative aspects of social policies are ultimately subordinated to, or even undermined by, the needs and values of the capitalist economy.

The limitations derive from a number of interrelated factors:

- Conflict between economic efficiency (reduction of costs) and social effectiveness (subsidised provision for disadvantaged or under-participating groups). The suggestion is that economic arguments ultimately dominate and that recreational welfare aspects of policy will always be subordinate.

- Attempts to reform leisure policy by the acceptance of multi-culturalism and 'relevant' provision fail to recognise that the differing needs of groups in society do not just reflect leisure issues but reflect fundamental patterns of social and economic inequalities (Clarke and Critcher, 1985). This may explain the relative failure of recreational welfare policies to achieve the desired levels of participation among certain groups. Such an analysis would suggest a wider ranging and more thoroughgoing definition of a 'leisure' policy than is currently accepted. For example it would take account of differential access to transport, housing conditions, income distribution and so on.

- The ideology of the capitalist market, with its emphasis on individualism, competition and profitability, serves to undermine the collective and altruistic purposes of welfare policies and to undermine the ability to provide for need (George and Wilding, 1976; Clarke and Critcher, 1985; Dower *et al.*, 1981).

- The liberative potential of leisure services is undermined by bureaucratic structures, 'managerialist' ideologies based on income maximising, facility-oriented approaches and the growing dominance of paternalistic professional groups in the determination of 'need' and 'relevant' provision. These all serve to produce restrictive definitions of 'appropriate' forms of behaviour and thereby effectively exclude particular sections of the community (Bacon, 1980; Clarke and Critcher, 1985; Coalter, 1988).

Many of these criticisms of public policies for leisure derive from more fundamental Marxist concerns with a democratic distribution of power and participation in decision making and resource allocation. For example, Clarke and Critcher (1985) wish to extend the definition of leisure beyond subjective feelings of 'freedom' and 'choice' to include the more objective, political concept of 'control'. They suggest that meaningful 'participation' must go beyond consumption of goods and services provided for profit by the commercial sector or determined by public sector professionals. It must include the opportunity to determine what is provided.

Some Marxists suggest that, because capitalism is an exploitative system based on the production of goods for exchange and profit, it cannot provide social and economic conditions for people to realise their true potential. In other words, capitalism cannot meet the higher order 'needs' of self-fulfilment and personal autonomy. As a consequence, the attempts to define and cater for 'needs' in leisure policy are doomed to failure.

However, others within this perspective acknowledge some potential in the present social and economic arrangements for extending welfare, making services more responsive and catering for 'need'. Their proposals tend to be a more radical and thoroughgoing version of the community recreation approach outlined in the previous section. The concern is to 'democratise' decision-making processes and delivery systems by extending community control over policy and provision, thereby undermining impersonal and bureaucratic forms of administration.

The major implication for leisure managers is that this perspective emphasises democratic participation in decision-making and implies the reduction, or even destruction, of the powers and privileges of the so-called 'leisure professionals'.

Such a role would require leisure services personnel to possess more than technical management, financial or marketing skills. Such a participative approach would require a range of 'political' skills such as interpersonal competence, negotiating skills, competence in committees, an awareness of different cultures and values and counselling skills. It would require the manager to be less of an expert provider and more of a partner and advocate for disadvantaged groups.

Feminism and Leisure Policy

Various elements of Fabian Socialist and Marxist analyses of failures of public leisure policies combine in feminist critiques of both leisure studies and leisure policy. Fabian Socialist proposals that leisure services have failed to cater for disadvantaged groups and proposed policies of positive discrimination are reinforced by feminist critics. They suggest that, in facilities and types of activities, leisure services have failed to recognise and cater for the special needs of women. Marxist concern with the democratisation of decision-making and the reduction of professional influence is reinforced by feminist concern about the absence of women from the male dominated field of leisure management (James, 1986; Deem, 1986a, 1986b). Further, feminists insist that an analysis of leisure needs and policies for women cannot be separated from a broader examination of women's economic and social position. As Deem insists, the issue of women's leisure 'is not an individualised problem which requires an individualised solution' (Deem, 1986a).

Despite some disagreement regarding the causes of, and the solutions to, the problems experienced by women, all are agreed that women generally occupy socially and economically disadvantaged positions. Crucial to feminist arguments is the claim that, in general, women are either economically disadvantaged when compared to men or are economically dependent on men. For example, in 1985 men in full time employment earned approximately 52% more than women in full time employment. Further, women are likely to be in poorly paid, part time work. Women who remain at home, as housewives and mothers, are economically dependent on their partners. Given that much leisure expenditure is dependent on discretionary income, that left over after necessities, this represents a major economic constraint on women's leisure choices.

For women, out-of-home employment is important because of the relative economic independence which it may ensure. Further evidence suggests that such women have a greater ability to compartmentalise their time and feel that they have a right to leisure time and to ensure that they achieve it.

The role of housewife and mother places both time constraints and ideological constraints on women's leisure. Socially constructed definitions of male and female gender roles largely restrict the domestic and child-caring roles to women. For women with young children this has the effect of fragmenting their leisure time. The presence of young children means that mothers are continually 'on call', unable either to obtain substantial blocks of time necessary for out-of-home leisure activities or to predict when 'free time' may become available. Research evidence (Wimbush, 1986) suggests that the ideology of motherhood further constrains many mothers, who have a feeling of guilt about leaving children to undertake leisure activities or feel that they do not have a right to leisure. Young children also act as a constraint on out-of-home leisure activities because of formal and informal restrictions placed on the presence of children in many public places and a failure to provide creches and childcare facilities in both public and commercial facilities.

More generally, sexist stereotypes and socialisation processes restrict women's choice of leisure activities as either appropriate or inappropriate for women. For example, Deem (1986a) and Scraton (1987) argue that within the education system, the curriculum tends to emphasise women's future destination as marriage and child-rearing. Further, girls' physical education tends to emphasise supposedly feminine values of passivity, attractiveness, and lack of physical strength, thereby implying that a range of sports and activities are not appropriate for women. The combination of restricted curriculum and particular definitions of appropriate physical activities combine to restrict the leisure experiences of young women and thereby restrict choice in later life. This is often reinforced by the stereotyped nature of activities provided for women (aerobics, keep fit).

Feminists propose a number of immediate policy responses to some of the problems of women's restricted leisure opportunities. These include:

- provision of creche facilities and not only for 'women's activities'
- women-only sessions to permit experimentation and confidence building
- improved transport provision to and from leisure facilities
- flexible programming that is responsive to the unpredictability of young mothers' free time
- recognition that payment for courses or programmes in advance might not be economically possible or, because of the problems of regular attendance, may be a disincentive (Deem, 1986a).

However, many suggest that the issue of women's leisure requires more fundamental social and ideological transformation. Many of the feminist analyses emphasise the importance of patriarchy in male control over women's public and private lives. They argue that major changes are required to destroy sexist stereotypes and the sexual division of labour. Men are required to recognise that their leisure lives often depend on women's domestic labour and to take equal responsibility for childcare and domestic tasks. However of more relevance to leisure management are the feminist proposals for transformations in the public sphere. Here the radical nature of the changes proposed are indicated by Deem (1986a) who states:

> The lesson which still needs to be learnt about women and leisure in public provision is that it isn't sufficient to recognise women as a target group or to provide what men think women need, under male control. Women actually need to be part of the politicking and planning process.

Feminists asks the question 'who decides what for whom?', which raises basic issues about the role of leisure managers. Feminists reject what they regard as the paternalist 'top-down' approach of traditional professional practice. They refuse to concede decision-making autonomy to leisure planners and managers. Rather than exercising their supposed technical and professional expertise to decide on the nature of leisure provision, they should adopt a more consultative, investigative role, acting in partnership with those for whom they seek to provide.

Although feminists are concerned about the 'paternalistic' nature of traditional professional approaches, they are more concerned with the male dominated, patriarchal nature of leisure management, and in some instances with the sexist nature of some sport and recreational activities. As Deem indicates, it is not enough for current (male) leisure managers to designate women as a 'target group' and to introduce policies of positive discrimination. What is required is positive discrimination in recruitment of women to management positions, and for women to be actively involved in planning and management rather than be passive recipients. Slade (1985) found that only 4.7 per cent of public sports centre managers in England were women. James (1986), commenting on the under-representation of women in leisure management jobs, suggests that the areas where they are represented tend to be in traditional female areas, like libraries, dance and drama and play leadership.

However, for some it is not simply a matter of 'more women leisure managers'. Such issues imply the need for a re-evaluation of the nature of management itself (see for example Chapter 7 in this volume). James (1986) suggests that in its membership, attitudes and values, management traditionally has been a male preserve. This is intensified in leisure management "where the very service being provided is associated with stereotyped male values and norms (outdoor sport; weight training)". From this perspective, traditional male attitudes (competitiveness, masculinity), seen to be inherent in management training and practice (and many types of sporting provision), need to be questioned and modified by the experiences and skills which women will bring to leisure management. This will affect not only the nature and context of provision but also the manner and style of management.

A Leisure Profession?

The first part of this chapter set out a range of 'consumption processes' through which services may be provided. Ranging on a continuum from collective consumption to individualised forms, each implies a different role for those involved in the planning and management of such services. Further, each of the perspectives on social policy has particular implications for the role of the so-called 'leisure professional'. These range from monitoring contracted service provision to being a social and community worker and counsellor. Such a spectrum of opinion about the actual or potential role of leisure planners and managers implies that the exact status of the occupation has yet to be decided.

In this final section we will therefore examine the debate concerning the nature of the 'leisure professional'. This raises a number of questions:

- How does a profession differ from an occupation?
- Is there such a thing as a leisure profession?
- Is the professional model appropriate for public leisure services?
- What are the implications of the 'professionalisation' of leisure services?

The traditional approach to defining a profession is referred to as the 'trait' approach. This consists of describing particular features regarded as constituting a profession, and measuring claims to the status of profession against this. The most common features, usually derived from the classic professions of law and medicine, are as follows:

- the practice of the occupation is founded on the basis of theoretical knowledge whose application is highly valued in sociaty
- the acquisition of this knowledge is founded on a long period of education and training
- the occupation subscribes to an ideal of altruistic public service rather than being motivated solely by profit
- the occupational group has control over recruitment and can regulate entry
- there is a well-organised colleague group which uses disciplinary powers to enforce an ethical code of practice.

Murphy (1986) used this traits model to evaluate the claims of public leisure service personnel to the status of a profession. Across the range of traits he found that such claims were largely unfounded. First, because of the wide variety of working environments (baths, parks, sports centres) and skills, he suggests that there is no integrated and coherent body of specialised knowledge characteristic of 'traditional professionals'. Secondly, leisure management is regarded as a practical, problem-solving job with little emphasis on formal academic qualifications as a pre-requisite for efficient job performance. Further, there were some who doubted that there was a specific job of 'leisure management', with the suggestion that 'a good manager can manage anything'. Thirdly, although the values associated with leisure – choice, self-fulfilment, autonomy – are highly socially valued, there is no evidence to suggest that leisure managers are essential to their achievement.

Fourthly, although many managers identified 'service to clients' as a primary goal and a source of job satisfaction, Murphy suggests that the use of 'client seeking' techniques such as marketing and targeting and the use of outreach strategies are not associated with professionals, who usually wait for clients to contact them. Fifthly, within the bureaucratic structures of local government the degree of autonomy to decide policy and procedures is extremely low, with managers often acting in the role of administrators of policy decided by their superiors. Many writers have suggested that bureaucratic norms and definitions of procedure within local government make it extremely unlikely that new occupational groups would be able to establish the degree of autonomy associated with professional practice. Sixthly, within the classic professional model the code of ethics establishes both a safeguard and criterion for success with regard to the professional–client relationship. However, in the so-called 'leisure profession', success may be established not by the quality of the individual manager–client relationship but by financial considerations and/or aggregate user statistics.

The last point concerning the definition of the criteria for professional performance is a crucial one for those attempting to develop a leisure profession, such as the Institute of Leisure and Amenity Management (ILAM). The major issues concern not just what are to be the performance criteria, but who is to decide what they will be. This raises broader issues of what might be referred to as the 'politics of professionalism' (Coalter, 1986).

Over the past decade the nature and functions of local government have been radically revised and it is within this set of changing circumstances that the emerging 'leisure profession' is struggling to establish itself and to construct an identity and purpose. The eventual nature of this occupational group will largely depend on the relationships it establishes with other local authority professional groups, local politicians and the general public and the type of service which emerges.

The claims of leisure service personnel to the status, autonomy and influence of a professional group need to be accepted as legitimate by other, longer established groupings within local government (planners, architects, accountants). However, many of these groups may not be committed to the development of leisure services or to the expansion of their welfare aspects. Their concerns may be with financial constraints, reduction of subsidies, income maximisation and the financially optimal use of facilities. Such pressures may produce an occupational grouping which concentrates on the development of facility-oriented, technical and management expertise, emphasising the efficient use of financial and physical resources. This approach would effectively ignore what the Yates Committee (DoE, 1984) referred to as 'philosophical problems' concerning the nature and social purpose of leisure services. Such a strategy might be better described as 'managerialism' rather than 'professionalism' and would seem to conform to the demands of both anti-collectivism and reluctant collectivism.

A second set of relationships which has implications for the future development of leisure services is that between leisure service personnel and local government politicians. Traditionally, professional groupings have gained autonomy because they possessed a high level of technical knowledge and expertise which was relatively inaccessible for non-professionally trained people. Local government members were dependent on the professional expertise of such officers. However, leisure is an area which is more accessible; it is a service which is open to general public use, located in the community and about which politicians feel able to make judgements on a day to day basis.

As a consequence, politicians may be unwilling to acknowledge that leisure service personnel have a special professional expertise (other than technical knowledge about such things as baths or horticulture). Such a development, and the growing direct influence of party-political policies in leisure services, mean that leisure services personnel may become more directly involved in political processes than has previously been the case. This may, of course, create tensions with the supposedly traditional role of the politically neutral expert, providing objective advice on the basis of professional expertise. The increasing influence of party policies on professional decisions has implications for the final set of relationships – those with the general public. Who is the leisure professional's client: local government employers or the local community?

We have seen that each of the social policy perspectives implies distinct roles for leisure service personnel, ranging from responding to expressed demand to acting as a 'helper' and 'advocate' (DoE, 1984). The traditional professional model is a 'top-down' one, in which an expert defines 'need' and provides a service on behalf of the 'client'. However, all the perspectives raise critical questions about such an approach, suggesting that a more 'consumer-led' approach to service delivery is required. Of course, the precise definition of such an approach differs between perspectives. Anti-collectivists and some reluctant collectivists would propose that expressed demand be the criterion. Others, such as Fabian Socialists, Marxists and feminists would suggest that the identification of 'need' is central.

The latter group express a concern that traditional facility-oriented approaches have failed to cater adequately for all social groups. Further, there is a more general view that 'leisure' policy is concerned not with objective, measurable needs but with individual choice. For example Murphy (1986) asks whether or not increased professionalism – with all the implications of privilege, status and lack of accountability – would detract 'from the desired social goal of a people-oriented activity'.

From such a perspective what is required is a greater knowledge of social problems, of public needs, aspirations and motivations. Many writers suggest that a research-based interactive and consultative approach is appropriate to leisure services, concerned as they are with such values as individual choice, freedom, opportunities and self-fulfilment. The growing unease with 'professionalism' in public services and the economic obstacles to service development may, paradoxically, represent an opportunity rather than a constraint. Although often treated with scepticism, the formal values said to underpin professionalism – public service, altruism, social welfare, liberal humanism – seem wholly appropriate to leisure services and improvement of the quality of life. They certainly seem appropriate values for Yates's categories of 'counsellor', 'helper' and 'advocate' (DoE, 1984).

Like many urban professionals operating within structures of bureaucratic and political accountability, the question of who is the 'client' is often difficult to resolve – politicians, corporate management, facility users or the recreationally disadvantaged? While not underestimating the real pressures from political or management processes, the status of a 'profession' depends not only on political patronage but also on what Yates refers to as a 'community sanction': the public acceptance of a professional role for recreation planning and management (Murphy, 1986). If this is so, in addition to developing technical and managerial functions, leisure service personnel must establish a broader social purpose.

However, as we have seen throughout this chapter, the definition of 'social purpose' varies widely, and depends in large part on more fundamental attitudes to the relative roles of the public and private sectors. The debate about leisure services and leisure management remains unresolved, and its possible resolution will depend on broader political and ideological forces.

Further Reading

The major arguments outlined in this chapter are considered in more detail in Coalter *et al.* (1986). For a discussion of political ideologies and their consequences for leisure see also Bramham and Henry (1985). Rosemary Deem (1986b) deals specifically with aspects of leisure policy and their implications for women. Finally in respect of local government leisure policy, Bennington and White (1988) provide an overview of the impact of contemporary forces of change on the nature of local policy and provision.

References

Bacon, W. (1980) *Social Planning, Research and the Provision of Leisure Services*, Centre for Leisure Studies, University of Salford.

Bennington, J. and White, J. (1986) *The Future Role and Organisation of Local Government Leisure*, Institute of Local Government Studies, University of Birmingham.

Bennington, J. and White, J. (1988) *The Future of Local Government Leisure Services*, London: Longman.

Bramham, P. and Henry, I. (1985) 'Political Ideology and Leisure Policy in the United Kingdom', Leisure Studies, 4 (1).

Bramley, G. (1985) *Grant-Related Expenditure and Recreation*, SAUS Working Paper, 51, School of Advanced Urban Studies, Bristol.

Carrington, J. and Leaman, O. (1982) 'Work for Some and Sport for All', *Youth and Policy*, 1 (3).

Clarke, J. and Critcher, C. (1985) *The Devil Makes Work: Leisure in Capitalist Britain*, London: Macmillan.

Coalter, F. (1986) 'A Leisure Profession? Definitions and Dilemmas', *Local Government Policy Making* (December).

Coalter, F. (1988) 'Leisure Policy: An Unresolvable Dualism?' in Rojek, C. (ed.), *Leisure for Leisure*, London: Routledge.

Coalter, F., with Long J. and Duffield B. (1986) *The Rationale for Public Sector Investment in Leisure*, London: Sports Council/ESRC.

Deem, R. (1986a) 'The Politics of Women's Leisure', in Coalter, F. (ed.), *The Politics of Leisure*, London: Leisure Studies Association.

Deem, R. (1986b) *All Work and No Play? The Sociology of Women and Leisure*, Milton Keynes: Open University Press.

Department of the Environment (1975) *Sport and Recreation*, London: HMSO.

Department of the Environment (1984) *Recreation Management Training Committee Final Report* (The Yates Committee), London: HMSO.

Department of the Environment (1987) *Competition in the Management of Local Authority Sport and Leisure Facilities*, London: HMSO.

Dower, M. *et al.* (1981) *Leisure Provision and People's Needs*, London: HMSO.

Dunleavy, P. (1980) *Urban Political Analysis*, London: Macmillan.

Friedman, M. (1962) *Capitalism and Freedom*, Chicago: University of Chicago Press.

George, V. and Wilding, P. (1976) *Ideology and Social Welfare*, London: Routledge.

Gratton, C. and Taylor, P. (1985) *Sport and Recreation: an Economic Analysis*, London: E & F. N. Spon.

Haywood, L. and Henry, I. (1986) 'Policy Developments in Community Leisure and Recreation', *Leisure Management*, 6 (7) and 6 (8).

Henry, I. (1986) *Alternative Futures for Leisure*, Working Paper 4:1, Institute of Local Government Studies, University of Birmingham.

Henry, I. and Bramham, P. (1986) 'Leisure the Local State and Social Order', *Leisure Studies*, 5 (2) May.

Hill, M. and Bramley, G. (1986) *Analysing Social Policy*, London: Blackwell.

Hoggett, P. and Bishop, J. (1985) *The Social Organisation of Leisure: A Study of Groups in their Voluntary Sector Context*, London: Sports Council/ESRC.

James, E. (1986) 'Management Development and Women in Leisure and Recreation', *Local Government Policy Making*, 13 (3) (December).

Limb, M. (1986) 'Community Involvement in Leisure Provision – Private Enterprise or Public Interest?' in Coalter, F. (ed.), *The Politics of Leisure*, London: Leisure Studies Association.

Maslow, A. (1954) *Motivation and Personality*, New York: Harper & Row.

Mennell, S. (1979) 'Theoretical Considerations on Cultural Needs', *Sociology*, 13 (2).

Mercer, D. (1979) 'The Concept of Recreational "Need"', *Journal of Leisure Research*, 5 (1).

Mishra, R. (1977) *Society and Social Policy: Theoretical Perspectives on Welfare*, London: Macmillan.

Murphy, W. (1986) 'Professionalism and Recreation Provision in Local Government and Industry', in Coalter, F. (ed.)., *The Politics of Leisure*, London: Leisure Studies Association.

Parry, N. and Johnson, D. (1974) *Leisure and Social Strucutre*, Hatfield Polytechnic, mimeo.

Rigg, M. (1986) *Action Sport: An Evaluation*, London: Sports Council.

Roberts, K. (1978) *Contemporary Society and the Growth of Leisure*, London: Longman.

Scraton, S. (1987) '"Boys Muscle in Where Angels Fear to Tread" – Girls' Subculture and Physical Activities', in Horne, J. *et al.* (eds.), *Sport, Leisure and Social Relations*, London: Routledge.

Slade, T. (1985) 'A Sociological Analysis of the Representation of Women Public

Sports Centre Managers in England', unpublished undergraduate dissertation, West Sussex Institute of Higher Education.

Sports Council, Greater London and South East (1988) *A Capital Prospect: A Strategy for London Sport*, London: London Council for Sport and Recreation.

Wimbush, E. (1986) *Women, Leisure and Well-Being. An Edinburgh-based study of the role and meaning of leisure in the lives of mothers with pre-school age children*, Scotland: Centre for Leisure Research.

7 Social Theory, Planning and Management

Ian Henry and John Spink

Introduction

This chapter aims to outline some of the major relationships between, on the one hand, leisure management and planning practice (and theories or explanations about how to practice), and on the other, explanations drawn from social theory which seek to account for the nature of social action and social structures in a wider context. The chapter will locate the primary perspectives on planning and management activity in relation to one another and to wider sociopolitical perspectives. Treatment of these perspectives will be necessarily brief and illustrative rather than forming a comprehensive critical guide. It will seek to provide guidance for further reading in a way which bridges the gap between the concerns of leisure management and those of social theory.

The typology, around which the commentary in this chapter develops, involves a characterisation of sociopolitical perspectives incorporating liberal individualism, pluralism(s), and structural marxism (see Figure 7.1). Two important points should be made in relation to the typology employed. The first is that this approach invariably implies some simplification of distinctions and similarities within and between the categories identified in the typology. The second is that the categories themselves should not be taken as exhaustive. We have chosen to discuss, for example, feminist analyses as ranging across the categories of social theory identified, although 'radical feminism' discussed below cannot be accomodated within Figure 7.1). Notwithstanding these difficulties, we suggest that the typology represents a useful way of conceptualising the range of perspectives in order to 'situate' discussion of approaches to management and planning.

Figure 7.1 Sociopolitical perspectives and their relationship to theories of leisure, management and planning

SOCIOPOLITICAL PERSPECTIVES	STRUCTURALIST MARXISM	PLURALISM			INDIVIDUALISM
Economic ideas	Marxist critique Economic Needs of Capital - accumulation - legitimacy - efficiency	Keynsian pluralism Economic management and planning to counteract disequilibrium Mixed economy, Public interest, Full employment			Free market; Monetarism Market mechanism achieves equilibrium Rational self-interest; Reduced inflation
Social ideas/ Problem explanations	Social structure	Class	Institutions	Area	Family	Individual
	(Exploitation)	(Values)	(Bureaucracy)	(Locality)	(Socialisation)	(Pathology)
Policy ideas	Collectivism Equity State responsibility Welfare rights Comprehensive state provision	Reluctant collectivism Communal responsibility Public interest Shared values Insurance			Anti-collectivism Individual responsibility Self-reliance Family life Law and order
Service provision	Universal eligibility	Pragmatic response to need			Reduced state provision Safety net provision
Political ideas	Marxism State reflects capitalist economy and social structure Class interests dominant - directly (instrumental) - indirectly (structural)	Reformism State acts to reduce inequality, redress imbalances in power Individuals partly constrained Support weak competitors	Conventional pluralism Plurality of interests Democratic expression Public interest Problem solving		New Right Laissez-faire Market competition Self-regulation; liberty efficiency
Ideas about the state	Aids capital - reproduces labour - social order State not neutral therefore 'capture or smash', replace with democratic institutions	Expansive state reform within the law Freedom by government action	State arbitration positive but neutral Economics and politics separate Open government, more information, more participation		Minimal state, passive, limited activity Existing state bureaucracy inefficient - so privatise

Ideas on political process	Democratic legitimation camouflage interests of economic elite	Government active accountable and responsive	Interest group competition	Expression of popular will; risk of government 'overload'
Feminist perspectives	Marxist feminism Sexual division of labour is functional for capitalism – unpaid labour of women reproduces workforce	Socialist feminism Patriarchy and capitalism combine to oppress women (and men); gender, class and race key sources of oppression	Liberal feminism Lobbying of government to redress gender inequalities through legislation	Socio-biology Biological differences Notion of individual overrides concern for collective interests of women: gender differences a result of biology not of social structure
Perspectives on leisure planning	State control of resources for public need Under capitalism leisure planning serves social order and economic efficiency	Reallocate resources for equity of opportunity	Resolution of conflicts in public interest Rational ordering and allocation	State intervention unnecessary and inefficient Market of 'free' consumers not plans
Perspectives on management theory	Anti-capitalist management approaches Co-operatives Anti-organisation theory	Worker participation Worker democracy	Human relations Contingency theory Worker motivation approaches	Scientific management/ Taylorism
Perceived role of leisure professionals	Professionals legitimate state's claim to represent interests of working class, but protect own interests and those of dominant group	Professionals act as animateurs, stimulators of 'inarticulate' groups Professionals also mistrusted as paternalist, promoting own cultural values	Professionals neutral technocrats, seeking most effective way to achieve consensual goals	Budget maximisers, empire builders
Concept of leisure 'needs', 'wants' or 'interests'	'Real' cultural needs exist which may not be perceived by the individual	Animation employed to help disadvantaged groups express their own interests	Leisure 'needs' identified by professionals as those which generate public/merit goods, and externalities	Leisure wants expressed by individuals through free market

Sociopolitical Perspectives: The Context for Theorising Leisure Planning and Management

The perspectives employed as a vehicle for discussion reflect different traditions in social, economic, and political thought. In this section we will therefore seek to identify the key implications of each perspective for analysis of social problems, as well as for policy solutions to such problems.

Individualism

This approach to understanding society and the economy is that which underpins what Coalter termed 'anti-collectivism' in Chapter 6. It is premised on the notion that society is made up of individuals with competing interests who seek to realise those interests in their own day to day and strategic activities. For the New Right (the political expression of modern liberal individualism) the notion of the 'public interest' or the 'common good' is limited in extent. Very few courses of action can rightly be said to reflect the interests of the majority of citizens. State activity, such as support for publicly owned council housing, implies taxation of some citizens to meet the needs of others and therefore cannot be said to be for the common good. In a situation in which resources are finite it is seen by the New Right as neither just nor prudent to meet the needs of some groups and not others, since this opens the way for further similar demands from those other groups.

There is a further difficulty to which individualists point, and that is that even where the interests of different groups are not incompatible, they are in practice incalculable. It is sufficiently difficult to attempt to summarise the interests of a small group or community, without considering those of a complex society. Thus, with the exception of policy areas such as policing and defence which guarantee the individual freedom to pursue his or her own interests, the state has a minimal role to play.

This line of thinking has implications for economic policy insofar as state intervention in the market is viewed negatively. Intervention, for example to reduce unemployment, is seen as counter-productive, since state subsidy for ailing industries or state employment can be funded only either by higher taxation or by printing money. Both increase costs for healthy industries, the former directly, the latter by inducing inflation, and both therefore render such industries less competitive, increasing the likelihood of industrial failure and therefore of unemployment, in the longer term. A free market is thus not only seen by the New Right as just, it also provides the medium by which strong companies are able to survive and flourish, with weaker businesses going to the wall sooner rather than later.

The individualist perspective also has implications for the analysis of social problems such as inner city deprivation. This phenomenon cannot be explained away as a failure of the state to act effectively, or as a failure of the market to allocate resources efficiently or justly. A minimalist state and a free market economy are seen by the New Right as logical concomitants of the emphasis on individual interests, and individual responsibility to meet those interests. The problems of the inner city are seen, not as a function of the way our system works, but rather as a failure on the part of the individual to operate effectively within that system. The 'blame' for failure is thus laid at the feet of the victim, to be remedied through, for example, life and social skills, or job training. Limited state intervention of this type, socialising individuals into modes of behaviour which will allow them to operate successfully in a free market economy, is seen as defensible (hence the New Right's willingness to fund some inner city recreation initiatives such as Action Sport). State intervention to mediate the impact of the free market in other respects is, by contrast, to be opposed.

Pluralist Perspectives

The term 'pluralism' has become unfashionable in debates about social and political theory, as political discourse has polarised around the radical critiques of the New Right and the New Urban Left. Nevertheless, the premises of pluralist theory continue to inform debates about policy. In contrast to individualist thinking or class-based analysis, pluralism conceptualises society as a 'polyarchy', a plurality of interest groups with overlapping memberships, rather than as a collection of individuals or an essentially economically stratified class system. Interest groups struggle with one another to secure their own ends, though such competition is invariably unequal since some groups have access to greater resources than others. However, where a group has few resources but feels sufficiently strongly about an issue it can effect change by putting greater effort into lobbying and other forms of collective action. For example, the urban disorders of the early 1980s might be conceived by pluralists as a set of interest groups with few resources resorting to collective action: 'social bargaining by riot'. Inaction by groups or individuals is generally deemed to imply acceptance of, or indifference to, the status quo or proposed changes.

Within this particular sociopolitical perspective (or more accurately this family of sociopolitical perspectives) the 'state' is not viewed as a monolith, a unified organisational framework, but rather as a set of linked organisation (which themselves have interests) such as local and central government, the judiciary, the liberal welfare professions, etc. The state is subject to checks and balances which prevent it from usurping control from its citizens. Principal among these checks and balances are voter control, organisational pluralism (e.g., the police, the judiciary, the armed forces, local government, etc. are not centrally controlled by a single unified command structure), and media pluralism (the media reflecting the whole range of public opinion acts as a watchdog on state activities). The effectiveness of each of these 'checks' has been challenged, however. Voter control seems ineffectual, particularly when a Conservative government, for which a minority of voters actually voted, can effect a programme of radical policy change. The notion of organisational pluralism has been challenged by the left, which points, for example, in the case of the miners' strike of the early 1980s, to the state machinery acting in concert (the National Coal Board, the cabinet, the police) to defeat the miners (Fine and Millar, 1985). Finally the notion of media pluralism has been undermined by the increasing concentration of ownership of media outlets in the hands of an oligopoly of multinationals.

Notwithstanding these difficulties for pluralist accounts, we should note an important distinction between two dominant types of pluralist thinking – between, that is, conventional pluralism, and reformist pluralism. Pluralist accounts see the state as essentially neutral, merely a vehicle for the expression of group wants and interests. The distinction between conventional and reformist pluralism hinges on key differences in the way the neutrality of the state is conceptualised. Dunleavy and O'Leary (1987) identify three levels of neutrality in order to illustrate these differences. The first type of neutrality is simply 'laissez-faire', the state merely acts as a conduit for the demands of interest groups without intervening at all in the interplay between such groups. The second type of neutrality involves the state in refereeing between interest groups according to agreed norms (e.g., in preventing cartels, or monopolies from imposing their wishes on consumers), and this is the form of neutrality normally associated with conventional pluralism. However there is a third concept of more active neutrality. Here the state is like the handicapper in a race trying to make the sides even in an unequal contest. The state, according to this notion of neutrality should actively seek to intervene in favour of those interest groups which have less access to resources for expressing and fighting for their interests. For example, when a planning objection is raised by a community group against a large scale industrial concern, state planners may act as advocates on behalf of the community group, on the grounds that the community does not have the resources to hire solicitors and planners to make its case.

Reformist pluralism casts the state professional – whether planner, leisure services officer or housing officer – in an advocacy role, yet some reformers mistrust the influence accorded to professional groups dominated by white, middle class males, reflecting the dispersed inequalities of wider society. Such groups have the power to structure the agenda of public policy debate in ways which will invariably reflect their own values.

Just as individualist thinking has implications for the way that social problems are conceptualised, so pluralism will also conceive of problems and solutions in particular ways. For pluralists, whether conventional or reformist, the key issue to be addressed in social or business policy or in leisure planning is the identification of effective mechanisms which will allow groups to 'speak for themselves', and influence outcomes. Thus in addressing inner city problems the focus of concern moves away from treatment of the individual, to a focus on 'institutions' such as local government or local business, and the ability of such institutions to act as vehicles for the expression of the needs and wants of interest groups. Where social problems manifest themselves, 'blame' is laid not at the feet of the individual, but tends to be attached to the workings of local institutions, whether recreation departments, housing offices, schools or clinics.

Pluralists are in Coalter's terms 'reluctant collectivists' (see Chapter 6 in this volume), intervening only when responsible institutions fail to act as vehicles for the expression of group interests.

Structuralist Marxist Perspectives

For Marxist theorists the key task of social analysis is to explain how capital is able to continue to extract profit based on the efforts of a labour force which acquiesces in an 'exploitative' relationship. Subordinate groups in society not only fail to oppose the interests of capital in overt ways by, for example, sustained industrial action to raise wages and improve working conditions, they may even support business interests through the ballot box. Working class acquiescence in the means of its own subordination is explained by structuralist Marxists by reference to the concept of false consciousness. Members of the working class fail to appreciate their own class interests because they are duped by the dominant ideology which successfully represents the interests of the dominant groups in capitalist society as those of society as a whole.

For structuralist Marxists the social structure functions in a way designed to 'reproduce' economic relations of subordination and dominance. The education system, the family structure, leisure, religion – in effect, all the cultural (non-economic) facets of social life in a capitalist society – are all seen as contributing to the physical and intellectual reproduction of labour, providing a fit, educated, healthy and therefore efficient workforce. The role of leisure in this process is to deflect working class interest from the political and to subtly reinforce the values of capitalism (cf. Brohm, 1977, Gruneau, 1983).

According to the structuralist Marxist account apparent advances in working class interests (by, for example, the development of a welfare state meeting working class demands for housing, health services, education and so on) are merely means of buying working class compliance. In other words, apparent advances in working class conditions are illusory since they serve to reinforce the status quo of systematic subordination.

The lines of argument traced out here leave structuralist Marxism with two central problems. The first, as Saunders (1981) points out, is that the notion that the state always functions in the interests of capital does not admit of any counter-example. Nothing could count as the state advancing working class interests at the expense of capital, since it is always open to the structuralist Marxist to explain such actions as capital 'buying off' resistance. (There is one case which could be taken as a counter-example, that is if the capitalist state overthrew capitalism, but as Saunders suggests this is a rather spurious case.) Since therefore the structuralist Marxist argument does not appear to admit of any set of circumstances which might constitute its failure (with the one exception cited), it is less than helpful. We cannot establish the conditions under which the structuralist Marxist thesis might be true because we are unable to cite the conditions under which it can be said to be false.

The second central difficulty for the structuralist Marxist case relates to the distinction it draws between 'reality' and 'ideology' (Althusser, 1969). The working class does not vote solidly for socialist parties, nor do owners of businesses, professionals and managers vote unanimously for parties representing business interests. This state of affairs is explained by reference to 'false consciousness', which is generated by ideology promoted through the cultural systems of our society (e.g., the education system, the media, the judiciary). These elements of cultural life promote a view of the world consistent with the interests of dominant groups, since dominant interests control policy and practice in such institutions. This is not to say that there need be any conscious conspiracy to suppress expression of the interests of working class groups, but rather that the view of the world which is perceived as 'natural' by the decision-makers is that which they invariable promote, while those which are inconsistent with their interests are dismissed as unreasonable or are marginalised. To return to our example of the miners' strike this, it is claimed, was reported largely in ways which reflected the point of view of the government, rather than those of some miners. Illegal picketing and use of violence by miners, are said to have been forefronted in the media, while illegal police action, taken to prevent pickets from gathering, and police volence were played down or treated as 'necessary evils' (Coulter *et al.*, 1984). The point being made here is not that one view is right and the other wrong (though structuralist Marxists would wish to make that claim), rather that one set of values was being favoured at the expense of others. For the structuralist Marxist such examples merely reflect the way the dominant ideology is perpetuated (cf. Abercrombie *et al.*, 1980).

The result of this promotion of the dominant iedology, Marxists claim, is that real class structures, and processes of domination and subordination, remain invisible to dominant and subordinate groups alike. There is an 'ideological blind' in operation, which individuals are unable to 'see through'. The solution to this dilemma is to employ scientific Marxist analysis which will allow the individual to highlight the inconsistencies in 'ideological' accounts of how society works and to grasp the real, structural conditions of class conflict inherent in capitalist societies. Since ideology, for Marxists, is not a reflection of reality but of capitalist interests, it will manifest inconsistencies which derive from the contradictions of capitalism. By analysing these contradictions the false nature of ideologically inspired accounts of society will be appreciated and reality grasped.

To illustrate this point, let us take a particular account of 'contradictions of capitalism' and how they manifest themselves. Castells (1976) attempts to explain the emerging difficulties of the local state in advanced capitalist societies as a consequence of the state's contradictory functions, meeting the needs of capital accumulation while responding to working class demands for increased expenditure on social provision. In seeking to sustain an increasing rate of profit, capital has traditionally 'socialised' the costs of reproduction of labour power. Nineteenth century factory owners may thus initially have provided housing, education, health provision and even leisure for their workers, but when competition squeezed profits, such forms of provision became the responsibility of the state, to be paid for collectively rather than by the individual employer. However, as increasing pressure is placed on capital it seeks to reduce its costs by pressing for lower taxation, while working class demands for expenditure on such forms of collective consumption increase. The costs of meeting the demand for collective consumption exceed the finance available from taxation, and this basic contradiction of capitalism manifests itself in the form of struggles around consumption issues. Thus by focusing on contradictions in the way the social and economic system operates, scientific Marxist analysis can explain the difficulties experienced in capitalist societies, highlighting the inconsistencies of 'ideological' explanations of such systems, undermining acceptance of the inequalities inherent in such a system, and promoting an understanding of the 'real' nature of structural relations and their consequences.

The difficulty with the structuralist Marxist claim is that it rests on the premise that while all views other than those based on scientific Marxist analysis are ideological and therefore inaccurate, the Marxist account is the only non-ideological explanation of social structure. This premise cannot be defended from the counter-claim that the Marxist account itself is simply the product of an ideologically influenced mode of analysis. The Marxist claim of privileged access to knowledge is simply an article of faith which, if rejected, undermines the whole edifice of the structuralist Marxist argument.

Of course not all Marxist analysis is structuralist (nor indeed is all structuralist analysis Marxist), and the appreciation of the two central difficulties highlighted here have led to a revision of the Althusserian emphasis on a dominant ideology. This revision is evident in the neo-Marxist work of commentators in leisure studies (Hargreaves, 1986) and in cultural studies (cf. CCCS, 1978) which draw on the concept of 'hegemony'. In contrast to the notion of a dominant ideology imposed by the structural requirements of the reproduction of capital, hegemony is a state of tension, negotiation and struggle between competing value systems for moral and political leadership. There are periods in the history of a society in which one set of values predominates, followed by periods of hegemonic struggle. Thus, for example, the political consensus which reigned in Britain from the late 1940s to the late 1960s reflecting broad support for a welfare state, funded from the marginal profits of economic growth, was challenged in the 1970s, and replaced in the 1980s by New Right arguments for rolling back the state, reducing taxation, and replacing state provision of welfare services with the notion of individual responsibility (see Figure 7.1).

However, a problem for such neo-Marxist accounts is that of differentiating such accounts from reformist pluralist explanations of the way the social system operates. If hegemony is really a state of struggle between dominant and subordinate groups, with the outcome undetermined, there is room (at least in principle) for subordinate groups to 'win'. What, then, is the significant difference between reformist pluralist accounts and neo-Marxist explanations of social struggles? Indeed some social theorists wish to claim that hegemony is a 'pluralist' concept (Dunleavy and O'Leary, 1987), with the implication that Marxism collapses into pluralism at this point. If, however, hegemony represents struggle which in the final analysis (or 'in the last instance' Poulantzas, 1973) is invariably to be won by dominant groups, then what is the significant difference between such neo-Marxist accounts and the structuralist Marxist analysis outlined above?

Despite the difficulties with structuralist accounts and the distinction between such accounts and neo-Marxist explanations, we should note that there are practical implications for the way in which social problems are viewed. Whereas individualists will seek to address solutions to inner city deprivation at the level of the individual, and pluralism implies a consideration of institutions, Marxists will focus on the economic system and its exploitation of subordinate groups as the source of such problems (see 'problem explanations' in Figure 7.1). Radical change of the system of market relations requires collective action, hence the attribution of the term 'collectivist' to its policy focus.

Feminist Analyses

One of the advances associated with the discussion of hegemony as a concept is its serious treatment of stratification and social struggle along dimensions other than class, and the importance of gender and race in any discussion of competing values, domination and subordination. Feminist analyses in particular have contributed to the undermining of the uni-dimensional model of society which structuralist Marxism represents, and have opened out lines of enquiry in social analysis in general, and leisure studies and management theory in particular.

In order to appreciate the contribution of feminist writings to such debates it is important to understand the range of thinking represented in such writings. To accomplish this we will make use of the framework of ideas reflected in Figure 7.1 and locate feminist analyses by reference to the premises underpinning individualism, pluralism and Marxism. Useful sources in this approach are works by Deem (1986), Scraton (1988), and Wimbush and Talbot (1988), each of which deals specifically with the application of a range of feminist analyses, to an understanding of leisure practices and/or leisure management and policy.

Individualism, the philosophy of the New Right, in rejecting analysis based on the structural characteristics of society, says little about the role of gender in shaping people's life chances. New Right thinking assumes that a free market will allow individuals to express their interests and neglects, therefore, to consider women's lack of influence and power in the economic sphere (as in others). Thus, in an important sense, feminist analysis and individualism are mutually incompatible. Gender differences will tend to be explained away as the corollary of biological differences, rather than as the product of structural inequalities in society.

What has been termed 'liberal feminism' refers largely to the work of social theorists, who explain the nature of women's disadvantage by reference to sex role stereotyping and socialisation into such sex roles. This approach seeks to encourage women to break free from such stereotypical roles, but fails to question why such stereotypes exist. They fail in other words to locate accounts of gender and disadvantage within wider explanations of the social, political and economic construction of power relations. We have located this school of feminist thought within the pluralist 'column' of Figure 7.1, because the implications for policy reflect pluralist concerns with institutions, in particular with changing legislation governing equal opportunities. Women are essentially conceived as a pressure group in such modes of analysis.

Marxist feminism takes the feminist critique a stage further, outlining how the sexual division of labour is functional for capitalism (Barrett, 1980), with the reproduction of labour being undertaken within the private sphere, largely through the unpaid domestic labour of women. While it is clear that the public–private division (allocating childcare and housework to an unpaid female workforce within the home) is functional for capital, it is also in an important sense functional for men. The male worker may gain free time and material benefits from such unpaid labour. Marxist accounts which explain such conditions by reference to the needs of capital alone are therefore limited. Furthermore, accounts based on explanations of the needs of capital alone fail to explain other crucial aspects of women's experience, in particular the fear of harassment and violence. Explanations which go beyond the economic dimension are therefore required, to accommodate such phenomena.

Radical feminists have focused predominantly on the concept of 'patriarchy' – systematic domination of women by men – as a prerequisite for understanding women's oppression. Central to such accounts is the analysis of sexuality. Male sexuality (or heterosexuality), it is argued, requires female sexual submission which is the foundation of gender inequality. How women are restricted in terms of space, time, work, leisure, physical appearance, and social relationships with one another as well as with men, is seen as controlled by the requirement to conform to dominant modes of heterosexual behaviour. The way to challenge such dominant modes of thinking, for some radical feminists, is to adopt a separatist stance, with the development for women of separate work and leisure forms of organisation and behaviour.

As Scraton (1988) points out, however, such radical feminist accounts fail to consider factors other than gender which influence women's life chances. Women's work, leisure, and education, are influenced not simply by gender but also by other factors, in particular their class position and race. In the same way as social explanation based predominantly on class fails to explain differences between men and women in terms of lived experience, so also explanations which focus solely on gender fail to account for the markedly different experiences of, for example, black working class and white middle class women in contemporary Britain. Scraton therefore argues for adoption of socialist feminism which takes account of the ways in which patriarchy and capitalism shape social relations between gender, class and race groups.

Structure and Agency

A crucial debate in social theory has related to the nature of human behaviour as freely chosen by the individual, or constrained by social structures. Individualist accounts tend to stress at their crudest, the freedom of the individual in a meritocracy to reap the rewards for her or his own efforts. A naive structuralist Marxist account portrays the freedom of the individual as illusory, with action shaped by the functional requirements of capitalism (see 'problem definition' in Figure 7.1). Structuration theory seeks a synthesis of these two polarised positions, pointing out that our freedom of action is constrained by limitations in our access to resources for action, but also that as individual agents we do have freedom to choose ways in which we might use whatever resources are available to us (Giddens, 1979).

Adopting a structurationist approach, the role of social theory is to identify the key dimensions of social structure (most notably gender, class and race), to analyse the resources and constraints (material, and cultural) which particular positions in the social structure generate or provide access to, and to analyse and explain individual and group behaviour within such contexts, at particular moments in time and in particular locations. To examine social structure without reference to agents is to deny, by implication, the freedom of individuals to elect for particular courses of action. Conversely to restrict social analysis to evaluating the action of individuals without reference to their structural location is to ignore the constraints and opportunities which such locations reflect.

In summary, what has been attempted in the foregoing sections of this chapter is a characterisation of key approaches to socipolitical theory, and the assumptions on which such approaches rest. Within this context, the discussion of leisure planning and of management theory which follows seeks to identify the assumptions on which different approaches to planning and management are founded, and to trace the links between such approaches and the sociopolitical perspectives identified.

Leisure Planning and Social Theory

All individuals and organisations 'plan' when they consciously organise their actions for the future. However, differing sociopolitical perspectives imply widely differing attidues towards state involvement in planning of resources or people, in leisure, as in all other aspects of life (Dunleavy and O'Leary, 1987).

Leisure Planning and the New Right

Criticism of planned intervention by government comes from both ends of the political spectrum. The New Right, with its support of individualism, free markets, and private enterprise, sees little justification for state involvement in most areas of public life. If the market is believed to be the best device for allocation of resources, there can be no justification for state intervention which can only distort its operation. Bureaucratic allocation, the alternative to a free market, inevitably implies reallocation of resources, with consequent inefficiencies and diseconomies. Commentators even adopt a moral dimension for their argument. Reallocation from individuals who have 'earned' their rewards through enterprise, efficiency and imagination, to others less materially successful is seen not only as unjust, but ultimately debilitating to the recipients of 'unearned' benefits who become weakened by continued dependence upon the state.

Within this perspective there is recognition of only a restricted role for the state, in some cases barely enlarging upon Adam Smith's conception of defence of the realm and maintenance of contract. Provision in leisure, welfare, employment and all other aspects of life becomes the responsibility of the individual or the family, but not of a wider collectivity.

Anti-collectivists see no role for centralised planning which usurps the functions of the market and the responsibility of the individual. Lifting this 'burden' has been the aim of New Right administrations, along with fostering personal independence and self-reliance. Echoes of a Victorian ethos of morality and laissez-faire, and a return to what is perceived as a 'golden age' of limited bureaucratic 'red tape' and government interference are central to these conceptions. Essentially the stance is that of non-planning by the state and limited intervention. The reality of hidden subsidies, whether in mortgage tax-relief or Enterprise Zones allowances, may be far from the ideal model of such political philosophy. However, the general attitude of reducing direct state involvement, whether in economic or personal life, in reversing support for fiscal controls and subsidies consumption, and in opposing collectivised provision of public facilities and their non-market operation, remains a dominant and continuing theme. It finds expression in the encouragement of private management to run publicly-owned leisure facilities, in the privatisation of some public sector contracts, in competitive tendering to increase efficiency in public staffs, and in the gradual enlargement of the private sector at the expense of the public and collective sector.

Structuralist Marxist Approaches to Leisure Planning

For the extreme 'left' of the political spectrum the desired dominance of the state in owning and allocating all national resources means that conscious planning is essential and inevitable. The state should be as committed to the organisation and structuring of leisure, and to its provision and planning, as it is in all other significant sectors of economy and society. Linked to centralised systems of government, as in the Eastern bloc, such approaches generate national 5 or 10 year plans which attempt to distribute resources comprehensively and organise towards centrally determined ends. The power of the state is reflected in the all-pervasive nature of established plans, which are possible only because of nationalised resources under unified control. From such a political perspective, planning in capitalist or mixed economies is of limited effectiveness since critical aspects of finance, materials, and strategy are removed from control of the planners. Government planning in capitalist dominated economies is seen as necessarily partial and limited in scope. The essential areas of economy or property are removed from the direct influence of government and many, if not most, market-based decisions may run counter to the intention of government, centrally, regionally or locally. Planning still has a role in such states but its major function may not be readily apparent or explicitly stated (Kirk, 1980).

Marxist critics of government planning in the UK consider that it inevitably serves the interests of capitalist class domination. Some aspects enhance capital, as when planning restrictions on land development, like Green Belts, effectively limit supply of available sites and hence increase land prices. Rational justification of planning decisions (see Chapter 2 in this volume) tends to reinforce the current organisation of investment and society and so protects established interests through zoning, conservation, or policy decisions. Industry gains state subsidies and improved plant or infrastructure; householders receive mortgage assistance and zoning protection; just as established sports achieve protection for their facilities and financial support. To Marxists, the planning structures which provide this assistance work to maintain established order in society and perpetuate its inequalities and injustices (Paris, 1982).

The existence of complex planning agencies further obscures the workings of state and capital, providing an apparent semblance of order and rationality for decisions which are ultimately determined by the needs of capital. Planning, from this perspective, becomes another of the mechanisms by which society is controlled, physically and ideologically, and social order maintained for more efficient exploitation by capital. The organised provision of recreation facilities serves twin ends of encouraging the complicity of an effective workforce and of providing for an acceptable dissipation of energy by potentially disruptive elements in society.

Pluralism and Leisure Planning

Planning as a necessary adjunct of government activity has always been part of pluralist notions of politics. Recognition of the presence of a range of competing, and in some cases contradictory, interests has implied the presence of government agencies attempting to resolve conflicts in the 'public interest'. In this way a plurality of interests can co-exist in an ordered and orderly way. Awareness of the presence of conflict and competition in society and of the imperfections and injustices of reliance on a purely market-based system provides the rationale for a pluralist approach to planning and collective action. In some cases pluralists may see intervention as an unfortunate necessity and do so only with reluctance, but the need to act in the public or national interest assumes superiority over the absolute rights of individuals. The vision of a collectivity in society with the state as a neutral arbiter of competing claims legitimates pluralist action in planning and legislation.

Traditionally, this has been the stance of successive British governments and the centre ground of political consensus. Reasonable interference with individual rights based on recognition of a wider public interest or duty has been the justification for planned intervention in British society from the nineteenth century. It has led to the creation of a development plans system for land-use (discussed in Chapter 2 in this volume) and to the establishment of agencies like the Sports Council and the Arts Council with the specific aims of redirecting taxation revenue and state policy towards explicit ends in aspects of leisure and recreation. By legislation, policy, funding and protection the state has assumed, and is seen to have a legitimate interest in, the leisure of its people. Pluralist ideas of interest and collectivity defend such intervention which individualists would dismiss as unnecessarily intrusive.

The reality of planned intervention has often been criticised by pluralists. Too often the agencies involved, whether local authorities or national sport or recreation bodies, have been seen as dominated by a white, male, middle class bureaucracy and governed by such values. In this case the criticism is not a questioning of the need to provide facilities, or to correct inequalities in opportunity, or deficiencies in resources, but is based on practical shortcomings in operation. Some criticisms from this pluralist perspective may be termed managerialist.

Critical analysis of operation of organisations has focused in the work of Pahl and others on the extent to which agencies and officials serve their own ends rather than the 'public interest'. The protection of professional interests and the creation of departmental empires can be seen to work against the ideal of rational efficiency, neutral service delivery and fulfilment of public interest. From this standpoint the Recreation Department is seen to have a principal aim of increasing its own size and status, while the Leisure Manager becomes most concerned about professional recognition and a suitable career structure. Public service delivery assumes far less significance than the instrumental concerns of the officials or service providers (Pahl, 1970).

As Pahl has recognised, this managerialist critique has at times over-emphasised the power of officials as 'gatekeepers', vested with the allocation of public resources or access to benefits. The apparently all-powerful bureaucrats of the 1960s are seen to have much less power or autonomy in the constrained economic climate of the 1980s. Despite the limits on power, some elements of influence remain firmly with decision-making professionals, albeit that most resources have shifted from the public domain of local authority or government agencies to those of the private sector and commercial bodies. The real influence of some managers remains, it is simply that their prejudices and predilections are governed by market rather than public sector political concerns.

Concentration of power and influence within the hands of any relatively 'elite' group remains a concern for pluralist theory and in part reflects the problems of too fundamental an assumption of equality of influence between interest groups. Recognition of the fundamental inequalities in developed economies and democracies encourages notions of reformism, when the influence of the state in planning is seen as essential for redressing some of the power imbalances within society. Such conceptions envisage a more proactive role for public interest planning which might be categorised as 'indicative' in setting goals and objectives and in actively co-ordinating their attainment by including the private sector in programmes of development (McKay and Cox, 1979). The work of the Countryside

Commission in rural areas and the plans drawn up by Regional Councils for Sport and Recreation in urban areas, or by the regional tourist boards, acting in association with local authorities and private interests, fulfil this general approach to an interventionist leisure strategy.

Less reformist approaches to planning adopt a far more regulatory approach, whereby initiative remains firmly within the private sector and is simply modified in accordance with pre-established guidelines representing the public interest. Regulatory planning has been the traditional Conservative party approach to town and country planning in the UK and fits a traditional pluralist model emphasising free competition between interests, with limited state direction or interference. In such circumstances local authorities operate in a largely passive, often negative role, responding to private initiatives in leisure and other spheres, using policy guidelines from local or national politicians, and committing few resources on their own behalf.

Naive pluralist ideas of relative equality of access to decision-making and to political influence in democratic societies have been criticised increasingly in recent years. Many citizens find equity hard to visualise, when compared with pervasive and often deepening inequalities based on race, gender, class and disability. Feminist critics in particular have identified structures and processes in society which tend to reinforce patterns of male dominance and exploitation through patriarchy. Planning based on historic trends or contemporary organisational forms reflects a gender bias in personnel, ideology and structure. Critics point to the male dominance of establishment committees like the Sports Council, Arts Council, Countryside Commission, and a wide range of formal and voluntary governing bodies in sport, recreation and leisure. These have major responsibility for policy formulation while remaining unrepresentative of the population at large or of many active participants. Whether within local government, built environments, leisure provision, or the media, the processes seem constructed to perpetuate male dominance and its conceptions of female roles and aspirations. The focus of the vast majority of public policy is on the public sphere of activity, though for many women, the private sphere is the locus of most significant oppression. From such a viewpoint whichever broad political stance is adopted is largely irrelevant without reform of fundamental structures of gender dominance (Deem, 1986).

Failure to reflect adequately the less powerful, less vocal or minority interests, remains a problem of pluralist planning. Attempts to increase public involvement and participation by widening representation have had only limited success. Minorities in leisure and recreation whether by nature of the activity or by disadvantage through race, class, gender, age or disability, tend to be neglected in policy-making and resource allocation. Alternative approaches like advocacy planning (where professionals cast themselves in the role of advocate for disadvantaged groups) seem only to reinforce the basic distribution of power within organisations and to provide limited and perhaps patronising assistance to groups combatting the machinations of the rest of the profession. Without real changes in the distribution of power such activities remain only marginal and the pervasive nature of professional power remains largely unchecked.

Until some of these crucial issues of power, representation and allocation, which political theory explores, are resolved, planning in leisure, as in all other aspects of society will be seen as reinforcing and reproducing existing patterns rather than radically reforming present relationships. Reliance on existing structures, personnel, professional values and programmes seems likely to reproduce the present order of society rather than to transform it. For critics of current circumstances such perpetuation is unacceptable. Models of political philosophy, practice and process may provide some direction as to possible ways of achieving goals for leisure management and for public participants.

Management Prescription, Social Theory and Political Values

Sociopolitical perspectives have implications not simply for planning and public policy, however, but also for management theory and practices. In Chapter 3 in this volume a range of prescriptions for the management of human resources were reviewed. This section will consider the relationships between the adoption of these prescriptions, the values or premises on which such prescriptions are based and the values or ideology underlying the perspectives on society identified in Figure 7.1.

Individualism and Scientific Management

Scientific management was introduced as a feature of early industrialisation in the USA, when Taylor sought to identify the single, 'most efficient' way of achieving output. This he did through the introduction of a piece-rate system with jobs subdivided into their simplest elements which could be accomplished most quickly, with least error, at least cost. This approach is seen as likely to be welcomed by the workforce, since wages can be raised with increases in efficiency. Such an approach also implies a clear division of labour between management and the workforce, with the latter being motivated solely by monetary rewards and therefore happy to accept a clearly prescribed task since this will facilitate the maximisation of wage levels. This 'prescription' is handed down by management since it is charged with the responsibility for planning work, the workforce is merely required to carry it out. Trades unions were seen by Taylor as unnecessary since workers would recognise that their interests lay in following management prescriptions, thereby maximising their incomes.

Some of the flaws in scientific management as a prescription are rehearsed in Chapter 3. Central to the difficulties associated with implementing the approach is its failure to recognise the alienation of the workforce, which results from deskilling jobs and the loss of control or influence on the part of workers in planning how work should be carried out. However, elements of scientific management thinking are reemerging in the 1980s in a way which is linked to changing social values. This is in part a function of wider political change and economic recession. Management is simply in a much stronger position to impose working arrangements than was the case in the immediate post-war period of relative growth and affluence. Multinational capital which is so prominent in developed economies, seeks in times of recession to continue to increase its return on investment. It can accomplish this in one of three ways, finding cheaper sources of raw materials, reducing wage costs by transferring production to low wage economies, or reducing wage costs by automation. Although the first of these options has worked in favour of UK employment in the form of North Sea oil and gas, the last two resulted in a net outflow of jobs in the late 1970s and early 1980s, and to the further deskilling of many of the jobs which are left, as a result of the introduction of automation. In such a situation where workers may be competing with one another for jobs, the deskilling process is complemented by a reduction in the power of labour to negotiate working conditions, and there has been a steady reduction in the number of trades unionists in this country, reflecting this. The imposition of management devised working conditions and practices, which is characteristic of the scientific management approach, has become an increasingly evident feature of industrial relations in the 1980s in Britain.

Key features of liberal individualist thinking are reflected in the scientific management approach. A fundamental assumption which is shared by the political philosophy and the management prescription is the dismissal of the notion of collective interests: individuals should be left free to pursue what they perceive as their own individual interests through the mechanism of the free market. A related concept employed by scientific management is that of the rational individual acting instrumentally, seeking to maximise income at work at the cost of intrinsic interest in the task itself, and at the cost of social and economic solidarity with co-workers. The increase in scientific management approaches to work situations is thus a reflection of, and reinforces, the emergence of a New Right ideology in the political field in the 1970s and 1980s.

As has been suggested in Chapter 6 in this volume, the New Right view of the role of the professional or manager in public sector service delivery is one of a pressure group, seeking to promote its own interests, by legitimating claims for the expansion of its service, on the basis of professional expertise in analysing the public interest. Public sector professionals are empire builders, or budget maximisers whose actions account for much of the growth in public sector budgets which has led to higher levels of taxation, 'burdening' private capital. By contrast, the role of the leisure manager in the private sector is regarded positively, since it fosters efficiency in the free market, allowing individuals to meet their own leisure 'needs' more readily.

Traditional Pluralism and 'Consensual' Management Theories

In the same way as the distinction between traditional and reformist pluralism carries with it different implications for the role of the state, so also it is consonant with different brands of management theory. The human relations tradition in management theory shares the main assumptions of the conventional pluralist mode of analysis. It is premised on the assumption that competing interest groups may have different goals, but that they can come to some compromise or consensus over what constitutes legitimate action for the management and workforce of an organisation. As we noted in Chapter 3, the Hawthorne experiments may have been flawed in design and may have generated dubious conclusions, but there is little doubt of the considerable ideological influence of the 'employee-centred' approach to management which this theoretical tradition exerted. In the same way as traditional pluralism admits of the possibility of the state identifying and acting in the public interest (a possibility largely denied by liberal individualists) so the human relations approach implies the possibility of management identifying the interests of 'the organisation'. This is accomplished by identifying those conditions under which the workforce will co-operate in generating a satisfactory return on investment. In the case of the Hawthorne experiments this involved predominantly social factors such as group cohesion and external recognition of the importance of the work group's contribution. Contingency theories – and to an extent theories of employee motivation – take this one step further in suggesting that not simply social factors, but any of the variables at play in the work situation, might be manipulated to effect the achievement of managerial goals.

Both conventional pluralism and the management traditions of the human relations school and contingency theory share the same inherent conservatism. Traditional pluralism does not seek to address the problems of unequal competition in society but simply reflects this as an inevitable feature of 'free' societies. The criticism that some groups in an unequal society may not be regarded as free, since they have few resources to exercise that freedom, is problematic for this mode of social explanation. The interests of society are thus treated as synonymous with the status quo. Similarly the management traditions of human relations, motivation, and contingency theorists make the assumption that the goals of the organisation are, and should be, those of management. In the same way as conventional pluralism implicitly defends the interests of the more powerful groups by seeking to sustain the conditions under which they have enjoyed power, so also these approaches to management seek to sustain relations of power within organisations, which promote the interests of management and/or ownership.

Reformist Pluralism and Worker Democracy

However, just as reformist pluralism represents an attempt to challenge the status quo (within certain circumscribed limits), by seeking to represent the interests of disadvantaged groups in the social system, so certain approaches to management represent attempts within a capitalist framework to empower the workforce, providing it with a share in decision-making processes and rewards. Experiments in worker participation and worker democracy are premised on just such arguments. Worker representatives sit on boards of directors, representing the interests of the workforce, but also symbolising the responsibility of the workforce, with management, for the success or failure of the organisation. Such approaches have not been without problems even in socialised economies (Seibel and Damachi, 1982) and they vary in the level of responsibility and power they may wish to devolve to workers.

Such worker-oriented approaches to organisation contral are attacked by both the Marxist left and the New Right. The former argues that 'democracy' is merely tokenism, because control ultimately rests with management which can outvote workers at board level, and because the organisation is still forced to follow the logic of capitalism, seeking to provide an attractive rate of return on capital invested in order to secure continued investment. The latter argues that worker ownership (in the form of share ownership) might be desirable, but that interposing a structure which seeks to reflect worker interests in an organisation is a recipe for inefficiency and therefore economic disaster.

Structuralist Marxism and Alternative Management Theories

Invariably Marxist theoreticians have rejected traditional management prescriptions, arguing that they play an 'ideological' role, masking reality in three principal ways (Clegg and Dunkerley, 1980). First, management theories represent problems of conflicting interest in organisations as potentially soluble, given 'rational', 'technical', 'objective' analysis by managers. Secondly, they represent the interests and problems of management as those of the organisation, thereby undermining consideration of the interests of the workforce, which may be in conflict with those of management. Thirdly, management can legitimate their favoured position in the organisation by reference to their role as technocratic experts, charged with solving the problems of the organisation.

The notion of a neutral state, ensuring fair competition in business with managers as rational, technical experts in competing organisations being rewarded for their effective and consensual solutions to organisational problems is rejected at every level. The state is not regarded as neutral (Poulantzas, 1973). Competitive capitalism is a myth. The markets that matter are dominated by multinationals which dictate the conditions under which competition will be conducted (Baran and Sweezy, 1968). Management theory is not neutral, but by purporting to be so, buys acquiescence from the workforce (Braverman, 1974).

The response of structuralist Marxism to ideologically inspired management theory is to advocate alternative organisational forms to those associated with capitalism. Co-operatives, in which rewards are not hierarchically dispersed, and influence more evenly spread, constitute organisational forms which are designed in rejection of hierarchical rewards and privilege. A number of examples of worker self-management sprang up in the UK in the 1970s as businesses found themselves in trouble because of the recession. Among the best known were the Clydeside Shipbuilders who took over the shipyards in response to closure threats in 1971, the Meridan Motorcycle factory, which with a lower interest loan operated 'successfully' for seven years, with equal pay for all and at one stage an expanding workforce, and the *Scottish Daily News*. The eventual 'failure' of such organisations is explained by Marxists as an inevitable consequence of the operation of isolated socialist organisations in a wider capitalist system (cf. Burrell and Morgan, 1979).

Feminist Analyses and Management Theory

The principal weakness of the approaches to organisation theory discussed above for feminists has been their failure to explain how the interests of women are systematically suppressed in work organisations. There is considerable evidence to illustrate that there are fewer women in positions of (managerial) power in organisations generally and in leisure organisations in particular (White, 1988). The response to this has varied across the spectrum of feminist thought. Liberal feminists have sought through equal opportunities legislation to change recruitment and employment practices not only to increase the number of women in managerial positions (a dismal 8.5 per cent in 1982), but also to improve the working conditions of all women within work organisations. Marxist feminists point to the wider role of the sexual division of labour, arguing that change within organisations is of limited value since in a wider sense this still condemns women to reproduce the workforce by unpaid labour in the private sphere, and to act as a reserve army of labour on which capital can draw. Changing the position of women for Marxist feminists therefore implies a fundamental shift in the nature of social structure. A step in this direction is the establishment of feminist co-operatives which reject both the capitalist system based on self-interest, and the subordinate role which women play within that system. The response of radical feminists to this line of argument is that separatism is essential not simply as a response to capitalism, but also as a response to patriarchy. If male sexuality functions to control women, making them conform to a female role of submissive deferrence, then modes of organisation which are exclusively female are needed not simply to combat the function for capital of sexually differentiated labour, but also to break the ideological dominance of patriarchy.

However, there are dangers in this separatist strategy. One of the building blocks of feminist analysis is challenging the dominant notions of feminine traits in our society as a 'natural' extension of biological differences between sexes. Gender roles are socially constructed. The notion of males as more assertive, self-confident, competitive, aggressive, physically and emotionally 'tougher' than females, who are more likely to be submissive, compliant, caring and co-operative, is the reflection of expectations associated with gender roles into which we are socialised. They are not a reflection of innate, biologically endowed characteristics of the sexes. Men have the potential to manifest behaviour 'characteristic' of the feminine and women that which is 'characteristic' of the masculine. Indeed it is the appeal to 'natural', 'biological' differences between males and females which is used to legitimate patriarchal practices (e.g., 'women are better at child-care because they tend to be more compassionate and caring'). Feminists reject the appeal to 'natural' differences between the sexes, the social construction of such practices being one of the foundations of patriarchy. In supporting separatist strategies in work organisations, however, there is an implication that differences between the sexes are enduring, and cannot be successfully challenged. Scraton makes the point in another context:

> While this [separatism] is a realistic and perhaps inevitable short-term political strategy . . . there is a danger that at a theoretical level it reinforces unwittingly a biological reductionist explanation of gender divisions. It suggests that there is a separate women's culture and specific female values. With such an analysis it is difficult to divorce the debate from arguments of biological differences between women and men and at a political level provides pessimistic forecasts for . . . the future in a world which is not separatist in most spheres. (Scraton, 1988, p. 11)

In contrast both to a separatist strategy, and to the approach of liberal feminists, who argue that women can be as successful in manifesting the (masculine) characteristics associated in the popular imagination with effective management, is a third strategy consistent with socialist feminism. This suggests that the positive traits traditionally associated with the feminine should be combined with those positive traits associated with masculinity in an effective manager. Thus, for example, a sensitivity to the needs of organisational members, an awareness of the alienation of the powerless, a willingness to establish a collective consensus – traits associated with the feminine – are seen as essential characteristics in management as an activity, if it is to be truly emancipatory, rather than simply reinforcing existing power relations. Both female and male managers are to be encouraged to draw on these strengths and to eschew the worst features of autocratic masculine management styles.

Sociopolitical Perspectives and the Identification of Leisure Needs, Wants or Interests

Earlier sections of this chapter have explored the implications of sociopolitical ideas, and their consequent relevance as a context for both leisure planning and management practices. This section examines the many links between the ideas expressed within the sociopolitical typology (Figure 7.1) and their articulation in leisure policy, as it attempts to address particular conceptions of leisure 'needs' or 'wants'. It is at this level that the more abstract ideas of the typology become articulated in the identification and addressing of perceived 'real' needs by leisure professionals and/or politicians adopting one of the various stances identified earlier. The same spectrum of opinion, represented in Figure 7.1, encompasses a wide range of approaches to leisure needs, wants, and interests.

The New Right or individualist stance conforms to other elements of that political philosophy in emphasising that leisure should be earned and that leisure time, experiences and facilities are a 'reward' for effort or success in other sectors of life. The sense of leisure as being socially deserved, a meritocratic benefit to be achieved through one's own effort and abilities, conforms to the market-based and self-reliant approach to social policy in general, with leisure wants of individuals finding expression through the operation of the free market. The market is seen as the most efficient and effective device for responding to effective demand, which represents 'real' leisure wants of deserving citizens.

Pluralist interpretations propose greater intervention by a neutral state and its institutions, serving a discernible public interest. The 'public good' in leisure is served within the conventional pluralist approach by leisure professionals acting in the perceived and considered 'best interest' of their public client groups. Power remains a professional and managerial preser-

ve, and leisure needs are met through the prescriptions of leisure professionals, particularly in public sector organisations such as the Sports and
Arts Councils and local authorities.

More reformist conceptions recognise the impact of social inequalities
and the need for action to redress imbalance in the existing distribution of
leisure opportunities and resources. In this more proactive stance, animateurs can operate to develop the interest of particular target groups,
focusing on the most disadvantaged and using state and public resources to
redress some of the inequalities of the market place. Such approaches
follow politically 'left wing' recognition of 'rights' in leisure as in other
areas of social welfare, which are identifiable and inalienable. The pursuit
of leisure rights and the redistribution of resources to attain them becomes
seen as the function of state intervention in leisure policy. In a context of
changing living standards and lifestyles, such a pursuit carries a danger for
the New Right of an endless prescription for further intervention. Most
notions of 'leisure rights' imply socially relative defintions of need and can
thus be revised upwards as wider society changes (Townsend, 1979). In an
unequal society the reformist concept of continuing intervention and
redistribution becomes the 'nightmare of state run inefficiency' of the New
Right.

A wholly more radical approach exists within Marxist approaches which
theorise the difficulty of identifying the 'real' needs of individuals in a
capitalist society dominated by exploitation and its supportive ideology. In
the view of many structuralist Marxists and those of the Frankfurt School
(see below), 'real' cultural needs may not be perceived by the individual
experiencing 'false consciousness' within capitalist society. Such groups
lack awareness or power and are subject to the pressures of a dominant
ideology. Subjectivity – the thoughts and feelings of the individual – is
thus no basis for appreciating individual needs, in leisure as in other
aspects of social and welfare policy, since all have to be viewed in the
context of capitalist structures of power and dominance.

Notions of power have invariably been central to attempts to theorise
leisure wants, needs and interests. Power has been seen as significant in the
ability of individuals and groups to define and realise their own wants,
needs and interests, and also in terms of the ability of professionals to
define them on behalf of client groups. In his seminal review of concepts of
power, Stephen Lukes (1974) identifies the three principal ways in which
power has been treated in the literature, and characterises these as the
three 'dimensions' of power. The first dimension is evident in the pluralist
writings of Dahl (1961) and others who, in local government contexts,
locate power by focusing on decisions across a range of issues to establish
who is influencing policy. This approach, in the Weberian tradition, views
power as the ability of an actor or group to 'realise their own will even
against the opposition of others'.

The second dimension of power, for Lukes, is exemplified in the work of
Bachrach and Baratz (1970) who focus not simply on struggles around

particular issues, but also on the logically prior concern of how policy issues find their way onto the policy agenda (and how many do not) – the exercise of power in 'non-decisions'. In particular politicians, professionals and others may act as gatekeepers to the formal agenda of local authority policy debate, and thereby exclude issues of relevance to the needs of particular groups. As with Lukes's first dimension, this notion of power is voluntaristic in the sense that it locates power at the level of individual action (whether this be in making decisions or in agenda control) rather than deriving an explanation of power as the product of the social structures within which it is exercised.

The third dimension of power which Lukes goes on to identify, in contrast reflects not the exercise of individual or collective will, but rather invokes the notion of 'interests', arguing that an individual or group can be said to have power (irrespective of its actions) when it is able to secure economic, political or social outcomes which are consistent with its 'real' interests. As we have noted, structuralist Marxist theorists, such as Althusser (1969) and Poulantzas (1973) have argued that individuals in a capitalist society are unlikely to be aware of their 'real' interests, a state of affairs which is explained by reference to the effects of ideology generating 'false consciousness', and therefore are unable to struggle to realise those interests. Power is conceptualised in this tradition as a function of the systemic needs of capital. 'Culturalist' Marxist accounts, however, focus upon classes and class fractions which in theory have the ability to break down ideological barriers, to recognise their own interests, and have the power to act to realise those interests. Nevertheless, in practice this may rarely happen. As Gramsci (1971) argues, so complete is the political and economic hegemony of the dominant group in capitalist society that workers will come to appreciate their real interests only under conditions of overt struggle with capital. Lukes draws on this argument to promote the view that the insistence on identifying power in the context of individual and/or group behaviour is unduly limiting:

> The trouble seems to be that both Bachrach and Baratz and the pluralists suppose that because power, as they conceptualise it, only shows up in cases of actual conflict, it follows that actual conflict is necessary to power. But this is to ignore the point that the most effective and insidious use of power is to prevent such conflict arising in the first place. (Lukes, 1974, p. 23)

In the same way as Marxist theorists wish to argue that it is in the interests of subordinate economic and political groups to oppose the interests of capital even though members of such subordinate groups may not be conscious of those interests, radical feminists promote the argument that women do not recognise their own interests as requiring them to oppose patriarchal practices. Radical feminism therefore sees power being exercised over women through the influence of the dominant patriarchal ideology.

There are, however, fundamental difficulties with this Marxist concept of power and its radical feminist counterpart. The conceptualisation of power as uniquely a function of structural factors without reference to individual wants, needs, or action is one which is difficult to sustain. Indeed, as Giddens argues, there would seem to be no logical connection between power and interests. Luke's formulation of the third dimension of power as the ability of an actor or party to influence another in a manner contrary to that other's interests presumes that power may not be used, for example, to influence people to act in their own interests, or to act in ways neutral to their interests.

Stephen Mennell (1979), drawing on Lukes's analysis of power, has attempted to establish parallels between the three dimensions of political–economic power and three dimensions of cultural need. The first category of cultural need identified as the equivalent of Lukes's first dimension of power is what Mennell terms 'administrative cultural democracy'. The cultural democracy approach involves identifying what people want (rather than what experts say they 'need') and ensuring that such experiences are made available either by publicly provided facilities and services or through the voluntary or commercial sectors. Such an approach is essentially what Roberts (1978) refers to in his description of sociocultural pluralism. Mennell is able to cite examples of this approach in practice from a number of EEC countries, drawn from an earlier comparative policy study (Mennell, 1976).

The second dimension of cultural need identified is what Mennell terms 'animation'. Here, however, the parallel with Lukes becomes more problematic than Mennell acknowledges. In discussing the shortcomings of the first dimension of cultural need, Mennell points out that pluralism presupposes that cultural needs will be expressed either through participation or through the articulation of requests for provision. Sociopolitical animation, however, is aimed at identifying needs which are not expressed (principally because certain groups are unable to articulate their wants) and with stimulating demand among such groups:

> Animateurs . . . may not seem so different from traditional attempts to popularise the arts, except that animateurs try particularly to involve people actively, not just as spectators, and in trying to find out what appeals most to people, modify their activities accordingly, whether or not that conforms to prior cultural standards (Mennell, 1979, p. 25).

This characterisation of cultural policy glosses over a tension in cultural democracy concerning the role of the professional. Professionals can be a positive factor in promoting animation, or they can operate as a barrier, reflecting their own values or preferences through their control of access to the policy agenda. Power in defining and meeting cultural needs at this second level is therefore seen either in professionals acting as facilitators (animateurs) helping people to recognise their interests (i.e., to discover ways of realising their wants) or in professionals controlling the policy agenda, promoting policies consistent with their own values. While the former is evidenced in the sociocultural animation movement, the latter is illustrated in, for example, Robert Hutchinson's (1982) account of the development of Arts Council policy, which represents a form of professionally determined analysis of need, and may well result in some form of policy for the 'democratisation of culture'.

The third 'dimension of cultural need' specified by Mennell employs the concept of 'real need' identified by the theorists of the Frankfurt school. Here the parallel with Lukes is clearly drawn. In the same way as Althusser, Poulantzas and Gramsci argue that we are normally unable to perceive our real political and economic interests, so critical theorists such as Marcuse, Adorno and Horkheimer contend that capitalist societies engender in their members false needs, which are evident in mass culture with its commodity fetishism, and its cultural forms which are crassly repetitive and unoriginal (e.g., soap operas) and often degenerate (e.g., video nasties). The function of such cultural forms is to divert interest from political activity. Cultural forms which are, by contrast, truly in the interests of subordinate groups are those which raise the consciousness of the population, sensitising it to the injustices inherent in capitalist societies. What is being promoted here is the notion of a form of cultural elitism which is not a reflection of professional values, but rather is a function of the 'real interests' of society (as identified by critical theorists).

However, the advocacy of elite cultural forms which meet 'real cultural needs' suffers from a difficulty which is analogous to that identified earlier in relation to the claims for 'real' political and economic interests. Although some criticisms of mass culture may be admissible, the implied and sometimes explicit claims of superiority for other cultural forms have not been supported. Roberts (1978) promotes a cogent argument against such claims for the high arts. He cites Wright's (1975) argument that all aesthetic judgements are culturally relative, and goes on to point out that even if aesthetic judgements were not culturally relative, the case for the superiority of certain art forms would have to evaluated, and that such a case has not been satisfactorily constructed:

> it is unnecessary to insist that objective aesthetic judgements were possible in principle, the fact would remain that we have no objective evidence whatsoever, in the ordinary meaning of the term, proving that high culture is especially effective in promoting well-being. Critics of popular culture offer only opinions . . . No one has yet offered convincing evidence that the quality of experience at symphony concerts is superior to that obtained at pop festivals. (Roberts, 1978, p. 56)

This argument highlights the central difficulty for critical theorists (and structural Marxists and radical feminists) in relation to their claims about 'false' needs and interests. Their argument is based on an unjustifiable premise that they have privileged knowledge of what constitutes the 'real' cultural needs of the population, while all other modes of analysis succumb

Figure 7.2 Relationship between concepts of power and the defining of 'cultural needs'

	LUKES'S DIMENSIONS OF POWER (MODIFIED)	MENNELL'S DEFINITION OF CULTURAL NEED
LEVEL 1	Power exercised in decision-making	The ability of the individual or group to define own cultural needs; sociocultural pluralism/administrative cultural democracy
LEVEL 2	Power exercised in the mobilisation of bias, unquestioned practices, and non-decision-making	(1) Sociocultural animation; professionals facilitate the recognition of ways of realising wants – facilitating cultural democracy (2) Professionals control policy agenda – administrative democratisation of culture
LEVEL 3	Power as a function of the ability of one group to influence another to act contrary to its own ('real') interests	People's perception of their cultural needs shaped by (1) capitalism or by (2) patriarchy Real cultural needs can be identified only by 'critical reasoning'

to the influence of false consciousness. Figure 7.2 on page 207 these concepts.

The corollary of tracing out the parallels between theoretical perspectives on power and notions of cultural need is that a rejection of some concepts of power requires a reconsideration of some concepts of cultural or leisure need. If, however, we wish to dismiss the notion of cultural interests of the structuralist Marxist (or radical feminist) does this mean that we are required to reject all explanations which refer to 'unconscious interests'? This is a significant question for the leisure professional. Are leisure professionals to be reduced simply to providing those leisure services for which there is a manifest demand by potential clients? The answer to this is depends on the definition of interests employed. Giddens (1979), for example, argues that although our interests cannot be legitimately said to be independent of our conscious wants, this does not necessarily mean that individuals are always conscious of their own interests:

> Wants (or wanting) are the 'basis' of interests: to say that A has an interest in a given course of action, occurrence, or state of affairs, is to say that the course of action, etc. facilitates the possibility of A achieving his or her wants. To be aware of one's interests, therefore, is more than to be aware of a want or wants; it is to know how one can set about realising them. (Giddens, 1979, p. 189)

If we accept this line of argument, we can argue against the individualist who would suggest that there are no 'interests' beyond the individual's conscious desires. The professional will have a role to play in highlighting courses of action which will lead to the fulfilment of consciously acknowledged wants on the part of the individual or group. Thus, for example, promoting the idea of a women's health group for which there is no manifest demand, may be defensible where the professional sees this as a means for meeting other expressed demands for social involvement for 'housebound' mothers. The professional's role is one of making individuals and groups conscious of their interests – that is, conscious of the means by which they may realise their own wants.

Conclusion

In this chapter we have attempted to illustrate how social theory is related directly to styles and approaches in leisure management, policy and planning. We have employed as the vehicle for our argument a typology which invariably describes schools of thought in ideal typical terms. Trying to fit individual commentators within the 'compartments' we have constructed may be difficult: their deviation from the prescription may be of more interest than their conformity to the particular schools of thought to which they may be assigned. Nevertheless, the framework offered here should provide a template with which to begin to identify the basic premises of the arguments advanced by particular commentators.

One of the tasks which has not been undertaken within the chapter is the mapping out of positions of individual authors in the leisure studies field against the framework provided. To what extent does Clarke and Critcher's (1985) cultural Marxism successfully avoid the criticisms levelled at structuralist Marxism? What kind of feminist analysis is Deem (1986) promoting? Is Roberts's (1978) brand of sociocultural pluralism most appropriately described as conventional or reformist? The frameworks employed here should provide some of the tools with which to address these questions.

Further Reading

There is a useful discussion of the range of sociopolitical theories provided in Dunleavy and O'Leary (1987), though this does not consider feminist analyses. For an overview of feminist analyses see Walby (1986).

The implications of these perspectives for management and planning are less evident in the literature. Gwynneth Kirk's (1980) book does consider a range of perspectives on planning (though not specifically leisure planning).

In relation to leisure, Clarke and Critcher (1985) explicitly address the question of the nature of alternative perspectives to their own neo-Marxist analysis, in particular those represented in the writings of pluralists such as Roberts (1978). Deem (1986) goes further, locating her own and other feminist work in the leisure area in the context of a critique of the work of pluralists and Marxists alike. Deem's work has the further benefit of considering management and planning strategies from her own feminist perspective.

References

Abercrombie, N., Hill, S. and Turner, B. S. (1980) *The Dominant Ideology Thesis*, London: Allen & Unwin.

Althusser, L. (1969) *For Marx*, London: Allen Lane.

Bachrach, P. and Baratz, M. (1970) *Power and Poverty*, New York: Oxford University Press.

Baran, P. and Sweezy, P. (1968) *Monopoly Capital*, Harmondsworth: Penguin.

Barrett, M. (1980) *Women's Oppression Today: Problems in Marxist Feminist Analysis*, London: Verso.

Braverman, H. (1974) *Labor and Monopoly Capital: The Degradation of Work in the Twentieth Century*, New York: Monthly Review Press.

Brohm, J. M. (1977) *Sport: a Prison of Measured Time*, London: Ink Links.

Burrell, G. and Morgan. G. (1979) *Sociological Paradigms and Organisational Analysis*, London: Heinemann.

Castells, M. (1976) *The Urban Question*, London: Edward Arnold.

Centre for Contemporary Cultural Studies (CCCS) (1978) *On Ideology*, London: Hutchinson.

Clarke, J. and Critcher, C. (1985) *The Devil Makes Work: Leisure in Capitalist Britain*, London: Macmillan.

Clegg, S. and Dunkerley, D. (1980) *Organisation, Class and Control*, London: Routledge & Kegan Paul.

Coulter, J., Miller, S. and Walker, M. (1984) *A State of Siege*, London: Canary Press.

Dahl, R. (1961) *Who Governs?*, New Haven: Yale University Press.

Deem, R. (1986) *All Work and No Play? The Sociology of Women and Leisure*, Milton Keynes: Open University Press.

Donald, J. and Hall, S. (1986) *Politics and Ideology: a Reader*, Milton Keynes: Open University.

Dunleavy, P. and O'Leary, B. (1987) *Theories of the State: the Politics of Liberal Democracies*, London: Macmillan.

Fine, B. and Millar, R. (eds) (1985) *Policing the Miners' Strike*, Edinburgh: Lawrence & Wishart.

Giddens, A. (1979) *Central Problems in Social Theory: Action, Structure and Contradictions in Social Analysis*, London: Macmillan.

Gramsci, A. (1971) *Selections from the Prison Notebooks*, Edinburgh: Lawrence & Wishart.

Gruneau, R. (1983) *Class, Sports and Social Development*, Cambridge, Mass.: University of Massachusetts Press.

Hargreaves, J. 91986) *Sport, Power and Culture*, London: Polity Press.

Hutchinson, R. (1982) *The Politics of the Arts Council*, London: Sinclair Brown.

Kirk, G. (1980) *Urban Planning in a Capitalist Society*, London: Croom Helm.

Lukes, S. (1974) *Power: a Radical View*, London: Macmillan.

McKay, D. H. and Cox, A. W. (1979) *The Politics of Urban Change*, London: Croom Helm.

Mennell, S. (1976) *Cultural Policy in Towns*, Strasbourg: Council of Europe.

Mennell, S. (1979) *Social Research and the Study of Cultural Needs*, in Zuzaneck, J. (ed.), *Social Research and Cultural Policy*, Ontario: Otium Publications.

Pahl, R. (1970) *Whose City?*, Harmondsworth: Penguin Books.

Paris, C. (ed.) (1982) *Critical Readings in Planning Theory*, Oxford: Pergamon Press.

Poulantzas, N. (1973) *Political Power and Classes*, London: New Left Books.

Roberts, K. (1978) *Contemporary Society and the Growth of Leisure*, London: Longman.

Saunders, P. (1981) *Social Theory and the Urban Question*, London: Hutchinson.

Scraton, S. (1988) 'Feminist Critiques and Reconstructions in the Sociology of Sport', paper delivered to the Olympic Scientific Congress, Dankook University, Seoul, South Korea.

Seibel, H. D. and Damachi, U. (1982) *Self Management in Yugoslavia and the Developing World*, London: Macmillan.

Townsend, P. (1979) *Poverty in the United Kingdom*, Harmondsworth: Penguin Books.

Walby, S. (1986) *Patriarchy at Work*, London: Polity.

White, J. (1988) 'Women in Leisure Service Management', in Wimbush and Talbot, *Relative Freedoms*.

Wimbush, E. and Talbot, M. (1980) *Relative Freedoms*, Milton Keynes: Open University Press.

Wright, D. F. (1975) 'Musical Meaning and its Social Determinants', *Sociology* No. 9, pp. 419–435.

Index of Authors

Index of Subjects